GATEWAY
to the
MAJORS

GATEWAY
— to the —
MAJORS

Williamsport and Minor League Baseball

JAMES P. QUIGEL JR. *and* LOUIS E. HUNSINGER JR.

The Pennsylvania State University Press
University Park, Pennsylvania

A Keystone Book

A Keystone Book is so designated to distinguish it from the typical scholarly monograph that a university press publishes. It is a book intended to serve the citizens of Pennsylvania by educating them and others, in an entertaining way, about aspects of the history, culture, society, and environment of the state as part of the Middle Atlantic region.

Library of Congress Cataloging-in-Publication Data

Quigel, James P., 1954–
    Gateway to the majors : Williamsport and minor league baseball / James P. Quigel, Jr., Louis E. Hunsinger, Jr.
      p.   cm.
    Includes bibliographical references and index.
    ISBN 0-271-02098-9 (cloth : alk. paper)
    1. Minor league baseball—Pennsylvania—Williamsport—History.   2. Minor league baseball—Social aspects—Pennsylvania—Williamsport.   I. Hunsinger, Louis E., 1957– . II. Title.

GV863.P372 W554   2001
796.357'64'0974851—dc21   00-064973

———

THIS BOOK IS DEDICATED TO ALL OF
WILLIAMSPORT'S BASEBALL KRANKS,
THEN AND NOW

CONTENTS

List of Illustrations   ix

Acknowledgments   xiii

Introduction   1

1 Town Ball to Pro Ball: The City Adopts a Game   7

2 Boosters, Promoters, and Promotions   45

3 Bowman Field: Gateway to the Majors   77

4 The New York-Pennsylvania League Era to
   Wartime Baseball, 1923–1945   97

5 Postwar Boom to Short-Season Bust:
   Williamsport Baseball in Transition, 1946–1972   117

6 Twilight of the Eastern League   147

7 Welcome Back to the New York–Penn League   159

Note on Sources   169

Appendix   173

Index   177

LIST OF ILLUSTRATIONS

1. One of Williamsport's early amateur baseball teams, 1867   11
2. The Union Park Fairgrounds, 1890s   23
3. Williamsport's Athletic Park, 1905   32
4. Williamsport's Tri-State Championship team, 1905   34
5. Sheet music cover for "The Millionaires March Two-Step," 1908   38
6. Opening Day festivities at Athletic Park, 1909   39
7. Sheriff Thomas Gray, early 1920s
8. Glenn Killinger, J. Walton Bowman, and J. Roy Clunk, 1930   49
9. The Williamsport Grays club directors meeting, March 1933   51
10. New York Mets delegation to Williamsport, with Casey Stengel and
    William "Bill" Pickelner, January 1966   53
11. Williamsport's youth leagues assembled on the diamond with the
    Williamsport Tigers and the team's administrative officers, 1947   55
12. Spence Abbott and Tommy Richardson welcome the "Grand Old Man of
    Baseball," Connie Mack, to Bowman Field, 1941   59
13. Tommy Richardson, 1953   60
14. The "Cavalcade of Baseball," celebrating Williamsport's seventy-fifth
    baseball anniversary, 1939   62
15. A. Rankin Johnson Jr., 1946   65
16. Philadelphia Athletics pose with Williamsport fans, 1931   68
17. Williamsport Grays draw large crowds to Bowman Field for special
    promotions, 1930s   69
18. The erection of Memorial (Bowman) Field's steel and concrete foundation,
    winter 1926   79
19. Memorial Field prior to Opening Day, April 1926   80
20. Bowman Field, July 4, 1930   82
21. Memorial Park and Bowman Field during the 1936 flood   84
22. Interior of Bowman Field, 1947   86

23. Structural changes to Bowman Field, made in 1947, including the construction of new box seating area and the installation of seats from Detroit's Briggs Stadium   87
24. Aerial view of Bowman Field, 1955   88
25. Head groundskeeper Al Bellandi, 1955   92
26. Satchel Paige, with Frank Delycure, 1950   96
27. Team portrait, 1923   98
28. Williamsport Grays game at the Williamsport High School Athletic Field, 1924   100
29. The 1934 NYPL champion Williamsport Grays   105
30. Members of the Grays warm up at a practice session at Bowman Field, 1937   108
31. The Grays at Elmira's Dunn Field, 1941   110
32. Brawl between the Grays and the Wilkes-Barre Barons at Bowman Field, August 24, 1944   111
33. Cuban players receive their uniforms from manager Ray Kolp, May 1945   114
34. Williamsport Tigers first-baseman Frank Heller, 1948   119
35. From centerfield, a game in progress between the Williamsport Tigers and the Scranton Red Sox   120
36. Ollie Byers and Don Manno return to Bowman Field in the opposing uniforms of the Hartford Chiefs, 1946   121
37. Manager Lynwood "Schoolboy" Rowe, 1951   122
38. Williamsport Grays, a Pirate farm club, featuring future Pirate standout second-baseman Bill Mazeroski, 1955   124
39. Charles "Chet" Lucas and Paul Bailey coordinate the "Keep Ball Alive in '55" ticket drive   126
40. A Grays player is nipped at first base in a game against the Reading Indians at Bowman Field, 1955   127
41. Veteran Philadelphia Phillies pitcher Curt Simmons passes on tips to young Grays pitcher Bob "Gunner" Gontkosky, 1959   130
42. The "Go-Go Grays," co-champions of the Eastern League, featuring Danny Cater, 1960   132
43. Dick "Richie" Allen, 1962   135
44. The Williamsport Mets young pitching staff, including Bill Denehy, Jay Carden, Terry Christman, Jerry Craft, and Les Rohr, 1966   139
45. Hall-of-Famer Nolan Ryan during a brief stay in Williamsport, 1966   140
46. Williamsport Astros pitching coach Jim Walton gives mound tips to Pat Darcy, 1970   143
47. Future Boston Red Sox slugging star Jim Rice with his Billsox teammates, 1971   144
48. Pitching legend Bob Feller makes a promotional appearance at Bowman Field, 1976   150

49. Williamsport Bills catcher Dave Bresnahan, 1987   152
50. Williamsport Bills first-baseman Tino Martinez, 1989   153
51. The Williamsport Bills, featuring Tino Martinez, Jeff Nelson, Dave Burba,
    and Rich Delucia, 1989   154
52. Williamsport Bills slugger Jeromy Burnitz, 1991   156
53. Future Chicago Cubs pitcher Kerry Wood, 1995   161
54. The 1998 Williamsport Cubs   163
55. The 1999 Williamsport Crosscutters   164
56. Exterior of newly renovated Bowman Field, June 30, 2000   165

ACKNOWLEDGMENTS

The most gratifying aspect of finishing a book is the opportunity for the author—or authors in our case—to express thanks to those individuals and institutions that assisted in the endeavor. If writing a book can be compared to indentured servitude, then all authors are perpetual debtors. Our bills are long overdue and our list of collectors long. Both authors are grateful to the management, administrators, and staff of the James V. Brown Library, Lycoming County Historical Society, *Grit* Publishing Company, and the *Williamsport Sun-Gazette* for allowing us unfettered access to their valuable archival and photograph collections, and providing efficient reference assistance. Without their collective generosity and expertise this book would not have come to fruition.

The librarians and archival staff of the National Baseball Hall of Fame Library and Archives at Cooperstown, New York, kindly tracked down every request we made for research material documenting Williamsport's and Tommy Richardson's contributions to the minor league game. Our trip to baseball's national shrine was a well-earned perquisite, and we benefited greatly from the insights of knowledgeable curators and archivists who provided excellent reference service.

The use of oral history to reconstruct the halcyon days of Williamsport's minor league experience reaped many dividends. From the outset we thought it important to conduct taped interviews with long-time baseball fans, former players, front-office personnel, and surviving relatives of local baseball personalities long departed. These interviews yielded rich anecdotal material as well as a personal context for our book. We were warmly received by many Williamsport residents who invited us into their homes to share memories, stories, perceptions, and opinions on the subject at hand. Indeed, it was quite an education. Their recorded insights deeply impressed us, providing a perspective on Williamsport's social history beyond the scope of baseball. Through them we were able to reclaim a lost era when local baseball reigned supreme in the hearts and minds of city residents. We gratefully acknowledge the following interviewees: Max and Alta Border, William "Buck" Byham, Al Decker, "Bud" Jaffe, Rankin

Johnson, Frank Kitchen, Baney Levinson, Frank Luppachino, Don Manno, John Markley, Larry Maynard, Johnny Miller, Dorothy Parsons, Margarite Seiler, and Ev Rubendall. Regrettably, a few participants passed away before their spoken words appeared in print.

Special thanks are owed to Rankin Johnson and William "Buck" Byham for sharing their experiences covering eras and aspects of Williamsport baseball not documented in other sources. The late "Bud" Jaffe, son of prominent baseball booster Max Jaffe, spent a memorable winter's evening with us regaling in old stories of his experiences at Bowman Field.

If this project had not seen the light of day our efforts would have been justified by the salvaging of rare photographs from the *Grit* collection. During our research we discovered three ample files of baseball-related photographic prints dating from the turn of the century. In the midst of reorganization and closing down the *Grit's* Williamsport division, the new parent company transferred the photographs to its home office. Realizing that an important part of our history might be forever lost if the images were not returned, we contacted local *Grit* officials Michael Rafferty and John Brockway, who successfully pleaded our case to their national office. The files were subsequently donated to Williamsport's James V. Brown Library, where the prints and negatives have been inventoried and cataloged. These images constitute the richest photo documentary source for our book and the last visual link to baseball's bygone era in Williamsport. Wayne Palmer, of Palmer Multimedia Imaging, did masterful work restoring several images and preparing prints for inclusion in this book.

We learned much about local baseball history from informal chats with Evan R. Rosser Jr. and William "Bill" Pickelner, who freely imparted their knowledge and collective wisdom. Gabe Sinicropi and Doug Estes, representatives from the front office of the Williamsport Crosscutters (Williamsport's current minor league team), provided a modern perspective on the business administration of a minor league club and a rare behind-the-scenes look at stadium operations.

Our manuscript received a healthy dose of constructive criticism from several reviewers. Michael Rafferty and Reed Howard patiently read early drafts and suggested several editorial revisions on matters of style and content that improved our book. The late Al Decker, venerable sports scribe and clubhouse veteran, provided valuable journalistic insight. We also want to acknowledge the fine work of Peter Potter, our editor, Patricia Mitchell, our copyeditor, and the staff of the Penn State Press, who guided us through the entire publication process. For our first book, we were very fortunate to have been associated with the Penn State team.

Finally, we wish to acknowledge the late sportswriters, Ray Keyes and Michael Bernardi, who inspired us to undertake the writing of this book. Their encyclopedic knowledge of professional minor league baseball and its roots in Williamsport kept the embers burning in many a "hot-stove league" over the decades. Their love of baseball and understanding of its relationship to the character of the city was unsurpassed. Our book, in a sense, is a continuation of their work and the book they should have rightfully written.

James P. Quigel Jr.
Historical Collections and Labor Archives
Pennsylvania State University

Introduction

Williamsport has always been a baseball town. Participation and passage through the ranks of the city's organized and recreational baseball leagues has enhanced the quality of life of area residents and forged a distinctive municipal identity built upon the national pastime. Lifetime friendships, rivalries, and familial memories have revolved around the city's ball diamonds—cutting across racial, gender, class, and generation lines to bind the community in ways few social and leisure activities do today. T-ball, Little League and Babe Ruth League baseball, American Legion and semipro games, industrial, city, and church-sponsored softball teams, and competitive leagues for women and girls attest to the diversity and variants of baseball played within the Greater Williamsport Area. Over the years, city baseball leagues have been a crucible for honing the skills of several talented native sons (among them Don Manno, Dick Welteroth, Tracey "Kewpie Dick" Barrett, Tom O'Malley, and Mike Mussina) who played in the Major Leagues.

Moreover, several "Billtown" generations have shared in the collective experience of baseball as spectator sport. Williamsport's love for the game has been nurtured by a rich history as old as the "dead-ball" (or slow-pitch) era and steeped in local baseball lore. If the history of America and baseball are inseparably intertwined, as documentary filmmaker Ken Burns claims, then the history of baseball in Williamsport has paralleled the ebb and flow of the city's fortunes, providing a convenient marker for the passage of time and a comprehensible barometer of its social history.

Though celebrated for pastoral qualities, modern baseball evolved in an industrial and urban age. Nineteenth-century industrialism uprooted traditional patterns of work and play, and spawned a leisure revolution that catered to a growing urban and middle-class population. City residents embraced baseball to escape the factory whistle and work regimen imposed by the burgeoning industries, machine shops, tannery plants and logging mills situated along the Susquehanna River. Accumulated profits reaped by the city's "lumber barons" provided sufficient capital for baseball's transformation from an informal club sport to a professional game packaged for mass consumption. The genteel amateur game of dedicated sports enthusiasts evolved into a commercial endeavor, as evidenced by hired players, enclosed playing fields, and admission charges for spectators. By the late 1880s, the necessary preconditions for the emergence of the modern professional game were already in place.

Professional baseball in Williamsport evolved as a by-product of the "gospel of wealth." Besides building lavish opera houses and mansions as testaments to their wealth and influence, Williamsport millionaires donated land for playing fields and material for the construction of ballparks, financed players' salaries, underwrote baseball operations, and often absorbed gate losses in times of economic downturn. Baseball was their gift to the city, an extension of their civic and philanthropic duties as custodians of accumulated wealth. Andrew Carnegie bequeathed libraries. In Williamsport, the Bowman and Gleason families gave the people Bowman Field.

Competitive athletics assumed great social importance in an era ideologically dominated by Social Darwinism and civic boosterism and spurred by rampant economic development. Local scribes and "kranks" (the moniker for nineteenth-century baseball fans) perceived contests on the playing field as an extension of the struggle for economic, civic, and (oddly) cultural ascendancy among communities. A community with professional baseball—and a good team to boot—was viewed as a city on the rise. Too much was at stake to entrust the game to amateurs. Civic pride, gambling revenue (a ubiquitous feature of the early professional game), and receipts at the turnstile demanded the best team that money could buy. Williamsport's logging millionaires spared no expense in attracting top-notch talent to represent the city.

As countless baseball historians have documented, the game functioned as an important agent of acculturation and assimilation for immigrants. Experiences gained from the rough and tumble of sandlot games, coupled with the democratic nature of bleacher seating, facilitated the Americanization of Germans, Poles, Italians, and East European Jews who settled in Williamsport during the great immigration wave of 1890 to 1917.

Baseball coaxed the immigrant from the neighborhood enclave and allowed for a level of social interaction not possible in other spheres of daily life.

Tragically, Williamsport's baseball legacy was not immune from racial prejudice and intolerance that mirrored American society. Jim Crow baseball extended to the minor leagues as well. Talented local black teams had emerged in the city; and barnstorming teams composed of Negro League stars frequently played before predominately white crowds at Bowman Field. However, African Americans were denied access to the mainstream of professional baseball until the era ushered in by Jackie Robinson.

Though renowned as the birthplace of Little League Baseball and home to the annual Little League World Series, Williamsport has been heir to an even richer minor league tradition. From membership in the fledgling Pennsylvania State Association in the late nineteenth century to the current Williamsport Crosscutters of the Class A New York–Penn League, the city has enjoyed one of the longest periods of association with professional minor league baseball in the country. Historic Bowman Field, constructed in 1926 and once considered the gem of the Eastern League, remains the second-oldest operating minor league ballpark in the country. While other cities have had longer unbroken records of affiliation with their respective parent clubs, they are few in number. What distinguishes Williamsport's place in minor league history has been the city's ability to support and sustain professional baseball at the level that it has—specifically, membership in the Class AA Eastern League—for such an extended period, notwithstanding its small market size relative to other cities. Between 1926 and 1991 (with the exception of a ten-year hiatus and an odd year or two) Williamsport's Bowman Field served as a gateway to the Major Leagues and hosted some of the best minor league baseball played anywhere in America. During this period hundreds of players donned the uniforms and caps of the Williamsport Grays, Athletics, Tigers, Pirates, Phillies, Mets, Tomahawks, and Bills before advancing to the ranks of the Majors; some became future Hall of Famers.

While Carl Stotz's legacy to the founding of Little League has been well-chronicled, the history of professional minor league baseball in Williamsport has not received commensurate attention. This book is meant to redress that imbalance. We have attempted to write an informative yet colorful history of the professional game in Williamsport that spans the past century. Given the city's rich baseball history, discerning readers and local baseball historians might take issue with our choice of highlights and anecdotal material, as well as our, perhaps, unbalanced coverage of some seasons. Such is the risk with an expansive terrain and a subject dear to the hearts of knowledgeable fans.

Important historical antecedents provided a foundation for professional minor league baseball to flourish in Williamsport. Chapter One delves into the relatively unexamined dead-ball era of local baseball. The transition from club sport to semiprofessional teams in the late nineteenth century marked a critical step toward Williamsport's entry into professional league play. Local trolley-, railroad-, and corporate-sponsored baseball leagues fueled spectator interest in the game and provided the necessary base of fan support for Williamsport's later participation in the Tri-State League—a nonsanctioned, "outlaw" professional league of some notoriety.

Chapter Two provides the reader with a collective biography of the city's prominent baseball boosters, civic leaders, and team officials who contributed immeasurably to the financial and managerial administration of the game. This chapter also highlights early marketing and promotional strategies vital to the economic development of professional baseball in Williamsport over the past decades.

No book on the subject at hand would be complete without a chapter chronicling the most enduring symbol of Williamsport's proud baseball past, historic Bowman Field. Chapter Three examines the individuals and factors responsible for the construction of Williamsport's storied ballpark, notes the structural changes that altered Bowman Field's appearance over previous decades, and offers a fitting retrospective of major events and people that have shaped its unique history.

Chapters Four through Seven primarily examine Williamsport's long period of affiliation (1923–91) with the Eastern League and, to a lesser extent, the more recent short-season New York–Penn League years, from 1994 to the present. While the scope is comprehensive, we have attempted to organize our chapters around distinctive eras, corresponding to Williamsport's association with several Major League organizations. This history of the Eastern League years represents meticulous research and detailed attention to the ebb and flow of the city's minor league experience. Co-author Lou Hunsinger Jr. has compiled, for example, a definitive list of former Williamsport ball-players who have played in the Major Leagues (see Appendix), a welcome by-product of his membership in the Society for American Baseball Research (SABR).

How did this book come about? Ironically, our project originated in the disappointing baseball season of 1991. With the stunning mid-season announcement that Williamsport's baseball franchise had been sold to the New York Mets (with the team's relocation to Binghamton, New York, at the end of 1991 looming), the city's future in the Eastern League was nonexistent. Whether professional baseball would remain a fixture in the city or, in the words of a September 1991 *New York Times* article, "vanish from the hills like the lumber, steel mills, and millionaires," weighed heavy on the minds of devoted local fans.

Williamsport, despite drawing well on a per capita basis, no longer fit the demographic and market profile favored by Eastern League officials. Franchises were often uprooted to larger cities and market areas with the political and financial clout to construct lavish new ballparks. Eastern League owners cited that an average yearly attendance of 200,000 was necessary for most franchises to break even. The best Williamsport ever did was 100,000. Stringent facilities guidelines mandated by the 1992 agreement between the Major League and the National Association of Professional Baseball Leagues (the governing body of the minor leagues) literally taxed the resources of many communities to finance costly stadium renovations. Construction of a new ballpark in

Williamsport was out of the question. Moreover, pundits argued that local fans would not accept a drop in classification—from Class AA to short-season Class A—in order to secure a professional team. Members of New York–Penn League expansion and relocation committee grew weary with Williamsport's arrogance, particularly the assumption that professional baseball owed the city a franchise.

Throughout the 1991 Eastern League season, we felt that team management had failed to capitalize and market the Bills on the basis of historic Bowman Field and Williamsport's rich baseball past. Little had been done to publicize the sixty-fifth anniversary of Bowman Field, one of the oldest surviving minor league ballparks in the United States. A rich vein of local baseball history and folklore remained untapped. A series of retrospective articles on Williamsport minor league baseball by sports editor Jim Carpenter appeared in the *Williamsport Sun-Gazette* while the season was in progress. His work inspired us to undertake a more systematic and comprehensive study of the role that minor league baseball played in shaping Williamsport's municipal identity and social history. To our surprise, we found no existing manuscript-length work dealing with the professional minor league experience in Williamsport. Our task was then defined, to write the first book on the subject.

This book is intended to impress upon readers the importance of history to the continuity and survival of minor league baseball in Williamsport. Within the past decade the changing economic dynamics and structure of professional baseball have transformed the minor league landscape. Sadly, absentee owners and ownership groups have been responsible for the wholesale transfer of franchises from city to city. Their quest for the almighty dollar and pursuit of larger markets has led them to abandon cities possessing a loyal fan base and a long-established history of minor league ball. Stated simply, the quaint and charming ballparks of our parents and grandparents are few and far between these days. What we have in Williamsport is unique and worth preserving. But history can't fill the ballpark, only fans can.

receive the pitch before it bounced in the dirt. First-basemen also sported fielding gloves (thin strips of leather covering the palms of hands) to catch balls. By the 1890s, the use of baseball mitts by infielders and outfielders had become the norm.

Early baseball clubs operated like other fraternal organizations of the Victorian era. Most clubs were governed by a formal written constitution that prescribed the payment of dues and rules governing behavior on the playing field. As late as 1886, when professional baseball superseded the amateur game, the Williamsport club retained and enforced the player's code of the by-gone era. Prior to the opening of the 1886 season the Williamsport Baseball Association enumerated its players' rules in the *Williamsport Gazette & Bulletin (WG&B)*:

The Rules

1. They shall report for practice on the ballground at the hour of—1 P.M.
2. On days of games they shall report in uniform on the ballgrounds not later than 2 P.M. When on the field, they shall strictly observe the commands and directions of the captain and be solely under his control.
3. Drinking of intoxicating liquors is positively prohibited and anyone found under its influence will be severely dealt with.
4. On days of match games, smoking on the grounds while in uniform will not be permitted.
5. They shall be held responsible for such masks, gloves, and other property as may be furnished them by the association.
6. No taunting or slurring one by another will be allowed, as it is liable to breed bad feeling.
7. When away from home for the purpose of playing ball they shall report to the manager at the hotel where they are stopping at 10:00 P.M.
8. The captain shall report to the manager any violation of the above rules.
9. The above rules will be rigidly enforced and the person violating them will be subject to a fine of $2 or more, according to the nature of the offense.

The *WG&B* reported that "the Association believes that the players selected will at all times conduct themselves as gentlemen, and so recommends them to the public."

Beyond the need for discipline inherent within any organization, these rules reflected the Victorian era's obsession with the outward appearance of self-control and emotional restraint—an extension of the cult of "muscular Christianity" to the playing field. Players were expected to comport themselves in a manly and honorable manner and serve as role models for spectators. Sporting press accounts of fan behavior in the late nineteenth century cited numerous incidents of unruliness and a "mob" mentality unleashed by the crowd's passion for baseball. Gambling, drinking, and fighting were by-products of the nascent professional game taking root among "kranks" (nineteenth-century baseball fanatics) in larger cities.

Civil War veteran; Luther Otto, physician and Civil War veteran; H. Otto, lumber dealer; William Sloan, bank teller and Civil War veteran; A. D. Lundy, insurance; and William Norris, attorney and Civil War veteran. Thus, the membership of Williamsport's amateur baseball clubs included a blend of young men in professional occupations, returning veterans from the Civil War, and a few college graduates who had acquired some proficiency in the sport. By and large, these men had a respected socioeconomic standing within the community, and devoted their leisure time to the refinement of the game.

As befitting the "gentleman's game" of that era, the host club arranged and scheduled match games in accordance with its respective by-laws. The Williamsport Athletics issued formal written challenges to other teams and responded in kind to worthy opponents. By mutual consent, the contesting clubs adopted a common set of playing rules— usually the "New York rules," codified by Alexander Cartwright and popularized by the New York Knickerbockers Baseball Club. This entailed the use of a diamond-shaped playing field rather than the square configuration prescribed by the "Massachusetts game."

Match games usually lasted nine innings with no set run limit. When tie games occurred, extra innings were at the discretion of the respective team managers and captains. The home team assumed responsibility for securing impartial umpires to interpret the rules and resolve disputes arising over judgment calls. Teams generally observed the three-strike rule, just as today, but the number of balls required for a walk varied from nine to seven during the 1870s and 1880s. Even with the acceptance of the four-ball rule, umpires had the authority to warn a pitcher an unspecified number of times before officially charging a ball to the batting count. Few batters of the era, however, had the patience or desire to reach first base at the expense of the pitcher. It was not considered manly and honorable to reach base on a walk.

Each side fielded a starting team consisting of eight positioned players and one pitcher. With the exception of the pitcher and catcher, the positioning of the other players varied little from the modern game. Then, pitchers stood a mere forty-five feet from "home base," or home plate. Catchers, wearing no equipment save a rubber mouthpiece, fielded pitches on the bounce, a few paces behind the batter. On a two-strike count the receiver positioned himself closer to the batter in anticipation of catching a foul tip for the third strike.

In the late nineteenth century, several rule changes revolutionized the game. Organized baseball sanctioned overhand pitching for the first time in 1884, resulting in the fast-pitch game that is familiar to present-day fans. In 1893, the National League (organized baseball's governing body, founded in 1876) lengthened the distance between the mound and home plate to sixty feet and six inches to placate batters and restore balance to the game. In the wake of these changes, catchers wore padded gloves and protective equipment for the first time and positioned themselves directly behind the batter to baseball game ushered the city into the sports and leisure revolution sweeping countless urban and industrialized communities in America during the second half of the nine-teenth century.

The partisan nonpaying crowd saw its hometown nine, the Williamsport Athletic (Baseball) Club, play the Philadelphia and Erie (P&E) Railroad club to a 27-27 standoff. As reported by the *West Branch Bulletin*, the Athletics and Railroaders finished the nine-inning slugfest in two hours. The *Bulletin's* accompanying box score recorded a com-bined total of twenty-one fly-catches made by the teams but, oddly, no extra-base hits. There were no player substitutions for either team, with the Williamsport battery of Homer Martin (pitcher) and Dr. Luther M. Otto (catcher) going the full distance. Games of that era did not hinge upon a hurler's stamina or pitch count as pitchers delivered the ball in a slow underhanded arc, much like slow-pitch softball. The news-paper's printed box score resembled its modern counterpart save for two features: it observed the archaic practice of listing the names of the umpires and the game's official scorer and it did not record runs batted in (RBI)—a statistical measure not yet recognized by organized baseball.

A week later, on August 5, 1865, the P&E hosted a rematch and defeated the Wil-liamsport Athletics 26-15. Though the Athletics continued to hold practices and intra-squad games between the "first nine" (starters) and "second nine" (substitutes), important matches with visiting teams were few and far between. Between 1865 and 1866 only five games were recorded in the local newspapers. On September 19, 1865, Williamsport defeated the Keystones of Troy, New York 31-24, and manhandled the Erie City club 45-3 on the following morning. Playing an abbreviated schedule in 1866 the locals went undefeated. The season included one-sided victories over the Erie Excelsiors (48-24 and 62-16), and the first recorded extra-inning game involving a city team—a 4-3 thirteen-inning win over the Swiftford club of Philadelphia. After the 1866 season, press coverage of the team waned. Presumably, membership and fan interest in the Athletics dwindled or the club decided, for whatever reason, to host less publicized matches with local opponents. Williamsport's heated baseball rivalry with its upriver neighbor, Lock Haven, began in the late 1860s. This series facilitated the rise of local semiprofessional baseball during the next decade.

Many early ball clubs were organized as fraternal societies or gentlemen's clubs. Even the term "match game" implied the genteel nature of early baseball and its close associa-tion to the rival sport of cricket. A perusal of the lineups and rosters of Williamsport's amateur baseball teams during the 1860s reveals members from many of the city's lead-ing families—names such as Herdic, Campbell, Lundy, Otto, and Packer, among others. Occupational data, culled from city directories, provides some insight on the social composition of Williamsport's earliest amateur teams. Of the Athletics' starting nine listed in the *Bulletin's* first box score, occupations could be found for the following seven: Hyman Slate, accountant and Civil War veteran; John Eutermarks, attorney and

1

Town Ball to Pro Ball:
The City Adopts a Game

 On July 29, 1865, a sweltering Saturday afternoon, a throng of Williamsport spectators made its way by foot, horse-drawn trolley, and carriage to a green expanse situated below Academy Street, bordering the Susquehanna River. The procession to the city's "Pleasant Greens," accompanied by much pomp and fanfare, was motivated as much by the curiosity of the participants as by their civic pride. Along the perimeter of a crudely demarcated diamond-shaped field, the crowd stood, observing within two groups of stalwart young men attired in contrasting uniforms of woolen-flannel jerseys and knickers, stockings, and pillbox caps. Oblivious to the crowd, the men engaged in various drills in an atmosphere resembling a military regimental muster. Instead of muskets, however, they brandished wooden baseball bats. Elaborate fielding, throwing, and batting drills, honed to their own rhythms, replaced precision marching.

Those assembled witnessed the first recorded match game of baseball ever played in Williamsport. Though rounders and townball—early versions of baseball—had long been played upon the city's common grounds, this first

Fig. 1   One of Williamsport's early amateur baseball teams, 1867. Many of the city's nineteenth–century ball clubs functioned as fraternal societies. The young gentleman in the suit is probably the manager or the club secretary. (E. Stuart, Lycoming County Historical Society)

Members of amateur clubs took great pains to distinguish the "pureness" of their brand of baseball from the tarnished professional game. Internally, the Williamsport Baseball Association enforced strict regulations against betting and gambling of any kind and specifically outlawed the paying of players and recruitment of professionals. Touting the superiority of the amateur game, the *WG&B* noted, "Baseball is really the only American sport that is strongly divorced from gambling and drinking, and for this reason alone should be generously supported." Though this pronouncement ran counter to the reality of fan insobriety at many professional games, Williamsport's reputation as a dry baseball town was generally well-deserved. Club officers and the local press even encouraged the attendance of woman and children at games as a mitigating presence against drunkenness and fan hooliganism. Still, even for amateur team members, drinking was part and parcel of the early baseball-playing fraternity.

Formal written challenges to opponents often included an itinerary for the customary postgame celebration. Host clubs planned a banquet and libations usually followed the exchange of fraternal greetings by the respective club members. Central to the festivities was the presentation of a gilded game ball, inscribed with the score and date of the game, to the victors. These rituals cemented the reconciliation of the baseball brother-hood following intense competition. After defeating the Erie Excelsiors on August 18, 1866, the Williamsport club hosted an evening complimentary dinner for the visitors at the renowned Herdic Hotel. The postgame banquet was reported to have been a meal that "would tickle the most epicurean taste." Following innumerable toasts to their respective cities, the Erie team presented a team photograph to the Williamsport club, while the hosts responded with a "handsome set of engraved resolutions" for the Excel-siors.

While vestiges of amateur club baseball persisted well into the next decade, the game underwent a profound revolution in the 1870s with the ascendancy of professional teams and the emergence of baseball as a commercial endeavor. Spurred by the fanfare and commercial success of the Cincinnati Red Stockings (America's first truly all-pro-fessional baseball club) in 1869, several enterprising individuals believed that baseball could be successfully organized and operated like any other business. Foremost among them was Albert G. Spalding.

Born in Rockford, Illinois, Spalding gained fame as a young pitcher on the great Rockford team of 1870 and later with Boston. In 1875 he retired as an active player and moved to Chicago to establish the lucrative sporting goods trust and empire that secured his fortune. Spalding was an ardent proponent of the commercialization of baseball. His sporting goods monopoly secured his place within the inner councils of those club owners and directors desirous of reaping greater profits and bringing eco-nomic stability to the game. In partnership with William Hulbert (president of the National Association of Professional Baseball Players) and the owners of key western clubs—including Charles Fowle of St. Louis—Spalding plotted both the demise of the National Association and the establishment of a new professional league along more favorable entrepreneurial lines.

The founding of the National League of Professional Base Ball Clubs (or National League) in 1876 put baseball on the irrevocable path to a business endeavor. As the first Major League, its principal goal was to transfer power from the players to the owners through the instrumentality of player contracts and later the reserve clause. Operating under the motto "Baseball Is Business Now," owners enclosed playing fields, charged admission prices for games, advertised promotions in local newspapers, and sold vending services. National League club directors took important steps to structure the game in conformity with modern business practices. Team and league schedules were now fixed, or at least regularized. The League also established a championship series to ensure additional revenue at the end of regular season play.

More important, owners attempted to control the baseball labor market by signing players to contracts and establishing rules for player transactions (trades) among teams.

Thus the National League's "reserve clause" was born in 1879, which bound players to their current team indefinitely, or until a team exercised its arbitrary authority to trade or release a player from his contract. The reserve clause curbed the practice of "revolving," whereby a player reneged on his current team contract (termed "jumping") and offered his services to a higher bidder. Designed to fix baseball's most variable labor cost—salaries—it effectively prohibited both a player's movement to another team and his ability to negotiate a more favorable contract.

Until the advent of free agency, the reserve clause was the legal linchpin governing baseball's management-player relations for one hundred years. The framework of the National League did not extend to the countless semiprofessional leagues and teams that thrived in smaller cities across America, however. These cities and their respective teams (the backbone of the future minor leagues) became embroiled in intensive bidding wars for players, including the raiding of other leagues to field more competitive teams. Williamsport experienced these growing pains in the transition from amateur to professional baseball.

A More Serious Game: The Semipros

By the early 1870s, encroaching professionalism had virtually supplanted the gentleman's game of the previous decade. The exploits of skilled professional players and teams such as the Cincinnati Red Stockings, publicized by the sporting press of the day, stoked fan interest in the professional game. Though Williamsport's amateur teams still played, their match games were sedate affairs when compared to the raucous barnstorming exploits of the Red Stockings and the skilled play of the pedigree New York City baseball clubs. In Williamsport, as elsewhere, local fans were now charged an admission price to games. As paying spectators, crowds demanded better teams and more highly skilled athletes to represent the city. As a result, fan interest in amateur clubs—especially the city's Athletics—waned.

The sporting press of the era reported on the financial affairs of local clubs and noted owners' concern about operational costs and arrangements for procuring enclosed playing grounds. Even the language and press coverage of the game reflected the transition afoot. Local beat reporters covering baseball dispensed with pastoral descriptions of games and embraced metaphors more commonly associated with the workplace. Players were described as plying their "craft" and "skills." Pitchers "efficiently" retired batters. Losing teams were castigated for their lack of a work ethic. Rookie players served an "apprenticeship" in picking up the "mysterious arts" of the game from veteran players.

Beginning in 1875, Williamsport fielded its first semiprofessional team. Though the team did not adopt a formal name, local sports writers dubbed them the "Portboys." Managed by Frank P. Guise, a young attorney, the local club played a highly competitive schedule against regional teams from Lock Haven, Danville, Bloomsburg, Sunbury, Elmira, and Harrisburg, as well as professional clubs representing Philadelphia (Athletics), Wilmington, Delaware, and Providence, Rhode Island. The 1875 Portboys included Thomas W. Lloyd (later Colonel Lloyd), and Ed Faries, as the battery, "Dad" Covert at shortstop, Larry Ruch, Fred Powell and Garrett Tinsman in the infield, and Ed Page, Eli Hemperly, and "Monk" Ellis in the outfield. All hailed from the city and had previously played as junior members of the Athletics or on other area amateur clubs. None of the Williamsport players received a living wage as such, but it was customary for local benefactors to pay players on a per-game basis and cover their equipment and travel expenses. Players often accepted seasonal jobs from merchants, industrialists, and lumber barons in exchange for their baseball services.

Williamsport's intense baseball rivalry with Lock Haven provided much of the impetus for local adoption of the semiprofessional game. Annual games of the mid-1860s gave way to a five-game series that commenced in 1875. Each city hosted two games, and a coin flip decided the location of the final game. Though playing schedules were erratic with teams disbanding at the slightest whim, the Williamsport–Lock Haven series constituted the highlight of the season for local kranks. Large fan contingents from both towns traveled by railroad to attend games, and substantial money was wagered on the outcome of the series. William Baldwin, then general superintendent of the Pennsylvania Railroad at Williamsport, was renowned for rolling out his private rail car and inviting friends to accompany him on the road trip to Lock Haven. To accommodate larger crowds, the Portboys relocated from the Pleasant Green to the infield concourse of the Old Oak (Herdic) Park racetrack—located between present-day High Street and Louisa Street, east of Campbell. Fans flocked to the new confines to witness some of the best baseball played in the north central tier of Pennsylvania.

Williamsport and Lock Haven scouted and recruited the best available local sandlot talent. After suffering an early 27-19 defeat to Lock Haven in 1875, the Portboys recruited its first overhand pitcher from Danville, "Cannonball" Aten. Because few of his teammates could catch the "fireballer," Williamsport signed a slick fielding catcher from Hughesville, Howard Lyon, who became one of the most popular players on the team. Roster additions in 1876 included the battery of Lafferty and Crowley from the disbanded Wilmington Quicksteps (one of Delaware's best semipro baseball teams) and the acquisition of second-baseman Harold McClure. All three later played professionally and McClure further distinguished himself as a judge in the Union County courts. The employment of "ringers" (nonroster players recruited from out of town) to gain an edge over opponents was quite common. In Williamsport's case the strategy succeeded brilliantly as the locals swept the five-game series with Lock Haven in 1876.

The Portboys 1877 season was notable, if for no other reason than the rise to stardom of Harry Stovey, whose real name was Harry Stowe, and John Montgomery "Monty" Ward. Stovey originally joined the club as a pitcher and was reputed to have been one of the fastest hurlers in the game. After breaking his batterymate's hand in one game, he was switched to first base as no one could catch him. Stovey took to his adopted position and developed into one of the best first-basemen of his era. He later played professionally for the Philadelphia Athletics. Although he has not yet been enshrined in Baseball's Hall of Fame (an injustice that many baseball historians hope to rectify one day), Stovey was generally regarded as one of the greatest players of the nineteenth century.

Monty Ward, a budding college pitcher, had played for a number of area amateur teams—including Renovo, Lock Haven, and Bellefonte—before making his pro debut with the Portboys. Ward introduced the mysteries of the curveball to Williamsport baseball fans and was master of control on the mound. His teammate Thomas Lloyd (later a sportswriter for the *WG&B*), noted that Ward "had opposing batters eating out of his hands." Ward gained a reputation as one of the best all-around players in the National League as a pitcher and shortstop for Providence, and later became a player-manager with the New York Giants. He pitched the second no-hit, no-run game in league history and later spearheaded a player's revolt in 1890 that failed to eradicate the infamous reserve clause.

Despite success on the field, the 1877 club abruptly disbanded in mid-season due to financial failure at the gate. The onset of the Panic of 1877, coupled with the Great Railroad Strike of that year, sealed the collapse of the semiprofessional game in Williamsport until prosperity returned in the early 1880s. While amateur city leagues and sandlot teams survived hard times, the professional game required major benefactors with capital reserves to spend lavishly on the national pastime. The expenses were such that Williamsport could only support one semiprofessional team.

The emergence of the city as a preeminent lumber producing center provided the necessary financial base to elevate the game to the next level. The surrounding forests of Bald Eagle Mountain and logging booms stringing the West Branch of the Susquehanna River produced millions for Williamsport's lumber barons. Spin-off industries such as tanneries, furniture factories, musical instruments manufacturing firms, and machinery and metal working shops soon fueled an economic revival in the 1880s. The city's *nouveau riche* built opulent mansions, underwrote the construction of schools, libraries, opera houses and theaters, and donated land for public parks. If baseball was representative of the city and its newfound wealth, the lumber barons intended to spend liberally on luring the best players. Around 1882 they began the movement to organize Williamsport's first professional baseball team. Their drive coincided with the proliferation of professional baseball leagues all across the country and the entry of smaller cities into the professional game during the 1880s.

In the wake of the National League's effort to bring structure and order to the growth of professional baseball (the 1883 national agreement involving the National League, the upstart American [Baseball] Association and Northwestern League), the professional game expanded and flourished in mid-sized cities all across the country. To regulate this growth and maintain the sanctity of the reserve clause, the National League formed the

League Alliance, which in effect, relegated all other professional leagues to the status of minor leagues. Members of the League Alliance acknowledged the National League as the only Major League and agreed to uphold the National League's reserve clause. In exchange, member cities were afforded protection from the raiding of their team rosters by rival leagues, and mutually agreed to enforce blacklists against players who jumped their contracts. Other benefits of membership included set season schedules and agreements on sharing gate revenues.

The League Alliance, though, covered only a small number of the new regional and state leagues that formed in the 1880s and 1890s. During this period, minor leagues appeared and disappeared at a rapid rate. According to the most reliable figures compiled by the Society for American Baseball Research, seventy minor leagues operated in the country between 1877 and 1900. Several new professional baseball leagues were established in Pennsylvania, such as the Pennsylvania State Association (1886), the Central Pennsylvania League (1887), the Keystone League (1891), and the Iron and Oil League (1895), among others. While the National League was preoccupied with subduing its chief competitor, the old American Association, these smaller leagues proliferated outside the governing body of organized baseball. They were also established in the shadow of more prominent leagues that later gave rise to the International, Pacific Coast, Southern, and Texas leagues that today constitute the upper echelon of the minors.

Between 1881 and 1882 the city's baseball scene was dominated by a handful of competitive amateur teams that played abbreviated schedules and did not have any league affiliation. After a dormant season in 1883 due to the lack of suitable playing grounds, city brahmins laid the foundation for Williamsport's first all-professional team. Their first action was to secure a suitable baseball venue for their enterprise. R. H. Crum, president and manager of the Williamsport club, organized a local stock company to finance the construction of a new enclosed ballpark situated along Packer Street (present-day Curtin Middle School) opposite the old city fairgrounds. Stock certificates were issued at $20.00 per share, with the Williamsport lumbermen "contributing freely of boards for the fencing." W. D. Richards was elected as treasurer and Major William P. Clarke served as the club's secretary and statistician. Clarke later became the city's foremost baseball historian and a permanent fixture on the local baseball circuit for the next forty years. He collected Williamsport's earliest baseball mementos and score books and contributed historical articles to local newspapers under the by-line "The Old Tymer." Known also as a "Figure Filbert," Clarke compiled statistics on the city's early professional clubs and wrote season reviews for the local press and *Spalding's Official Baseball Guide*.

With a new ballpark and new administration in place, club officers then assembled a team of salaried players, bound by contract to play for the duration of the 1884 season. The core of Williamsport's first professional team was recruited from the city's best amateur teams and the semipro Portboys. Playing an independent schedule in 1884 the Williamsport club (dubbed the "Billtowners" by the local press) took three games of a five-game series against York, split two games with the Lancaster Ironsides, and won two and tied one against Trenton, the champions of the old Eastern League that year. In a bold move to upgrade its short season, Williamsport scheduled late September exhibition games against several National League (NL) opponents—defeating Philadelphia 7-6, and losing to Providence (the NL championship team) 9-2. Among the more notable players on the 1884 Billtowners roster was Mike Tiernan, an outstanding pitcher and second-baseman. Tiernan graduated to the old Eastern League (forerunner of the present-day International League) and later played outfield for the New York Nationals.

The 1884 season constituted a watershed in Williamsport's baseball history as the Billtowners evolved into a true professional team in terms of contract signings and level of play. Crum and other club officials ambitiously explored affiliation possibilities with a number of fledgling professional leagues forming within the state. The team finished with a 33-22-4 record in its inaugural campaign.

The following season, Crum reported that the team had a total of sixteen players under contract but no more than eleven at any one time, owing to roster changes and the desire to limit players' salaries. Only six original contract signers finished out the 1885 season in a Billtowners uniform. Two players jumped and signed with other teams in mid-season. One homegrown talent, Dave Deshler, was released in order to cut expenses. As an independent team operating without league protection, Williamsport's players were vulnerable to offers of more money and other inducements by raiding teams. Not bound by the strictures of the reserve clause that governed the NL, several Williamsport players exercised their right to revolve, or sign with the highest bidding team—nineteenth-century baseball's version of free agency.

The team performed admirably in 1885, despite the accompanying growing pains associated with the business side of the professional game. Playing a seventy-three-game schedule Williamsport won fifty-four and lost nineteen. Seven of the Billtowners' losses were to NL ball clubs: Pittsburgh, Boston, and Philadelphia. The locals managed to defeat one of the weaker NL clubs, the Philadelphia Athletics 3-2. The city's rivalry with Lock Haven was particularly bitter that year, perhaps owing to an extended seventeen-game series between the warring clubs. According to an observer of the series, "All kinds of charges were hurled back and forth between the two clubs," as Williamsport won eleven of the games. Three of those games lasted only to the seventh inning, owing to frequent disputes that erupted on the field and in the stands.

Williamsport and the State Association

Williamsport entered professional league play for the first time in 1886 when the club joined Wilkes-Barre, Scranton, Lancaster, Lewistown, and Altoona as members of the

Pennsylvania State Association or Pennsylvania State League. Major William Clarke and other Williamsport Club officials played an instrumental role in establishing the state loop by initiating correspondence with prospective league members. Meeting at the Old City Hotel in Williamsport on April 1, 1886, team representatives hammered out a league agreement and adopted rules patterned after the rising American Association of Professional Clubs (forerunner of the American League). Clarke served as the Association's secretary-treasurer and had the unenviable task of putting the league on a solid financial footing. Membership had its price, of course, and, owing to a lack of solid financial backing, Lock Haven did not qualify for admittance into the Association. For the duration of the State Association's short existence, the Williamsport–Lock Haven series fell by the wayside.

Affiliation with the State Association purportedly afforded member clubs the same rights and protection governing players' contracts as stipulated by the National Baseball Agreement of 1882. That agreement had been brokered by the National League to avoid a costly bidding war with the upstart American Association over players. With the implementation of the reserve clause, local clubs could fine, suspend, or blackball their own players with impunity. Each member club was now obligated to honor the player contracts and reserve lists of other member teams. The *WG&B* reported at the time:

> Former organizations of this kind in Williamsport never had any protection or control over their players. They could jump contracts, disobey instructions, and in fact do anything they pleased . . . without fear of penalty. But with the situation and the protection now afforded, the clubs will play better ball than has ever been played in this city. The stockholders did not organize the present club for the purpose of making money, but are anxious that it will be self-sustaining, and if the public will give their support by attending the games the club will become a perpetual organization.

Members of Williamsport's 1886 squad included Briel, Guehrer, and Hasney as catchers; Rittenhouse, Kimber, and Drauby as pitchers; Foulkrod, shortstop; Fitzpatrick, Humphrey, and Rickley on the bases; and Baker anchoring the outfield with the two reserve catchers. Rittenhouse, a pitcher of great potential, was thought to be destined for the Majors but his playing career was short-lived owing to his ill temper and lack of discipline.

The Pennsylvania State Association garnered a reputation as a highly competitive league, with several teams producing Major League players. They included Altoona's Lave Cross, Jake Virtue, Charley Manlove, and Charles Faatz, as well as Scranton's John "Dasher" Troy. It was Wilkes-Barre, however, that won the 1886 State Association championship, with the Billtowners taking second place with a 42–35 record. Williamsport's finish was tarnished by the fact that only four teams completed the season.

Ironically, the protection sought by teams to prevent players from revolving did not extend to clubs jumping to other leagues. Franchise instability plagued many of the early professional leagues operating outside the National League. Rules governing league affiliation were liberally interpreted and many clubs exercised their option of exploring more lucrative opportunities. Clubs on the verge of financial collapse often dropped out of their respective leagues in mid-season, only to be replaced by other cities. Lancaster, for example, folded after playing only fourteen games in the State Association's inaugural season. Danville filled the vacancy but immediately fell behind its financial obligations to the Association treasury. When the league officers traveled to Danville to formally expel the team they found themselves the recipients of a temporary restraining order (served by a local sheriff at the rail station) that prevented them from taking any legal action. Within a few short weeks, however, Danville suspended baseball operations after compiling a dismal record and heavy losses at the turnstiles.

Unscrupulous owners frequently severed ties with one league in order to affiliate with a more prestigious league that covered a larger market area. Such was the case in 1887, when Scranton and Wilkes-Barre pulled up stakes in mid-season to join the International League. Notwithstanding the protests of Williamsport and other teams for legal retribution, the Pennsylvania State Association disbanded before the completion of the season. Thus the membership fees paid by State Association affiliates afforded little protection when club owners were enticed by more powerful and lucrative leagues. Nevertheless, Williamsport fans in 1887 witnessed the exceptional play of a fiery hell-brand pitcher named William "Kid" Gleason, who later became a famous second-baseman with the Philadelphia A's. Gleason, who played all nine positions in one game during his rookie year, later achieved notoriety as the manager of the tarnished Chicago "Black Sox." Fergy Malone, a former catcher with the Philadelphia A's, piloted the Billtowners in 1887. He was a favorite of local fans for his Irish wit and iron hand with the players.

The State Association died a quiet death on July 16, 1887, following Williamsport's pummeling of Altoona 15-6. Fittingly, the final game was played on a bizarre note when the home-plate umpire collapsed from heat exhaustion. After a lengthy delay, both teams agreed to substitute a local umpire, Dunbar Frey, to finish the ballgame. Two days later, the *WG&B* wrote the Association's obituary under the banner "No More Baseball":

> The Williamsport Baseball Club has disbanded. During the four years in which a professional club has been located here there has not been one in which the patronage has been sufficient to pay expenses. All sorts of devices have been resorted to, and finally the grounds were moved up town in the hope that it would increase attendance. A large sum of money was expended in putting the new grounds in shape and making them attractive, but still the public did not attend in paying numbers. The Wilkes-Barre club officers and directors were

dishonorable enough to violate all their pledges and desert to the International. This caused the State Association to be in a shaky condition and, fearing a loss through collapse, it was thought best to close the season with the Altoona series.

Williamsport's initial foray into professional league play had failed financially. Such failure became a recurring theme throughout the city's long affiliation with professional minor league baseball. Local interest in the national pastime ebbed and flowed, subject to the capricious nature of fan support. Interest and anticipation in the pro game peaked only after long periods of being denied a team. When the city was fortunate to attract a franchise, fans took the team for granted and counted on the largesse of the Williamsport lumber barons to sustain losses at the gate. With the demise of the Pennsylvania State Association, professional baseball remained dormant in the city until a revival under the aegis of the Tri-State League in 1904. In the interim, a new brand of local rough-and-tumble amateur and semiprofessional ball dominated the city sandlots during the 1890s.

City Teams and Corporate Ball, 1890–1902

The new decade ushered in Williamsport's golden age of independent baseball. Without a professional team to represent the city, amateur baseball again enjoyed a popular resurgence among fans and players. While the gentlemen's baseball club of an earlier era had become all but extinct, amateur baseball in the form of independent teams and city-sponsored leagues had managed to survive alongside the rise of the professional game throughout the nineteenth century. In place of formal clubs that subordinated the game to ritualized social functions, amateur teams kept their focus upon the diamond and gritty play. In time, the city's amateur leagues became a feeder system for later semiprofessional and corporate-sponsored baseball clubs that also flourished between 1890 and 1902. Thus, the late nineteenth-century baseball scene in Williamsport could be best characterized as a patchwork quilt of independent amateur teams coexisting with semiprofessional teams sponsored by many of the city's leading industries.

In their heyday, several city teams eclipsed the popularity of their professional predecessors. City championship games and contests with Lock Haven commonly attracted crowds of two thousand or more. The city's amateur baseball leagues provided a crucible for emerging sandlot talent. Many local ballplayers learned and refined their skills playing for city teams. Several graduated to the pro ranks and even played before the hometown crowd as members of Williamsport's later Tri-State League team. Moreover, the city league resuscitated fan interest and passion that had been absent with the professional game. Various city teams, representing the mosaic of Williamsport's socioeconomic classes and ethnic wards, built solid bases of fan support. City games engendered intense personal and familial rivalries as fans rallied behind teams associated with their neighborhood or place of work, or perhaps to support a playing family member. In some instances, this passion spilled over into fights between opposing teams and among spectators. Such intense fan loyalty was not always conducive to the best interests of the game.

During the 1890s the standard bearers of city baseball were the Demorests (sponsored by the Demorest Sewing Machine Company), the YMCA, and four teams affiliated with the City League—the Brandons, Lycoming Rubber Works, Printers, and the Keystones [Foundry] Team. Although the Demorests (a semiprofessional team) were heralded as the pride of the city and represented the town in regional play, the bulk of fan attention revolved around the city league rivalries, especially that between the Brandons and the Rubber Works. The City League was launched in 1889, with the Brandons capturing the first citywide championship series played in 1891. The Brandons were considered so strong a team that the semipro Demorests declined their offer of a three-game series. Hailing from the city's East End, near Brandon Park and "Dutch Hill," the team drew a large following among that ward's German-American residents. Members of the 1891 team included Joseph Mertz (later a county sheriff), John Lutz, Charley Kast, Jess Gohl, Dick O'Neill, Henry Schmidt, Lefty Willman, Bobby Searfoss, and Ed Willig. The Rubber Works team, still smarting after losing the regular season pennant to the Brandons, challenged their rivals to a three-game series. Despite "padding up" for the series (a nineteenth-century euphemism for the use of illegal players), the Rubber Workers lost to the champions. According to one local press account the series was bitter, marred by "frequent outbreaks of fistic display on the part of principals and patrons alike."

The local YMCA team, under the direction of its athletic director and coach William "Pop" Golden, also gained a reputation for fielding one of the strongest nine in north-central Pennsylvania. Considered the city's best judge of sandlot talent, he skillfully assembled the youngest competitive teams. Golden later distinguished himself as a football coach for the Pennsylvania State College (Penn State University) from 1900–1902, and established the college's first athletic department.

In its initial city league season the YMCA team was considered formidable enough to challenge the Demorests to a three-game series, which it promptly won two games to one. Although the YMCA team existed for two seasons only, it produced a number of prominent baseball prospects. From its ranks emerged Fred "Snitz" Applegate (pitcher) and his batterymate Charles "Mother" Booth, both of whom played in the Tri-State League for Williamsport. Several others played for the Demorests when the plant team tried to revive its fortunes during the latter part of the decade. YMCA club members included Allie More, Henry Willig, Harry "Hack" Clayton, Mickey Autters, Fred Plankenhorn, Ed Gass, Bill McMunn, and Howard Kiess. The YMCA team also challenged and defeated many of the area's state normal schools—Mansfield, Bloomsburg, Lock Haven, Penn State, Bucknell, and Susquehanna.

Throughout the 1890s City League games were played chiefly at the Union Park

---

Diamond located on Penn Street near the site of the present Armory complex. During its heyday the league included many other teams, perhaps less distinguished on the playing field but colorful nonetheless. City League affiliates in 1897 included the Dark-tones, the Keystones, the Kuban Joint Club, the Athletics, the Young Champions, Joe Ottenmiller's Brewery Colts, the Brownies, the Riversides, the Bankers, the Reporters, the Ramblers, the Clover Leaves, the Young Men's Republican Club, the City Hotel team, the Newberry team, the DuBoistown Stars, and the Turn Verein Vorwaerts. Clearly, players clustered around teams for a variety of reasons. Whatever the basis for the organization—whether ethnic, religious, fraternal or occupation—a team associa-tion provided a group identity in an increasingly impersonal urban society. In many cases, the formation of a ball club revolved around the support of a popular "watering hole," nothing more than an expression of the "drinking classes."

All city league teams measured their progress and success against the achievements of the Demorests, the pride of Williamsport baseball. Formed in 1890 by the management of the Demorest Sewing Machine Company, this semipro team quickly earned a reputa-tion as one of the state's leading independent clubs. Company baseball represented an early manifestation of corporate welfare-capitalism, an attempt to foster worker loyalty toward the company. Baseball also provided corporate sponsors with cheap advertising. David Spencer, plant superintendent and manager of the team, used company money to recruit both local and outside players under the banner of the Demorests. Players received a small stipend to defray their rent and other living expenses, but few were paid a living wage. According to a *Grit* account, the average monthly salary during the season for one of the team's stars amounted to $80, most of which was paid in company scrip. All players were offered employment in the sewing machine factory during the off-season.

The Demorests were renown for their gritty play and eagerness to "take on all com-ers." Considered Williamsport's best ball club, the team revived the old-time West Branch Susquehanna River regional rivalries—particularly with Lock Haven—dormant since 1887. In 1893 the Demorests joined a loose affiliation with Renovo, Tyrone, and Bellefonte to form the River League. Led by temperamental pitching star "Popp" Case, the Demorests finished in second place by a percentage of .010. In a postseason exhibi-tion game with the stellar New York Giants, the locals held their own against pitching ace Amos Rusie before losing 8-3.

Renewal of the city's bitter rivalry with Lock Haven between 1893 and 1895 prompted an outbreak of fan hooliganism that even surpassed that of the previous series. A new twist was added when the teams scheduled special morning-afternoon double-headers on holidays. Fans attended the morning game in Williamsport and then traveled with the team by rail to Lock Haven for the "return" game. As in the past, large bets were placed on the series and it was not uncommon for hats to be passed around the stands while the game was in progress. In some instances fans avoided middlemen and threw money directly onto the diamond to reward players who made key hits or out-

Fig. 2 The Union Park Fairgrounds hosted some the city's best semiprofessional baseball teams during the 1890s. Among the clubs that played here were the Demorests, Lycoming Rubber Works, the Keystones, and Joe Ottenmiller's Brewery Colts. (D. Vincent Smith Collection, Lycoming County Historical Society)

standing plays in the field. Overzealous fans forced the suspension of the Williamsport–Lock Haven series in 1894 when fights in the stands poured out onto the playing field during one game. In 1896, the Demorests joined the professional Central Pennsylvania League for one season, playing against Sunbury, Shamokin, Milton, and Bloomsburg. The local team finished third in the loop. After 1896, the Demorests played an independent schedule with many leading Pennsylvania and New York clubs.

The fortunes of the Demorests waned after 1896, but the team had provided fans with some of the best baseball played in the area until the rise of the Tri-State League in the early 1900s. Though organized baseball had not yet instituted a classification system for the minor leagues, knowledgeable fans and baseball historians rate the Demorests' level of competition as comparable to that of the present-day Class A professional leagues. The most colorful member of the Demorests was Ossie Schreckengost, a strapping unorthodox catcher who played for the Philadelphia Athletics by the time the 1897 season ended. Dubbed the "Rocking Horse" because of his unusual catching stance, Schrekengost achieved fame as one of the few catchers who could control the eccentric and mercurial Athletics ace "Rube" Waddell. Together Schrekengost and Waddell formed perhaps baseball's oddest battery. Other notable Demorests included Charles "Mother" Booth and Eddie Sales, the latter called out of retirement to fill the team's dwindling roster in 1897. Sales had been a member of Williamsport's first semi-pro club of 1875 and well past his prime when he donned the togs of the Demorests.

Unable to retain their best player and escape the league cellar, the Demorests finally disbanded at the end of the 1897 season. Their collapse ended the first chapter of Williamsport's golden age of amateur and semiprofessional baseball. The spirit of that era would subsequently be revived and embodied in the Trolley League and the Pennsylvania Railroad baseball games that were played in the interval (1911–23) between Williamsport's affiliation with the Tri-State League and New York–Pennsylvania League.

Restructuring the Minor Leagues

In the immediate years after 1900, momentous changes in organized professional baseball occurred at the national level, causing a restructuring of the Major Leagues and formalization of relations with the established minor leagues. These changes ushered in the modern era of baseball and propelled Williamsport into the arena of professional minor league baseball. While city amateur leagues and corporate teams continued to operate within the confines of Williamsport during the 1890s, the rapid growth of professional minor league baseball in the country continued unabated. The professional game had a powerful hold on fans, even withstanding periodic economic depressions in the late nineteenth century. Despite the broad popular appeal for amateur and semipro teams, local fans still hungered for the return of seasoned professional ballplayers who could carry the city's banner in regional and interstate competition. Williamsport, along with other moderately sized Pennsylvania cities, desired to join the professional baseball cavalcade. This growth spurt of the minor leagues, however, was not accomplished without accompanying growing pains.

The impetus for establishing and structuring an administrative body to govern relations among minor leagues came against the backdrop of the war between the National League and the upstart American League, led by Ban Johnson and a group of free-spending club owners. In 1901 Johnson and his associates claimed Major League status for the new American League, touching off a bidding war for baseball talent. Competition for players was so intense that the National League abrogated the 1883 National Agreement and conducted wholesale raids on minor league rosters. With little protection, the minor leagues initiated the first step toward establishing a self-governing agency to chart their future course. On September 5, 1901, eleven representatives from the organized professional leagues (including seven league presidents) met in Chicago to found the National Association of Professional Baseball Leagues (NAPBL), the organization that to this day governs the minor leagues.

This first meeting ostensibly addressed the issue of raiding by the two warring major leagues. The following year, the NAPBL adopted rules and operating procedures to stabilize the entire minor league establishment and formalize relations with the Major Leagues. Among the NAPBL's chief accomplishments was the creation of a classification system for the minors (A to D) based upon the market size of member cities and the level of play. Though modified in subsequent years with the emergence of baseball's farm system (whereby Major League teams established and operated their own minor league teams), the classification system is still intact.

Minimum and maximum salary limits for players were established for each classification level. The NAPBL observed a strict reserve clause, making it illegal for players to jump their contracts and join other member teams. Players who disregarded the sanctity of contracts were fined according the their classification level—the higher the league, the larger the fine. In this era, minor league free agency exacted a high price, as much as $1,000 for violations at the highest (Class A) level.

The major and minor league signatories to the 1901 NAPBL agreement constituted what was then called "organized baseball." Nineteen leagues were brought under the administrative umbrella of the agreement by 1903. Independent professional leagues operating outside the rules of NAPBL were branded outlaw leagues.

The great baseball impasse at the Major League level was finally resolved in 1903 with the National League's recognition of the American League as a legitimate Major League, although the moniker "junior circuit" forever haunted the younger league. On the heels of this truce the two leagues joined the NAPBL in signing a tripartite agreement to administer the professional game. The agreement addressed such outstanding issues as the protection of minor league players' contracts and the territorial rights of clubs. It also established a selection system to eliminate raiding (the arbitrary abrogation of a player's contract) by Major League teams. Under the system, minor league teams drew up a selected list of players eligible for a draft by the Major League clubs. The Majors then reimbursed minor league teams (usually a pre-arranged sum) for each eligible player chosen. This agreement, with necessary amendments made down through the years, remains the foundation of organized baseball.

Concurrent with these national developments, Williamsport's civic and athletic boosters sought to revive professional baseball in the city. In March 1902 William Abbot Witman, president of the Pennsylvania State League, met with local community leaders and made an on-site inspection of the city's newest baseball venue, Athletic Park (situated at the present-day site of the Cochran Elementary School). Witman pronounced the playing field "one of the finest base [ball] grounds in the state," and initiated negotiations leading to Williamsport's entry into the new state circuit. A stock company was established and capitalized at $5,000. Organized as the Williamsport Athletic Club, its principal directors and stockholders included many of the city's influential industrialists and business leaders—Frank C. Bowman, J. Walton Bowman, Carl and Peter Herdic, N. Burrows Bubb, M. C. Rhone, Thomas Gray, and George Breon, among others. The law office of M. C. Rhone served as the front office of the Williamsport Athletic Club.

Carl Herdic and manager Percy Stetler assembled a team that included talent of professional caliber drawn from outside the city, as well as veterans from city league and corporate teams during the previous decade. Nicknamed the "Billies," Williamsport's 1902 roster included such well-known veteran players as Charles "Mother" Booth, Jimmy Sebring, Fred "Snitz" Applegate, the Willig brothers—Lou and Henry—and two young college pitching prospects, Jack Maley and Johnny Lush.

Members of the Pennsy League included teams from Scranton, Wilkes-Barre, Hazelton, Reading, Lebanon, Lancaster, Mt. Carmel, and Williamsport. The inaugural season consisted of one hundred league games and allowed flexibility for the scheduling of games with independent clubs. Despite optimistic projections, the state loop quickly folded when a few teams canceled previously scheduled league games in order to pursue more lucrative contests against clubs in larger markets. In one instance, Reading's general manager informed the Billies front office, via telegram, that his team had "missed its train" for the scheduled game of May 15, 1902. Later that day, Reading played Lebanon, which in turn had been tardy for its scheduled road game with Wilkes-Barre. The *WG&B* caustically noted:

> It is apparent that there is a large size leak in the State League and Williamsport is getting the short end of the deal all around. If the lower end cities want to maintain a circuit throughout the season there needs [to] be a great improvement in the management of affairs. . . . More such treatment as that of yesterday and the whole shooting match will be knocked into a cocked hat. There were too many 'trains' missed to suit the local patrons of the game.

Faced with the prospect of a truncated season, the local club scheduled games with the remaining league members in good standing, and played area teams on other open dates. One of the memorable events of the 1902 season was an exhibition night baseball game with the Milton nine—the first night game in city history. Sixteen arc lights, gerry-rigged around the perimeter of the infield, illuminated Athletic Park for the 8 P.M. contest on May 14, 1902. The *WG&B* reported that a crowd of one thousand dodged the turnstile and pay booth to enjoy the beautiful open air and baseball. However, the game was another matter. The exhibition game quickly degenerated into a comic spectacle when fielders careened into poles and lost fly balls that went beyond the range of the lights. One reporter summed up the evening, "Though the game was not a howling success . . . with light hitting and fast fielding considerable good work was done, and the locals dispatched the visitors 12-5." Thirty years passed before a perfected lighting system ushered in the first night game at Bowman Field. In 1932, night baseball became a permanent fixture in Williamsport.

The Williamsport Athletic Club entered the 1903 season with the strongest financial and administrative support ever bestowed upon a Williamsport sporting endeavor up to that time. Club officers pledged an "open-purse" policy and Stetler assembled the nucleus of talent that solidified the city's reputation as an earnest baseball town. Early season stock subscriptions yielded $4,000 before a ball was ever pitched. Yet, average monthly payroll expenses for the team amounted to $3,500, often exceeding gate revenue. "Despite hearty patronage on the part of the public," the *WG&B* reported, "it was necessary for the stockholders to reach down into their pockets to meet expenses." Competitive bidding for players in higher classification levels drove the payroll increasingly upward. Still, club officials bore the financial burden and refused to gouge the public. The general admission price was ten cents, reserve seating cost a mere quarter, and ladies who attended the first home game received free passes to a future game.

Playing as an independent club in 1903, the Billies scheduled a slate of 127 games. Their opponents included many strong independent teams in the eastern region, area colleges, and Major League clubs—the St. Louis Americans, Pittsburgh, Brooklyn, the New York Giants, and the Chicagos of the National League. To regulate the affairs of the independents, club representatives from across the country formed the National Association of Independent Clubs. This organization implemented many of the governing principles embodied in the NAPBL agreement but only those applicable to signatory teams without league affiliation. Williamsport's own M. C. Rhone was elected as the organization's first president.

On their barnstorming tours of the early 1900s, several stellar black professional teams—the Cuban X-Giants, All Cubans, and Philadelphia Giants—played against Williamsport's professional club. The Cuban Giants—featuring such stars as Clarence Williams, Shep Trusty, and William Whyte—were frequent visitors to Williamsport's Athletic Park. Despite the obvious disparity in talent, Williamsport held its own against the legendary team. In 1903 the Williamsport Billies won six and lost three against the

Cuban X-Giants and Philadelphia Giants. One of the best games featured Williamsport's Johnny Lush's four-hit, 2-1 win over the X-Giants. Lush outpitched future Hall-of-Fame pitcher Andrew "Rube" Foster. Calling the X-Giants "the dusky demons," the *WG&B* proclaimed, "The Cuban X-Giants are the fastest team on their feet that has been seen here this year." Between 1904 and 1910, the black barnstorming teams were regular features of the exhibition slate before Williamsport opened its Tri-State League season.

The 1903 Billies etched a place in history as one of the city's strongest independent clubs ever to take the field. Its ranks included catchers Jerry Donovan and Frank Bevier; "Blondy" Jackson, Johnny Lush, Jack Maley, and "Rube" Bressler on the mound; Sandherr at shortstop; "Scoops" Scudder at first base; Lou Willig at second; Schultz at third; and Edgar Maitland, "Dutch" Clymer, and one of the pitchers in the outfield. Williamsport compiled a record of eighty-eight wins, thirty-eight losses, and one tie. In head-to-head competition with Major League clubs the locals lost to the St. Louis Americans 3-2, fell to Detroit (with Wild Bill Donovan pitching) 5-0, but defeated Brooklyn twice and tied the New York Giants 5-5. Rube Bressler established himself as a franchise player, compiling a 22-10 record as a pitcher—including a perfect game against Reading, 5 two-hitters, and a total of 8 shutouts. He also played right field and batted .364 over the course of 103 games.

Williamsport's strong showing in 1903 elevated the city into the elite membership of the newly established Tri-State League the following year. Its period of affiliation with this outlaw league (1904–10) constituted the golden age of baseball in Williamsport, replete with championship pennants and baseball lore.

Outlaws to Millionaires: The Tri-State League Years

The origin of the Tri-State League can be traced to a championship series sponsored by the *Philadelphia Inquirer* in 1903. Theodore A. Creamer, representing the paper, proposed a challenge-cup series in Philadelphia pitting representative clubs from the tri-state region of Delaware, New Jersey, and Pennsylvania. Wilmington, Camden, and Harrisburg (Williamsport's main rival) heeded the call. Over fourteen thousand fans witnessed Harrisburg's decisive win over Camden to notch the cup. The success of the series spurred Creamer and W. C. Farnsworth (an eminent Harrisburg attorney and baseball booster) to establish a new league encompassing the most profitable and successful independent baseball clubs in the Tri-State region. Plans were laid for a seven-team loop—Altoona, Williamsport, Harrisburg, York, Lebanon, Camden, and Wilmington—to begin play in 1904. When Farnsworth stepped down from the league presidency, he lent his name to the championship cup.

The fledgling league experienced the usual growing pains. Franchise instability

(Camden folded during the first season) and squabbles over revenue dominated the first year of operation. The surviving clubs drew splendidly at the gate for league games but suffered losses on the independent portion of their schedules. In 1905 the Tri-State League prohibited member teams from playing exhibition games until the conclusion of the championship series in early September—thereafter, clubs could schedule as many nonleague games as desired.

Though operating outside the National Baseball Agreement of 1903, the league modeled it schedule and financial arrangements after the Major Leagues. The new league distinguished itself by its lucrative spending and aggressive recruiting of baseball talent. Early on, "outlaw league" became synonymous with the Tri-State League. During its years of operation outside the organized baseball establishment (1904–7), the league became a thorn in the side of the Major Leagues and the NAPBL. Often dubbed the "third Major League," the Tri-State League, perhaps it is truer to say, presented the stiffest challenge to the big leagues until the formation of the short-lived Federal League in 1914.

Owners and boosters of Tri-State teams believed that they had every right to secure the highest caliber baseball talent that money could buy, irrespective of market size and the strictures of the NAPBL agreement. Though recognizing the principle of the sanctity of players' contracts among its own members, Tri-State League officers and team owners refused to honor Major League baseball's reserve clause. Tri-State teams raided the reserve lists of Major League clubs and the higher minors to stock their own rosters, in effect, inducing players to jump contracts. Contemporary observers, intimate with the league's financial and player transactions, noted that just as many Major League players jumped to join Tri-State teams as those who bolted the Tri-State for the Majors.

Players often exploited this window of free agency by fueling the bidding war for their services. The "Old Tymer," writing for the *WG&B* in later years, described how the baseball mercenaries operated:

> A favorite game in organized ball was for players to telegraph a Tri-State manager asking him what he would pay the sender of the telegram to jump from his team. If it brought a reply that reply was taken to the big league manager who had no knowledge of the original telegram, and it was presented to him as an offer to jump and was [almost always] accompanied by a request for more salary.

Because of the intense competition among teams to secure the best baseball talent, the Tri-State League legitimately earned the title of the "salary suicide circuit." One reporter of the day noted, "The league played big league ball and paid big league salaries." Tri-State owners and boosters spent lavish sums on their teams and gave their respective general managers carte blanche to pursue the Farnsworth Cup. Despite efforts to impose a salary cap, the baseball barons circumvented the spirit of the agreement by paying players additional sums for traveling, living expenses, and under-the-table bonuses. Initially, Altoona's railroad tycoons and Harrisburg's politicos matched the Billtown lumbermen dollar for dollar. But the spending gap became evident in later seasons when Williamsport financed championship caliber teams.

Williamsport's Tri-State opener against Lebanon occurred on May 5, 1904, as two thousand spectators rooted the locals to a 5-1 victory. Before the game, the city's Newton Band escorted the teams and city and club officials through the town's principal streets on the way to Athletic Park. At the park, "the teams marched down the baselines, met at second base, and came up to [the] grandstand in line." There, Mayor Laedlein officially opened the season by throwing out the first baseball. Opening Day parades and pennant celebrations became woven into the city's social fabric and remained so until the custom waned in the 1940s.

In their inaugural season the Williamsport Billies battled down to the wire for possession of the coveted Farnsworth Cup, but finished in second place behind York. The club roster included the nucleus of the previous season's state league entry: catchers Jerry "Ironman" Donovan and Barton; pitchers "Rube" Bressler, Johnny Lush, "Blondy" Jackson, and "Lurid Lou" Ritchie; and outfielders Edgar Maitland and Mullen. Completing the roster were pitchers McHale and McIlveen, Charley Moss at short, and Bob Lindemann, Curt Weigand (the team captain), and Mike Mowrey on the bases. Bressler achieved a respectable pitching record of 16-7 and batted .354 in seventy-one games.

The succeeding year produced one of the most memorable and exciting pennant races in all of organized baseball, attracting national attention in the press. In 1905 Williamsport's financial backers made a firm commitment to bring home the pennant and cup, and they spared no expense in scouting and procuring talent. Manager Max Lindheimer assumed the reins of the team and bolstered the roster with proven Major League players. Among them were the marquee pitcher Fred "Snitz" Applegate (later a member of the Philadelphia A's), the future Major League battery of Walter "Rube" Manning and catcher Walter Blair, and outfielder Bill Hinchman.

York, the front runner, had occupied first place for much of the 1905 season, with Williamsport ensconced in fourth place as late as August 12. By mid-season the White Roses had come under fire because of the use of hometown umpires and the short right-field fence of its home ballpark—tailormade to accommodate a heavy hitting left-handed lineup. When other teams fell from contention, their fans rallied behind the Billies as the league dark horse.

Frustrated by his team's failure to close ground on York, the Billies principal owner, J. Walton Bowman, instructed general manager Sheriff Thomas Gray to lure Jimmy Sebring from the Cincinnati Reds. Sebring, a slugging outfielder, had played for both the Reds and the Pittsburgh Pirates. He had gained some fame as the first player to hit a home run (for Pittsburgh) in the inaugural World Series of 1903. After severing ties with the Reds, Sebring signed a $1,000 contract to play the remainder of the season with Williamsport. The acquisition of Sebring inspired the team to play the greatest spurt of baseball ever witnessed by local fans. Sebring possessed what one scribe called "the essence of ginger, which he freely . . . imparted in large and small doses [to team-mates] before and after meals, and the medicine agreed with the players."

With Sebring on board in early August, Williamsport began an unprecedented pennant drive to overtake York. The pennant race began inauspiciously when the Billies won a hard-earned split of a doubleheader with the Roses on August 2. Thereafter, the Billies scorched opponents, winning thirty-five of forty-six games over a seven-week stretch. The team received superb fielding and timely hitting from Sebring (.329), Lush (.326), and Hinchman (.283). Moreover, the pitching rotation of Ritchie (24-9), Manning (17-11), and Lush (16-13) converged at the most opportune time. By league consensus, the Billies possessed the best pitching staff.

The pennant drive included several extra-inning affairs, most notably consecutive twelve- and fifteen-inning victories over Coatesville. Despite early defeats at the hands of the White Roses, Williamsport beat York (11-5) on September 8 (one week before the season's conclusion) to even the season series and dislodge the champions from first place. The Billies received additional support from the Johnstown club that had been a thorn in the side of York all season long. The Johnnies routed the Roses and quickly became one of the more popular visiting teams among area fans. When the dust settled the Billies finished a half-game, 78-46 (.629), ahead of Johnstown (78-47) (.624). York fell to third place. Because the Tri-State League did not sanction postseason playoff games, Williamsport won the Farnsworth Cup outright.

To mark the season's finale at Athletic Park, an overflow crowd estimated at 8,500 jammed the friendly confines to witness the unfurling of the pennant and formal presentation of the cup. Before the scheduled game with Harrisburg, city and club officials planned a massive celebration replete with an automobile parade led by the town's Repasz Band. Every owner of an automobile was urged to participate in this outpour of affection for the team. The *Grit* reported:

> Automobile row was so crowded that the motor carriages filled the roadway and overflowed way past center field. Beyond that a solid wall of humanity afoot, in carriages and every other way but horseback, stretched in a circle to the woods, where it met another equally large overflow. In front of the bleachers in both fields there were double rows of spectators sitting on the bank and on the grass, something never before seen in Athletic Park. Deadhead Hill was also occupied as never before and the usual array of delivery wagons afforded places of vantage to several scores of men and boys who either did not have the price of admission or did not want to spend it if they had it. But inside and out-side—on bleachers or in grandstands—in automobiles or carriages—there were Williamsporters with leather lungs ready to shout for the Champions at the proper time, or any other time.

Fig. 3 Williamsport's Athletic Park served as the home of the Williamsport Billies and Williamsport Millionaires during the halcyon years of the Tri-State League (1904–10). The Tri-State League played big league ball and paid big league salaries. (Postcard image, Lycoming County Historical Society)

Accompanied by band music, a procession led by Williamsport Athletic Association officials, manager Lindheimer, Tri-State League president Creamer, and W. C. Farnsworth marched to the center-field flag pole and grandstand area to raise the pennant and formally bestow the Farnsworth Cup upon the team. The pennant, "an exquisitely ornamented bunting of navy blue measuring 30 x 8 feet was unfurled with the inscription 'TRI-STATE CHAMPIONS—1905,' visible for miles." Whereupon, "ten thousand joyous whoops mingled in one and sent out a greeting which was heard in York, Altoona, Harrisburg, Johnstown, Shamokin, Wilmington, and Lancaster." N. Burrows Bubb, representing the Association stockholders, presented pitcher Rube Bressler and groundskeeper William Myers with gold watches; manager Lindheimer received a diamond ring. As a finale, Farnsworth formally presented the league cup to Bubb, and as the Repasz band played "There'll be a Hot Time in the Old Town Tonight," the crowd erupted in a frenzied cheer. Needless to say, the final game was anticlimactic, as the locals lost to Harrisburg 2-1 before a spent crowd.

Despite fielding an even stronger team in 1906, the "Millionaires"—so-renamed by the Harrisburg and Altoona sporting press because of the salaries it could pay its players—failed to repeat as champions, as the Yorkies captured the pennant. Nothing short of another championship would have placated the local kranks who could not fathom second place after the euphoric finish of 1905. Sebring shared player-manager responsibilities with Harry Wolverton. Additions to the 1906 roster were catcher Charles "Gabby" Street, pitchers Frank "Fiddler" Corridon and Frank Dessau, former Milwaukee first-baseman Bob Unglaub, "Kid" Charles at second, Harry "Rabbit" Gleason at short, Wolverton at third, and Joe Delahanty in left field. One of the highlights of the 1906 season was Rube Bressler's ironman performance in a sixteen-inning game against Johnstown in which he pitched eleven scoreless innings before losing a 2-1 decision. Charles set a record of nineteen put-outs without an error during the marathon. Bob Unglaub led the league in homers with fourteen and Joe Delahanty had seventeen triples to pace the league in that category.

Williamsport's ruthless bidding wars against other teams engendered much bitterness in the Tri-State League. In addition to signing Sebring, the Billies outbid the Reds and Boston for the services of Unglaub. The slugging first-baseman spurned a two-year contract offer of $4,500 from the Red Sox to earn more money with the Billies. Such extravagance united the league's other contenders against the Williamsport Millionaires. But the symbol of the top hat, cane, and white gloves soon became a badge of honor to Williamsport followers. Responding to the charge that the team's fiscal "rule or ruin" practices would ultimately bankrupt the Tri-State League, Williamsport's club directors countered that the signing of accomplished players enhanced the league's outlaw image and attracted fans to the ballpark. Williamsport had been one of the league's biggest drawing cards on the road. The Tri-State League later suffered a precipitous decline in attendance and revenue when the Millionaire team disbanded after the 1910 season.

While critics and opponents looked for signs of organizational weakness within the

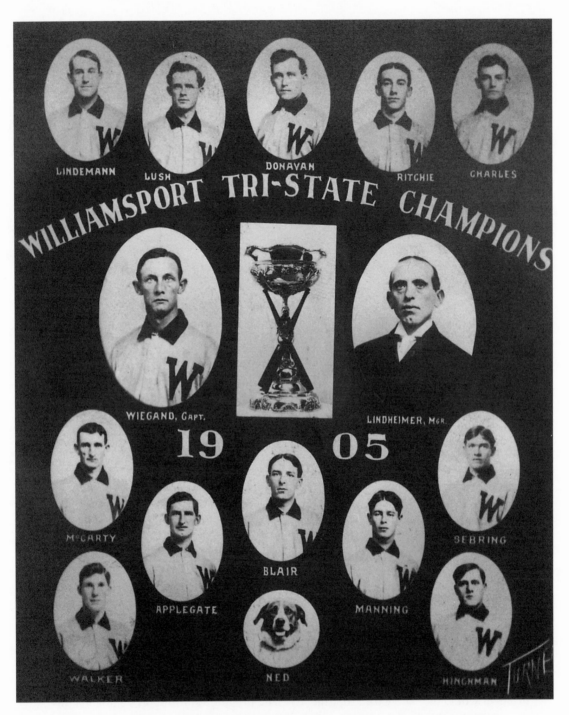

Fig. 4 Williamsport's 1905 Tri-State Championship team was captured in this unique cameo portrait. Fred "Snitz" Applegate, a city native, and Major League slugger Jimmy Sebring were members of the team. This portrait also included the Billies mascot "Ned," and the coveted Farnsworth Cup. (*Grit*)

Williamsport Millionaires, it soon became apparent that those teams unwilling to maintain high salaries would fall by the wayside. The Tri-State League's newer franchises displaced the bankrupted clubs and quickly gained parity with the free-spending Millionaires. Within a year, the hated White Roses of York folded and were replaced by Reading. In 1907, despite some mild protestations on the part of those owners who held out for favorable concessions, the Tri-State League returned to the fold of organized baseball by entering into the National Agreement. On the heels of the agreement came a movement by Williamsport's opponents to impose a salary cap on players and strict enforcement of the reserve clause. These measures were designed to circumscribe Williamsport's ability to lure players from other teams and leagues.

Concurrent with this development, it was widely reported in the baseball press that the Cincinnati club had made overtures to Wolverton and Unglaub to jump their Williamsport contracts. The *Cleveland Plain Dealer* printed the following account:

> Harry Wolverton, who is managing the Williamsport club, was . . . approached to quit the Tri-State, but he declined, and will once again handle the Portboys in 1907. Other offers of big salaries have been made to players in the [league] but in most cases they were turned down, the players apparently being satisfied to stick to the mining towns.

The Millionaires signed veteran players before the league's imposition of a salary cap and entered the 1907 season with a squad composed almost exclusively of former Major League players. The team had definite sights on recapturing the pennant. New pitchers Birdie Cree, Jimmy Whalen, Rube Vickers, and "Slim" Sallee anchored the rotation, while the infield was strengthened by the acquisition of Charles Wolverton (Harry's brother) and Mert Whitney. The "Erin outfield" of Tom O'Hara, Joe Delahanty, and Joe Hennessey complemented Sebring.

Harrisburg jumped out to an early lead in the standings but the Millionaires closed ranks as the season progressed. Steady pitching and the hitting of Wolverton, Delahanty, and O'Hara propelled the team past the Senators. This troika led the Tri-State in batting, hitting .359, .350, and .346, respectively. Pitcher Rube Vickers led the league in wins with twenty-five and Sallee topped the league in winning percentage with an outstanding 22-5 mark. Williamsport finished with a record of eighty-six wins and thirty-eight losses. Its winning percentage of .694 was nearly seventy points above the Senators' mark of .627. The championship was even more gratifying from the standpoint that the team had overcome injuries to the infield that had necessitated shifting players to secondary positions.

Williamsport celebrated its second Tri-State championship with nearly the same ardor as in 1905. Six thousand fans poured through the turnstiles of Athletic Park on September 14, 1907, to watch the Millionaires end the season with a victory over Lancaster by the score of 4-2. Once again, the Repasz Band led a parade through the city, attended by thousands who lined Pine, Third, and Fourth streets along the parade route. Charles F. Carpenter, the Tri-State League president, presented the blue pennant and Farnsworth Cup to N. Burrows Bubb and the Athletic Association. Upon receiving the cup and acknowledging the sustained cheering and applause, Bubb declared, "I hope the emblem of Tri-State supremacy would never have cause to leave the city." Manager Wolverton received a diamond ring valued at $500 from the Association's directors. The ceremony drew good-natured ribbing as Carpenter had fined manager Wolverton $100 and levied a two-week suspension earlier in the season. As a nightcap, Wolverton's boys attended a postseason banquet at the Alpha Hotel dining room, where music and drink flowed freely for the newly crowned champs.

After achieving two championships and two second-place finishes in four years, Williamsport faced numerous challenges heading into the 1908 campaign. The Tri-State League's ability to attract Major League talent was severely curtailed by the National Agreement that prevented minor league teams from raiding the Major League reserve lists. Tri-State League managers faced the prospect of depleted rosters and diminished talent; owners braced themselves for a decline at the gate. Major William P. Clarke, Williamsport's leading baseball authority, feared such a dilution of talent. Before the Tri-State League entered into the National Agreement, he believed that any member team had a legitimate chance to compete with the Majors for the services of players. He opined that the number of former Tri-State players placed on the Majors' reserve list could have stocked a new eight-team Major League. Would fans, accustomed to a higher caliber of baseball, still support their teams? Local sports editorialists argued that fans had grown so accustomed to seeing the highest caliber of play that any dilution of talent might cost teams at the gate.

Williamsport was particularly affected by the peace with the Major Leagues, having only one third-baseman and one outfielder under contract from the 1907 championship team. Moreover, the outstanding battery of Rube Manning and Walter Blair left to join the New York Highlanders at the end of the season. Without a nucleus, Wolverton assembled a new team composed of veterans on the downhill slide and youngsters long on potential, but short on skill and professional experience. His ability as a crafty judge of baseball talent enabled the Millionaires to field a highly competitive team in line with the new salary structure and player transaction restrictions imposed upon the Tri-State.

Hit by drafts and the selling of players to the Major Leagues, Williamsport suffered through a horrible first month of the 1908 season. The new players—Townsend, Ollie Britton, Dave Shean, George Cockill, Foster, Jack Flater, Jack Warhop, and Edgar Maitland—failed to adjust to their new surroundings. However, Wolverton succeeded in re-signing Cree to join the stalwarts O'Hara and Hennessey in the outfield. By early June, the newspapers in Altoona, Harrisburg, and Lancaster had all but buried the Millionaires. However, no front-runner emerged and the league lead changed several times in the course of the early season.

Within a month, Williamsport crawled from fourth place to grab the lead from Harrisburg on July 10, a lead that it never relinquished on the way to the team's third Tri-State title in five years. Cockill, fresh from the Bucknell University varsity baseball team, played exceptionally well at first base, while Harry Wolverton, the player-manager, captured the batting crown with a hefty .349 average. The Millionaires pitching staff was led by Jack Warhop (who won a season-high twenty-nine games) and Flater. Both kept the club afloat during the early part of the season. By all accounts, the 1908 Williamsport team was what Major William P. Clarke called a "second-division bunch" that had overcome adversity through hustle and heady play.

The 1908 pennant celebration was a more subdued affair. The celebration attracted a smaller crowd of five thousand and there was no Farnsworth Cup presentation as the Millionaires possessed the coveted prize from the previous season. After the parade to Athletic Park and the raising of the pennant, Williamsport's most famous bandleader and musician, John Hazel ("the Wizard Cornetist"), serenaded a hushed crowd with two ballads, "The Wearing of the Green" and "Love's Old Sweet Song." Wolverton received a cut-glass punch bowl from the Millionaires directors, and the venerable Frank Bowman received a gold cigar from the players. For the first time in recent years, the Tri-State president failed to attend the festivities. It was a harbinger of things to come.

The years 1907–8 were the high-water mark of Williamsport's affiliation with the Tri-State. Unfortunately, success and familiarity bred contempt. Other league members, with Harrisburg and Altoona in the vanguard, initiated a campaign to legislate Williamsport out of the loop. Clubs pooled their resources to monitor Williamsport's player transactions and followed any rumor or innuendo involving the illegal procurement of players and under-the-table payments that violated the new salary cap. They found their opportunity in 1909.

Williamsport's prospects for 1909 looked uncertain as a new manger, Bill Coughlin, assumed the helm of the Millionaires. Again there was very little carry-over in terms of personnel, and the club immediately had to rebuild under the stringent guidelines of the league salary cap. The club signed retreads Applegate, Britton, "Red" Porter, and Townsend as pitchers. Applegate, no longer able to throw his fastball, was released and signed by Wilkes-Barre. Williamsport's one bright pitching prospect was Ralph "Sailor" Stroud, who posted a record of 20-10 in the 1909 campaign and later became an established Major Leaguer in New York. The Millionaires were led by first-baseman Pete Lister (a former member of the Cleveland Indians), who captured the Tri-State batting crown with an average of .350 in 116 games. Virgil Cannell and Tom O'Hara tied for the league lead in hits with 145. The club as a whole finished second in the league in batting average (.273) and club fielding. Thick in the pack of a four-way chase for the pennant, Williamsport became embroiled in a league investigation that resulted in the forfeiture of five games, and any chance of capturing another Farnsworth Cup.

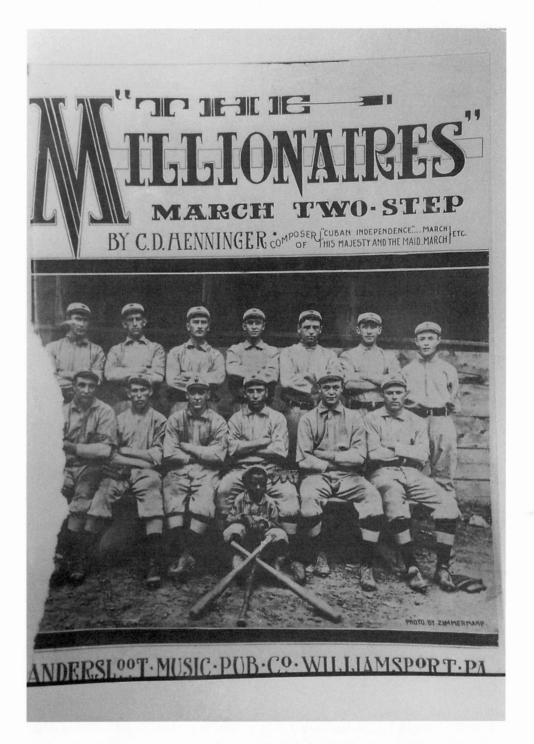

Fig. 5 To celebrate the Williamsport Millionaires championship season of 1908, C. D. Henninger composed "The Millionaires March Two-Step," and approached the Vandersloot Music Publishing Company to produce and sell the sheet music. This is the only surviving image of the 1908 Tri-State champions. (James V. Brown Library)

Fig. 6 The opening of a new baseball season was always cause for celebration in Williamsport. This image captures the 1909 Opening Day festivities at Athletic Park, with the 1908 Tri-State Championship Pennant proudly on display. (*Grit*, Courtesy of the *Williamsport Sun-Gazette*)

The ruling by Tri-State League president Carpenter stemmed from an incident that became known as the "Crane affair." A young free agent named Crane had contacted the Williamsport club, hoping to sign a lucrative contract well above the salary cap imposed by the league. In order to give the player a trial, one team booster (not a club official) agreed to pay Crane a supplemental bonus to cover incidental travel and housing expenses until a contract was issued. When Crane was released to Harrisburg, he immediately registered an official complaint with the president's office. Though Williamsport claimed it had no "official financial contact" with Crane, a league investigation concluded that the spirit of the salary cap had been violated. Though the Tri-State rules specifically imposed a fine for such infractions, the league saw fit to impose a five-game forfeiture on the Millionaires. Effectively eliminated from pennant contention, the Millionaires finished the season in third place.

The cumulative animosity generated by the Crane affair, combined with declining attendance and rising operational costs, cast a pall over the 1910 season. Success on the field did not automatically balance the club's account ledger, and annual debts accumulated. Despite large crowds of 3,000 to 4,000 for important games with Harrisburg and Altoona, Williamsport's average game attendance hovered around 1,500—remarkably on par with the attendance figures for the present-day Williamsport franchise. Seldom did the Williamsport Athletic Club stockholders break even on their investment.

The 1910 team made a spirited chase for the Tri-State title but ended a distant third behind Altoona and Lancaster. Indicative of the team's misfortune was the broken arm suffered by Coughlin (the player-manager) only thirty-five games into the season. Veteran Jack Stansbury replaced Coughlin at third base for the remainder of the season. Other team members included Tony Marhefka at shortstop; Keister at second; Virgil "Rip" Cannell, Weeks, and Madigan in the outfield; George Therre behind the plate; and Jack Ness at first. Cannell won the Tri-State batting title hitting .355, and tied for the league lead in hits with 129. Among the pitchers, Ollie Britton stood out, winning sixteen games and losing fourteen.

By 1910 Williamsport's baseball talent pool had dried up. Moreover, constant friction with the Tri-State League and the poor financial state of the franchise dissipated the will of the Millionaires directors. In November the *WG&B* reported that the directors had put up the Williamsport franchise for sale at the price of $3,000, "carrying with it the players under contract and reserve." The public bid did not include a stipulation requiring the potential buyer to maintain the franchise within the city. Citing rising costs and declining fan support, Millionaires president J. Walton Bowman declared:

> The action taken by the board last week does not mean that the men on it will have nothing whatever to do with baseball in the future . . . we are simply tired of running the team. In the first place we are weary of having to face constant deficits. Each one of us put in money at the beginning of the season, most of us a little more in the middle, and then we have to go down in our pockets to make up the deficit at the end. This latter feature is what we are tired of. Williamsport has not supported a team as it should have, especially in the last two or three years.

Thus ended the city's most successful era of minor league professional baseball. While famous players and other championship teams later represented the city under the banner of the New York–Pennsylvania League (NYPL) and Eastern League (EL), they did not rival the level of competition and excitement that Williamsport fans experienced during the city's membership in the outlaw Tri-State League. The level of play during the years of Tri-State affiliation (1904–10) was perhaps the best in the city's illustrious minor league history. During its seven-year membership in the league, the Millionaires captured three pennants, finished second twice, and never fell below .500 in the final standings. Many established Major League players and future stars dotted the rosters of the Billies and Millionaires from 1904 to 1910. If Williamsport can legitimately claim the title of Gateway to the Majors, that title was certainly earned during the golden years of the Tri-State League.

Trolley League and Boomer Baseball

Between 1911 and 1923 amateur and corporate-sponsored baseball enjoyed a resurgence in Williamsport. In the absence of the professional game, the city Trolley League, Pennsylvania Railroad League, and church-sponsored baseball attracted a wide following. Similar to the decade of the 1890s, amateur and semipro baseball monopolized the city's baseball landscape. Trolley League games spawned popular team rivalries and generated much fan interest. The Railroad League's popular Grand Division Championship Series attracted crowds that often exceeded the attendance figures of the old Tri-State League games. This level of support motivated the old baseball boosters, especially J. Walton Bowman, to open up their checkbooks once again in the pursuit of a professional baseball franchise for the city. Williamsport's eventual return to the minor league fold in 1923 was a direct outgrowth of the highly competitive Pennsylvania Railroad League.

Though dormant during the Tri-State era, semiprofessional and corporate-sponsored baseball flourished in Williamsport during the second decade of the twentieth century. Sandlot veterans from the 1890s played a prominent role in the organization of new teams, the establishment of new leagues, and the procurement of playing fields and sponsors. Sheriff Joseph Mertz, a former ballplayer, was arguably the leading figure associated with the revival of amateur baseball. Following the collapse of the Millionaires, Mertz organized and managed the Vallamont Athletics, a team that "took on all sandlot [comers] in the district" ("The Old Tymer," *WG&B*). In 1912 Mertz took his Vallamonts into the Trolley League along with several of the city's best amateur ball clubs. The Trolley League operated from 1912 to 1916, with J. J. Heinz as president and W. Herbert Poff as secretary-treasurer. League members included Newberry, the Hermance Machine Company, the Brandons, and Montoursville. Later, West End replaced Hermance and South Side took the place of Montoursville when that team folded.

Though not on par with the great Tri-State League, competition within the Trolley League was nevertheless intense. The Newberry–West End series of 1914 generated much excitement within the city as large crowds flocked to the Grier Street diamond (located on the present-day corner of Grier and High Streets) to root on the team of choice. Trolley League teams recruited the best local high school and college talent available and added a few seasoned veterans to balance out their respective rosters. Because teams played only one game a week (Saturday morning), most relied upon one pitching ace and a lone reliever. Trolley League stars included: Jim Dugan of Newberry, Pete Godfrey of the Brandons, Ray Hanner representing the West End, Bill McVaugh of South Side, "Blondy" Strauss of Montoursville, and "Weldy" Wyckoff. Wyckoff later pitched for the Philadelphia A's and the Boston Red Sox in the Major Leagues.

After 1916 the baseball scene shifted to the new Williamsport High School Athletic Field, located at the corner of West Third and Susquehanna Streets. There, city league and company-sponsored teams revived the old rough-and-tumble rivalries of the 1890s. The Keystone team, city champions in 1917, acquired the services of old Tri-State veterans—Gabby Street and Rube Manning—in the county championship series against the Jersey Shore Centrals. The Industrial League and West Branch League were also established in 1917 and 1918, respectively. Around that time, the Pennsylvania Railroad League (PRL) emerged as the preeminent baseball league in the region. The PRL consisted of teams and players recruited by the various divisions of the Pennsylvania Railroad. In 1919 Williamsport's "Pennsy" team brought home its first Central Grand Division Railroad title.

Other prominent company-sponsored teams included the Lycoming Foundry, the United States Rubber Company (named the Keds), and Lycoming Motors. These teams featured many prominent players and boosters later associated with Williamsport minor league baseball—Max Bishop, Joe Boley, Clyde Barnhart, Roy Clunk, Jack Walton, and Joseph Mosser. Semipro baseball reached its zenith in 1920 when Williamsport's railroad team won the system-wide PRL championship and Lycoming Motors swept through its independent schedule with other regional corporate teams. In a challenge series played before crowds estimated at upward of five thousand, Lycoming swept the railroad boomers in three straight games.

No series, however, captured the interest and passion of Williamsport fans more than the Pennsylvania Railroad's Grand Division Championship series, particularly when Williamsport was involved. The PRL championship series provided a much-needed diversion in the wake of World War I and the Black Sox scandal of 1919. Perhaps the greatest game ever played within the city pitted Williamsport against the Pitcairn team of Altoona for the Grand Division Championship of 1920. Before an estimated crowd of ten thousand that engulfed the High School Athletic Field, Williamsport defeated the visitors in a riveting 1-0 game dominated by superb pitching. With the victory, the city's railroad team captured the PRL's President's Cup—symbolic of baseball suprem-acy "east, west, north and south, or any other old way" (*WG&B*). Bands representing the two communities ignited their respective fans to unprecedented noise levels during the entire contest. Afterward, the Williamsport marching band celebrated the victory with a procession down Third Street into the heart of town. Photographs of the victori-ous team, as well as a movie picture of the cup presentations, were made for posterity.

The railroad championship series of 1920 once again renewed fan interest for professional minor league baseball. And many former baseball directors and boosters associated with the Millionaires teams of the Tri-State era recognized that the longing and support for professional ball remained strong. They intended to secure a permanent professional baseball franchise for the city. In 1923 they got their chance with an offer to join the New York–Pennsylvania League.

2

Boosters, Promoters, and Promotions

 In a tradition that dated back to the 1870s, Williamsport's semipro and professional minor league teams received financial backing from local prominent businessmen and civic boosters. Lumber barons and financiers associated with the area's largest industrial concerns were among the earliest baseball boosters. Several well-known civic figures—among them Peter Herdic Jr., R. H. Crum, J. Walton Bowman, Frank Bowman, and N. Burrows Bubb—laid the groundwork and financed the professional teams that represented the city during the late nineteenth and early twentieth centuries. These influential investors spent lavishly on baseball, starting with their support of semipro teams and culminating in the "free-market spending" associated with Williamsport's Tri-State League teams. Though later baseball promoters were not as profligate, they carried on the tradition of covering the financial shortfall when franchises teetered on the brink of collapse.

Boosters

Despite the popular perception to the contrary, few if any of the early professional teams returned sufficient profit to justify the exorbitant sums of money invested in baseball. The question begs, why did so many prominent citizens invest in the endeavor? Clearly, the spirit of philanthropy and civic pride motivated them, as epitomized by Chamber of Commerce president Carl Williner's remarks celebrating his organization's booster night at Bowman Field on August 18, 1926:

> The Chamber of Commerce with the cooperation of public spirited men brought about the organization of the Williamsport Baseball Club. The public often fails to recognize the necessity of ample entertainment features for the people of this city. The Williamsport Baseball Club was organized to meet this need. It was not the expectation of the organizers to look for profit but to furnish high-class baseball games. This they do as a rule. The new baseball park [Memorial Field] was financed by these same public spirited men, not for their own personal profit, but for the advertising and entertainment value to the city. . . . A venture of this kind must be self-supporting if it is to continue the class of entertainment desired.

When the Williamsport Baseball Club entered the New York–Pennsylvania League (NYPL) as a charter member in 1923, the team inherited two of the principal backers associated with the old Williamsport Millionaires of the Tri-State League era, J. Walton Bowman and Sheriff Thomas Gray. Both men represented Williamsport at the charter meeting of the NYPL held in Binghamton, New York, in March 1923. They were prime movers in coordinating business and community support for Williamsport's entry into the league and marshalling the organizational talent needed to operate a minor league franchise. Gray also assisted NYPL president John Farrell in establishing the league on firm footing.

Appointed Lycoming County deputy sheriff in 1902, and elected sheriff outright in 1919, Gray achieved distinction as a fair-minded and even-tempered law enforcement administrator. He was an influential member of the State Republican Committee and one of Williamsport's most respected civic leaders. Despite his immersion in daily political and municipal affairs, Gray devoted much energy to securing the city's future in professional baseball. He served as secretary-treasurer of the Williamsport Millionaire team during its entire period of affiliation with the Tri-State League, from 1904 to 1910. Under his administration, Williamsport gained a reputation as one of the best operated (if over-financed) professional ball clubs in the league.

Gray's contribution to Williamsport baseball history was duly noted after his premature death (of a heart attack) in August 1923. Among the many tributes paid to him, perhaps none exemplified his legacy more than a *Williamsport Gazette & Bulletin*

(*WG&B*) sports editorial entitled, "Baseball's Tribute to Tom Gray." It read in part, "No baseball history of the city will ever be written in which 'Tom' will not have a commanding place . . . no more fitting tribute can be paid him than to say he knew baseball thru and thru and was as big and clean as the game which ranks unchallenged as the national game."

The ultimate posthumous tribute to Gray came in the spring of 1924 when the *WG&B* sponsored a contest to name the new Williamsport baseball club. On May 10, 1924, following the submission of 197 different nicknames, the baseball club adopted "Grays" in honor of the deceased sheriff. That team name (with only a few minor exceptions owing to periodic affiliation changes) survived until 1962.

J. Walton Bowman also occupies a secure place in Williamsport's baseball pantheon. One of the chief financial backers of Williamsport's old Tri-State League team, he championed the return of professional baseball in Williamsport in 1923. Bowman accumulated a fortune as a wealthy lumber dealer, manufacturer, and banker, and had the distinction of purchasing the first automobile in Williamsport in 1899. He was an active member of the Williamsport Masonic Order and an accomplished cornet player. Bowman founded the Imperial Teteques Band, one of the earliest Masonic bands in America. A devoted sports enthusiast and former cyclist, he channeled his competitive energies into securing professional baseball for the city.

In 1926 Bowman became president of the Williamsport Baseball Club and spearheaded the construction of the Memorial Park ballfield that would later bear his name. He also provided the funds to balance the club's financial ledger in lean years. Unlike Gray, Bowman received deserved recognition before his death. On June 26, 1929, Memorial Field was formally renamed and dedicated in his honor as "Bowman Field." When he passed away on February 14, 1931, Bowman received fulsome praise from the Williamsport Grays club directors and the local press. The Grays directors issued a statement that declared: "Baseball in Williamsport has suffered the loss of its sincerest friend and staunchest supporter in J. Walton Bowman." An editorial appearing in the February 16, 1931, edition of the *WG&B* read in part:

> His love for baseball was an outstanding trait, and it was due to him more than any other one man that Williamsport was and is represented in the New York–Pennsylvania League. He keenly enjoyed the national pastime and it was because of this enjoyment that he wished his friends and acquaintances, and all others so inclined to enjoy it also.

Bowman and Gray united diverse business and civic groups, and possessed the financial acumen to operate professional baseball in the city. Moreover, they established the administrative model adopted by later directors to guide the affairs of Williamsport's minor league clubs down to the present day. It is impossible within the limited scope of

Fig. 7 Sheriff Thomas Gray, influential civic leader, baseball administrator, and namesake of the Williamsport Grays. Gray guided Williamsport into the professional Class B New York–Pennsylvania League in 1923. (*Grit,* Courtesy of the *Williamsport Sun-Gazette*)

this book to mention all the people responsible for making professional baseball a success in the city. However, a number of prominent individuals merit discussion.

Nathaniel Burrows Bubb, businessman, entrepreneur, and former secretary of the Williamsport Board of Trade (forerunner of the Chamber of Commerce) was counted among the city's millionaire baseball boosters. As vice-president of Williamsport's Tri-State League team, he (along with Frank and J. Walton Bowman) contributed to the pot that secured the high-caliber players needed to compete in the salary suicide circuit. Bubb served as Williamsport's first club president when it entered the New York–Pennsylvania League in 1923, and held that post until his death on January 19, 1925.

Irvin W. and James B. Gleason were also substantial contributors to Williamsport baseball and took active roles in the administration of ball clubs—especially during the Great Depression. The Gleason family had earned a fortune in the leather tanning busi-

Fig. 8 (Left to right) Grays manager Glenn Killinger, club president J. Walton Bowman, and business manager J. Roy Clunk. Bowman was Williamsport's most prominent booster and investor in minor league baseball from 1900 to 1930. He established the Municipal Athletic Field Corporation to fund the construction of the ballpark that today still bears his name. (*Grit*)

ness and subsequently sold its tannery to the Armour Leather Company in 1917. Irvin Gleason was noted for his involvement in community affairs, and in 1942 received a *Grit* meritorious community service award for his lifetime dedication to bettering Williamsport. James, his younger brother, patented the Gleason leather polishing machines used in tanneries throughout the world. Both shared a passion for sports, particularly horses and horse racing, and gained national prominence as champion horse breeders. The Gleasons were among the business associates whom J. Walton Bowman approached to finance the construction of Memorial Field in 1926. Over the next two decades, the brothers tapped the family coffers to support the local baseball team.

James Gleason took a more active role in the daily operations of the Williamsport ball club than his brother. As club president from 1934 to 1940, he presided over the team's transition from an independent entity (purchasing player contracts from various major and minor league organizations to stock the team) to a de facto farm organization of the Philadelphia A's. Gleason remained a faithful backer of Grays baseball until his death on September 4, 1960, four days after his beloved Grays won their first Eastern League pennant since 1934—ironically, the first year of his presidency of the ballclub. J. Roy Clunk, long-time business manager of the Grays, remarked on Gleason, "When Jim was president he ran the whole thing and when he wasn't listed as president he was the big man behind the scenes. He was good for baseball." The *Williamsport Sun-Gazette* (*WS-G*) editorial on his passing stated, "His interest in baseball never waned and Williamsport owes much to Mr. Gleason for its reputation in this sport. Often he dug into his own pocket to sustain the sport."

The story of Max Jaffe, a Russian immigrant and rabbi's son, is the quintessential American success story. Arriving in America in 1894, the Jaffe family later settled in Williamsport. After finishing public school, Jaffe entered the clothing trade and established a business partnership with S. E. Ullman. In 1923 Jaffe formed his own business, Jaffe's Men's Store, Williamsport's premier men's clothing store. He also was instrumental in founding one of Williamsport's largest furniture stores—Wahl-Braun Furniture—that served area consumers for many decades.

Jaffe was among the original group of merchant-industrialists who launched the Grays in 1923. In addition to the outlay of capital, he contributed his considerable marketing and promotional acumen to the stewardship of Grays baseball. Irving "Bud" Jaffe, Max Jaffe's son, reminisced about the sales pitch that J. Walton Bowman made to his father, "Mr. Bowman once said he would give of his money if his friend Max would give of his time and his talent. They made a great pair." Jaffe became president of the Grays in 1933 and initiated many novel promotions that later became staples of Williamsport baseball and minor league baseball in general. Among Jaffe's firsts were the creation in 1933 of the "Knot-Hole Gang"—whereby boys fourteen years and under were admitted into games for free—and the inaugural Ladies Day, Boosters Day, and Bat Day promotions. He remained active in club affairs until his retirement to Florida in 1940. Jaffe passed away on November 23, 1966, at the age of eighty-two.

In terms of longevity and energy, few boosters rivaled Joseph H. Mosser. Rankin Johnson Jr., former Eastern League president, characterized Mosser as "the real backbone of baseball in Williamsport and a real credit to the Eastern League and to the game itself." Mosser's family had owned a lucrative tannery company (J. K. Mosser Tannery) before selling the business (like the Gleasons) to the Armour Leather Company. He then established his own tannery, the Joseph H. Mosser Leather Company. Mosser had attended Penn State University on a football scholarship and later played semiprofessional football on various Sunday town teams. Mosser participated in many civic activities and was a prominent figure in Pennsylvania Republican Party circles.

Mosser was also one of the original investors in the 1923 Grays. He coordinated

Fig. 9 The Williamsport Grays club directors met in March 1933 to pledge their continued support of the team despite heavy financial losses the previous season. Seated in the front row were the team's principal shareholders: (L–R) Edward Bullock, Tommy Richardson, Pat Thorne, J. Roy Clunk, and Max Jaffe. (*Grit*)

many key promotions vital to the stability of the Williamsport franchise and was also a skilled fundraiser in the construction campaign for Memorial Field. Mosser's persistence earned him the moniker "Groundskeeper." As he recalled, "I took such great pride in helping to lay out the new field that the fellows referred to me as Groundskeeper."

Though he often remained in the background, Mosser was often cited by insiders for his many contributions to the ballclub. Mosser's able administration of the Grays' financial affairs allowed the club to weather the Great Depression, the war years, and the downside of minor league baseball in the 1950s. Through it all he remained a believer in Williamsport's future in professional minor league baseball when others doubted the city's ability to support a franchise. Dubbed "Mr. Baseball" by local sportswriters in the 1950s, Mosser shunned the spotlight and was refreshingly unpretentious about his efforts on behalf of the game. He once remarked, "We're playing baseball, that's all that counts. What I have done means nothing to the fans. They want to see baseball."

Until his death on March 31, 1964, Mosser remained active in baseball administration. He served as honorary chairman of the Bowman Field Commission, the body established to administer the ballpark. William "Bill" Pickelner (long-time baseball booster and associate of Mosser) noted that "Without a doubt he was the greatest fan Williamsport baseball, in particular, and the Eastern League, in general, ever had. He was the most generous supporter ever known through the years. The figure would stagger you if known."

In the modern era, William "Bill" Pickelner has inherited Mosser's title as Williamsport's "Mr. Baseball." A successful coal and fuel oil magnate, civic philanthropist, and sports enthusiast, Pickelner has been synonymous with Williamsport minor league baseball over the past fifty-plus years. When the city rejoined the Eastern League for a brief period (1987–91), civic leaders named the new team the "Bills," in honor of Pickelner's contributions to Williamsport baseball over the decades.

Pickelner's passion for sports found an outlet in his sponsorship of local amateur baseball and softball teams, and his ownership of the Williamsport Billies professional basketball franchise of the old Eastern Basketball League. Moreover, his brother, Louis Pickelner, had been sports editor of the *WG&B* for many years. Above all, Pickelner loved Williamsport and minor league baseball. He spent much of his youth within the confines of Bowman Field during the heyday of the Eastern League.

An avid fan of the Williamsport Grays since the early 1920s, Pickelner became active in the affairs of the club during the late 1940s by his participation in B'nai B'rith Night—one of the biggest promotions of the baseball season. He later gained membership in the Community Baseball Association, a prominent booster organization that promoted and managed professional baseball in Williamsport. Pickelner also was a charter member of the Bowman Field Commission, the advisory body established in 1957 to oversee Bowman Field. He remains an active member of the commission. As chairman, Pickelner's counsel on matters pertaining to the ballpark and franchise has been invaluable in keeping minor league baseball alive in Williamsport. When the Nine-County Baseball Booster Association was formed in 1959 (the nonprofit organization that operated the Williamsport franchise), Pickelner served as its first president. This group guided Williamsport's minor league baseball affairs until 1972.

Over the years, Pickelner cultivated friendships and close working relationships with several Major League executives and front office personnel—particularly the Mets and Phillies—in an effort to bring professional baseball to Williamsport. His persistence and power of persuasion frequently paid off. When the city lost its working agreement with the Philadelphia Phillies at the end of the 1962 season, Pickelner negotiated a working agreement with the New York Mets for the 1964 season and beyond. After the depar-

Fig. 10 On the mend from hip surgery, the legendary Casey Stengel (second from left) headed a Mets delegation to Williamsport in January 1966 as part of the Winter Banquet program to promote the Williamsport Mets. William "Bill" Pickelner (third from right), chairman of the Nine-County Booster Association, arranged for the visit. (*Grit*)

ture of the Mets in 1967, he persuaded Erie businessman Joe Romano to relocate his New York–Penn League franchise to Williamsport in 1968.

Pickelner's dream of returning Class AA Eastern League baseball to Williamsport was finally achieved in the period from 1987 to 1991. With the relocation of the Waterbury franchise to Williamsport, and subsequent affiliations with the Indians, Mariners, and Mets, Williamsport enjoyed one last fling with the historic circuit. Following the 1991 season and the departure of the Mets, Pickelner initiated the hunt for a short-season Class A team to occupy Bowman Field, resulting in the move of the Geneva Cubs franchise to Williamsport in 1994. He continues to play a major role in galvanizing community support and financial resources for the maintenance of Bowman Field and minor league baseball in Williamsport. Pickelner remains the most important link in the long chain of philanthropic boosters who have given freely of their time and money to promote baseball within the community.

Promoters

While the city has always been blessed with men of financial means willing to field a ballclub for local fans, it has also drawn upon a local pool of baseball executives to administer the game. One of the more talented business managers was Robert "Bob" Steinhilper. Steinhilper started out as a newspaperman, working as the *WS-G's* sports editor for fifteen years, and later as city editor of the *WS-G*. In 1947 he was named business manager for the Williamsport Tigers and served in the same capacity when the Philadelphia A's took over Williamsport's working agreement in 1953. His tenure spanned the postwar boom period of minor league baseball until the early 1950s, when the game suffered due to competition with televised Major League baseball.

Steinhilper was imaginative and resourceful with respect to promotions, the lifeline of any successful minor league operation. He worked closely with various community groups and leaders to foster support for the special promotional nights—B'nai B'rith and Boosters Nights—that kept the Williamsport franchise on even keel during minor league baseball's downswing. Though the Williamsport Tigers and A's were perennial second-division dwellers, Steinhilper worked hard to maintain respectable attendance figures. In 1948 Williamsport drew more than 100,000 fans, one of only four seasons in the history of the franchise to draw as many. His considerable newspaper experience proved beneficial in promoting the team. Sportswriter Mike Bernardi noted, "He [Steinhilper] knew exactly what information a sportswriter sought and made sure that it was available to him." Steinhilper also founded the Williamsport Booster Club, one of the earliest fan-based organizations that supported both the parent Detroit Tigers and their Williamsport farmhands.

Noted for his compassion in a cutthroat business, Steinhilper often had the onerous task of releasing ballplayers. Rankin Johnson, who played for Williamsport during the 1940s, recalled how Steinhilper handled his own release in 1947:

> I was coming to the end of my career as a pitcher in 1947 when I was with the Grays. At the end of the season Bob called me into his office and gave me my release. It hurt him badly to do it. He showed it. I could sense it. Many times before I'd been released or sent down to a lower league. The business manager never showed any emotion. Bob did that night at Bowman Field. I [knew] that I was through and I felt badly that Bob hated the assignment of releasing me. He had a lot of feeling for his players. He is one of the best men that I have ever met in my career in baseball.

Steinhilper's efforts on behalf of the Tigers resulted in his advancement up the minor league ladder to Buffalo, New York, and Charleston, West Virginia. Finally, the parent Tigers rewarded Steinhilper with a front-office job in the ticket promotion department. He later became the assistant director of public relations for the Tigers. Steinhilper

Fig. 11   In 1947 Williamsport's love affair with baseball was the subject of a feature photo shoot courtesy of _Life Magazine_. This unique image shows all the city's youth leagues assembled on the diamond with the Williamsport Tigers and the team's administrative officers. (Putsee Vannucci Collection, Lycoming County Historical Society)

received high praise from many Tigers officials, including general manager Jim Campbell. He pursued his job with the Tigers in the same quiet professional manner that he had done in previous posts. Steinhilper succumbed to a fatal heart attack at his Tiger Stadium office on June 3, 1967, at the age of fifty-nine.

The cigar-chomping J. Roy Clunk was one of Williamsport's most durable and venerable business managers. He spent nearly a half-century in organized baseball as a player, manager, and executive, guiding the Grays front office, off and on, from 1927 to 1961. Clunk played professional baseball for Jersey City in 1909, and had been a member of various teams in the Virginia, South Atlantic, and Southeastern Leagues. He then embarked upon a managerial career with Knoxville in the Appalachian League, Hanover in the Blue Ridge League, and Gulfport in the Cotton States League. In 1918 Lycoming Motors recruited Clunk to manage its semipro baseball team in the City Industrial League. Several future Major League standouts—Joe Boley, George "Mule" Haas, Max Bishop, and Clyde Barnhart—cut their baseball teeth under Clunk's tutelage. Clunk produced several championship teams in the City League and in 1922 managed Williamsport's entry in the old Pennsylvania Railroad League.

Clunk became business manager of the Williamsport Grays in 1927 and quickly acquired a reputation as one of the most parsimonious members of the Grays front office. It was, however, a temperament sorely needed during the Depression and in later years when minor league baseball experienced periodic financial trouble. His thrift was legendary. In an interview given to sportswriter Ray Keyes (portions of which were published in Keyes's tribute to Clunk following the latter's death on November 9, 1961), Clunk embellished upon his ability to operate a ball club on a shoestring budget:

> We didn't have any money in those days. We had to skimp. I'd get mileage out of the baseball though. I'd take beat-up balls home, shine 'em up and soak 'em in milk and keep them overnight in the refrigerator. The other clubs thought we were using new balls.

Many local fans fondly recall Clunk's obsession with foul balls. In order to reduce expenses, he tried to induce fans to return foul balls and home runs with the promise of a ticket to a future game. Failing that, he grudgingly attempted to buy the ball back from the fan for the lowest possible price. Clunk loathed freeloaders. For daring fans not afraid of heights, the trees behind Bowman Field's left-field fence afforded an excellent viewing point to watch a baseball game for free. They were a source of constant irritation to Clunk who once tried to cut the trees down even though they were on private property. Above all, he detested giveaway nights and "freebie" promotions that became instant fan favorites and a staple of today's game. However, he was savvy enough to realize that such promotions contributed to a profitable franchise.

Clunk was reputed to be one of the most astute judges of baseball talent, no doubt a by-product of his earlier managing and playing days. Ray Keyes remarked that "men like the Gleasons, the Bowmans, and the Mossers poured money into the operation but it was Clunk who made sure that the money was spent wisely." Clunk possessed an encyclopedic knowledge of organized baseball's regulations and guidelines involving player contracts and transactions. He ran a tight-fisted organization and rarely made unfavorable trades that hurt the Grays. Under Clunk's stewardship, Williamsport was one of the most financially stable organizations in the Eastern League.

Despite his immersion in baseball, Clunk had other interests as well. An accomplished cigar-maker (a skill handed down from his father), he established a cottage industry in a small building near the back of his house that he maintained until a few years before his death. His son-in-law, former Williamsport Grays and Philadelphia A's pitcher Emil Roy, helped him market the cigars in New York City.

When Williamsport lost its franchise in 1943, Clunk became business manager of the Elmira Pioneers—a post that he held until the end of the 1940s. He returned to Williamsport in 1954 but was replaced the following year by a new general manager within the Pirates organization, Williamsport's new parent club. The franchise floundered in August 1956 and Clunk again heeded the call as a troubleshooter. After a dormant year in 1957, he laid a solid foundation for baseball's return to Williamsport in 1958 as a Phillies farm club. At the behest of Phillies, he managed the Grays front office until his retirement in 1961.

When Clunk's health declined, other directors shared the burden of managing the club's office affairs—yet he remained in the forefront of all major administrative decisions. In acknowledgment of years of loyal service to Williamsport baseball, fans and club officials honored Clunk with a special night on August 30, 1961. He received an engraved watch and a radio from the Grays. It marked Clunk's last hurrah. He retired at the end of the 1961 season and died on November 8, 1961, at the age of seventy-three.

Another giant figure in Williamsport's minor league history was the inimitable and irrepressible Thomas (Tommy) H. Richardson. This native Williamsporter served as Eastern League president for twenty-seven years and also had a short stint as International League president. Dubbed "Ambassador of Sunshine," and "Merry Minstrel Man of Baseball," Richardson was born on May 3, 1895, the son of a poor working-class Irish family that resided on Second Street. Following the death of his father, he quit school in the seventh grade to earn income for the family. Richardson recalled those hard times in a 1960 *WS-G* column by Ray Keyes, "I had four jobs at one time and made $8 a week out of all them. I delivered hats, painted signs, ushered in a theater, and made popcorn balls for a candy company . . . I was so poor that my family invented the open toe shoe."

Poverty aside, Richardson was recognized by his contemporaries to possess a "keen Irish wit" and the "gift of gab," traits that made him a natural fit for the budding entertainment field and vaudeville circuit. Graduating from singing and dancing on Williamsport street corners, the Richardson brothers (Tommy and Joe) parlayed their talents into a successful vaudeville act. After his vaudeville days and a hitch in the Navy during World War I, Tommy Richardson returned to Williamsport and entered the car business, opening his own Buick dealership, which he operated for over thirty years. Around this time, he also became a professional after-dinner speaker, toastmaster, and raconteur. Writer L. H. Addington noted:

> No baseball banquet is complete without the little imp of fun spouting his saucy stuff from the dais. He's done his stuff over the map, not only for [baseballers] but for civic and fraternal clubs and the like. . . . He was known by many as the man of a million stories.

This was a trade that Richardson excelled in right up until the time of his death. In his lifetime he had been an intimate of many show business luminaries, including Joe E. Brown and Bob Hope.

Tommy Richardson's interest in Williamsport minor league baseball can be traced to the city's NYPL team of 1923. He was one of the original directors of the Grays and later rose to the position of vice-president of the club in the late 1920s. It was at this time that Richardson cultivated a lasting friendship with baseball's grand old man, the beloved Connie Mack. This friendship had much bearing on the course of Williamsport's minor league baseball history.

Richardson traveled to Philadelphia in 1928 to consult with Mack on a variety of matters pertaining to player personnel. The two immediately took to one another and both recognized an Irish kinship that transcended their disparity in height and wealth. Mack conferred upon Richardson the sobriquet of "Ambassador of Sunshine," and hired him for three years as the team's roving goodwill ambassador. When the great A's teams of 1929, 1930, and 1931 went to the World Series, Richardson and his brother provided much-needed comic relief for Mack and his players. During one of his frequent visits to Williamsport in the early 1950s, Mack expressed his feelings about Richardson, "Tommy is without a doubt, one of the best-known figures in the sports world. I'm very proud to call him my friend."

Richardson's warm relationship with Mack yielded important dividends for the Williamsport ballclub. Between 1931 and 1953 (though not annually), Mack brought his Philadelphia A's to Bowman Field to play exhibition games against the Williamsport Grays. The revenue generated by these games enabled the Grays to earn a modest margin of profit and weather the throes of the Great Depression. Between 1934 and 1942 the Williamsport Grays established a formal working agreement with Philadelphia whereby the A's stocked the Williamsport team with players, and later purchased their respective contracts when the players were called up to the big leagues. The A's and Grays revived their relationship in 1953 after Detroit canceled its working agreement with Williamsport following the 1952 season.

By virtue of his administrative work with the Grays, and through Mack's influence,

Fig. 12 Grays manager Spence Abbott and Eastern League president Tommy Richardson welcomed the "Grand Old Man of Baseball," the legendary Connie Mack, to Bowman Field in 1941. Mack and Richardson were close friends, and the Williamsport Grays enjoyed a close working relationship with the Philadelphia A's. (Tommy Richardson Collection, Courtesy of Louis Hunsinger Jr.)

Richardson was elected president of the NYPL in November 1937. Upon entering office he gained approval for changing the name of the league to the Eastern League (EL), in recognition of the expanded geographic territory of the loop. By this time the league had franchises in Pennsylvania, New York, New Jersey, and Connecticut, and one planned for Massachusetts.

Richardson's talent for showmanship and promotions served him well in his new post. The Eastern League needed a charismatic innovator as attendance lagged during the 1937 season. In 1938, the first season under his administration, Eastern League

Fig. 13 Tommy Richardson was Williamsport's most influential baseball publicist and promoter of the minor league game. He also served as president of the Eastern League for twenty-seven years. Richardson is shown here outside the Tompkins News Agency, promoting himself and Williamsport Grays baseball. (*Grit*)

attendance neared the magic milestone of one million. The following year, the league reached that mark for the first time in its history. Richardson's off-beat and novel promotions, as well as his marketing talents, played a large role in attracting larger crowds to Bowman Field and the league overall.

One of his more outlandish promotions entailed the dropping a ball from an airplane as part of the Opening Day ceremonies around the league. In 1939, Richardson awarded a "President's Cup" trophy to the league franchise that achieved the highest paid Opening Day attendance. He pioneered and popularized many of the giveaway promotions (automobiles, bicycles, ponies) and community-sponsored booster nights that later became staples of minor league parks across the county. Richardson traveled the Eastern League circuit to observe special promotional nights and often performed as master of ceremonies when his schedule permitted. Richardson gave new promotions a trial run at Bowman Field before recommending their implementation by other league members. He grasped that fans, particularly families, came to the ballpark to be entertained and share a sense of belonging. Promotions added to fan's total enjoyment of the game. If a promotion played in Williamsport, it would play throughout the Eastern League.

Richardson's promotional acumen reaped rewards as the Eastern League survived the difficult days of World War II while other less fortunate leagues folded in droves. The Eastern League was one of only ten minor league circuits able to continue baseball during the war period. Baseball insiders acknowledged Tommy Richardson's role in saving his league.

Richardson was also one of Little League's earliest supporters and its best-known publicist. He sponsored a team, Richardson Buick, in Little League's second season, 1940. One of his more ingenious Bowman Field promotions entailed a Little League exhibition game played before the Grays' regular game in conjunction with "Bicycle and Suburban Night" in July 1939. Richardson worked both publicly and behind the scenes to help Carl Stotz promote Little League Baseball. He encouraged Williamsport Grays officials to include Little Leaguers in its August 23, 1939 pageant at Bowman Field commemorating the seventy-fifth anniversary of baseball in Williamsport. Richardson subsequently became a member of Little League's board of directors.

In 1946 Richardson openly campaigned for the presidency of the National Association of Professional Baseball Leagues, the minor leagues' governing body. But his outspoken support of independent club owners (at the expense of the Major League clubs that owned and operated a growing number of minor league teams) doomed his candidacy. Major League interests thwarted his election; and the NAPBL agreed to support a compromise candidate for the presidency. Richardson's influence, however, remained strong within the high councils of minor league baseball.

Few people recall that Richardson nearly became an owner of the Philadelphia A's. When Connie Mack decided to sell the team in 1954, Richardson was part of a group of investors who raised $3 million to purchase the franchise. Richardson recalled, "I practically had the club in my hands, but some American League owners took exception to the people associated with me so I lost out. We intended to move too, and we were going to stay in Philadelphia for one more season, then move to Los Angeles."

In 1961 Richardson became president of the International League (baseball's oldest operating minor league), succeeding the legendary Frank "Shag" Shaughnessey. He transferred the league's headquarters from Montreal, Quebec, to New York City and ran the office with the same firm hand as when he directed EL affairs. Richardson held the post for four years before being ousted. Wanting to regain his old EL presidency, Richardson then attempted to unseat his own handpicked successor—fellow Williams-

Calvacade of Baseball
Bowman field,
Williamsport, Penna,

Tommy Richardson
"Pres Eastern
Leag

Fig. 14 One of the most popular promotions of the 1939 season was Williamsport's celebration of its seventy-fifth baseball anniversary. The "Cavalcade of Baseball" included a marching band and drum corps, fans dressed in period costumes of the nineteenth century, and a reunion of players from Williamsport's Tri-State League era. (Tommy Richardson Collection, Courtesy of Louis Hunsinger Jr.)

porter Rankin Johnson. Richardson lost the race for the EL post in 1966. The following year, he used his extensive leverage—calling in a lifetime of debts and obligations owed by long-time league owners and associates—to defeat Johnson.

Richardson reassumed his duties in 1968 and served until failing health forced him to retire in 1970. Unfortunately, the man that *The Sporting News* hailed as "the Minor's Little Dynamo," had squandered his life's earnings on a lavish and jaunty lifestyle. Guided by his own credo, "If you couldn't be a millionaire, you could at least act like one," he died penniless. On November 13, 1970, Richardson succumbed to leukemia at the age of seventy-five.

With Richardson's passing, Williamsport lost a vital link to its baseball past and its most flamboyant civic publicist. The *WS-G* noted:

> His keen Irish wit and repertoire of jokes delighted hundreds of audiences for the past forty years. He carried the name of Williamsport far and wide. . . . A man not soon forgotten in Williamsport and certainly not likely to be duplicated in years to come—such was Tommy Richardson whose close friends are legion.

The *Grit* echoed, "As an ambassador of mirth he had a remarkable talent for spreading sunshine wherever he went. Williamsport won't be the same without Tommy Richardson."

The flamboyant, dapper man was honored posthumously in a manner befitting one of the city's most respected civic leaders. August 16, 1971, was designated "Tommy Richardson Day" in Williamsport. That evening, Bowman Field—Tommy's beloved ballpark—served as the backdrop for an emotional celebration of Richardson's life and legacy to minor league baseball. Proceeds from the New York–Penn League game between Williamsport and Niagara Falls were donated to the cancer treatment programs at the Williamsport and Divine Providence hospitals. A celebratory luncheon held earlier in the day at the Lycoming Hotel drew such notables as Monte Irvin (representing baseball commissioner Bowie Kuhn) and Elmer Valo of the old Philadelphia A's.

Richardson was honored again in July 1975 with his posthumous induction into the West Branch Valley chapter of the Pennsylvania Sports Hall of Fame. To mark the occasion letters poured in from all over the country, many from well-known sports personalities and front-office people who had a long association with Richardson. Bob Prince, the legendary Pittsburgh Pirates broadcaster wrote, "I'm sure that somewhere in heaven he [Tommy] is blowing his whistle saying, 'Lord, I've got one I'm sure you've never heard.' " Pittsburgh Pirate manager Danny Murtaugh offered a fitting epitaph for Richardson when he wrote, "Tommy was baseball's all-time goodwill ambassador." Richardson also received recognition at the National Baseball Hall of Fame in Cooperstown, New York. In an exhibit area devoted to the leading executives and players of minor league baseball, a picture portrait and capsule biography of Richardson has been mounted.

When discussing baseball executives who have served Williamsport and baseball at large, the name of Adam Rankin Johnson Jr., should not be overlooked. Johnson's career in organized baseball spanned nearly forty years—from batboy to minor league and Major League player, and from Williamsport business manager to the EL presidency.

Adam Rankin Johnson Jr., was born on March 1, 1917, in Hayden, Arizona, but spent his formative years in the Burnet-Marble Falls area of Texas near Austin. Born and bred into a baseball family, his father, Adam Rankin Johnson Sr., had played professionally as a pitcher. The elder Johnson saw action with the Boston Red Sox and St. Louis Cardinals, as well as the Chicago Whales and Baltimore Terrapins of the old Federal League. He later embarked upon a managerial career in the minors, including a stint with the Harrisburg Senators in 1925. His son, Rankin Jr., worked as the team batboy and often accompanied his father on road trips to Williamsport. To this day, Rankin Jr. fondly recalls the team's stay at the fabled Old Park Hotel (the present-day Park Home). He learned the fundamentals of baseball literally at the knee of his father, a knowledge that came in handy when Johnson began his own baseball career in 1935.

Signed by the Yankees to a minor league contract, Adam Rankin Johnson Jr. was farmed out to Akron of the Middle Atlantic League, and later to Washington, Pennsylvania, of the old Penn State Association. There, he came under the tutelage of Benny Bengough, a catcher and former member of the 1927 Yankees. Johnson also had a short stint with the Chicago Cubs organization and remembers his spring training days on Catalina Island, California, with the 1938 World Series team. Johnson was later traded to the Philadelphia A's where he came under the watchful eye of Connie Mack. He saw some Major League action with the A's in 1941. Johnson's made his Major League debut at Yankee Stadium as a reliever against the Yankees. Eventually, he was sent down to the minors, ending up in Williamsport. There, he met and dated his future wife, Joan, whom he married while on leave from the Navy in 1943.

When the war intervened, Johnson enlisted in the Navy and served for four years (including eighteen months of sea duty). Following his tour of duty, Johnson honed his pitching skills, playing on the Honolulu submarine base's baseball team. In 1945 his team played in the Pacific Fleet championship game against the Kanahoe Bay Naval Air Station before an estimated crowd of thirty thousand servicemen. Both teams included established Major League and minor league players. Johnson fondly recalls relieving Detroit Tiger standout pitcher "Schoolboy" Rowe to pick up the victory for his team: "To pitch and win such a championship game, especially before thousands of servicemen . . . was quite an experience."

Johnson returned stateside in 1946 and hooked up with the Chattanooga Lookouts of the Southern League, operated by the legendary minor league entrepreneur Joe Engel, who was known as "Baseball's Barnum" for his many unusual promotional schemes. After his contract was sold back to Connie Mack's A's, Johnson found himself playing ball once again in his adopted home town of Williamsport. He played for Wil-

Fig. 15 Pitcher A. Rankin Johnson Jr. played for
the 1941 and 1946 Williamsport Grays and later
served as president of the Eastern League from 1961
to 1968. (Courtesy of A. Rankin Johnson Jr.)

liamsport mid-way through the 1947 season before given his release. Shortly thereafter,
Johnson entered the automobile business, working at his father-in-law's car dealership.

In 1953 Tommy Richardson hired Johnson as his personal secretary. Richardson
tapped Johnson's extensive baseball background to assist him in running the day-to-day
operations of the Eastern League. Johnson split his work between the Eastern League
office and the Grays front office. When Grays directors decided to lessen the workload
of the ailing Roy Clunk, they appointed Johnson as his assistant, in charge of promotions.

With Richardson's departure to the International League in 1961, Rankin Johnson
Jr. became president of the Eastern League. Johnson's extensive baseball background
served him well in administering the affairs of the league. The 1960s proved to be a
very challenging time for the EL, as well as all minor leagues. Johnson encountered

difficulty in finding cities willing to support minor league franchises, and ironing out working agreements with Major League affiliates. For much of the decade, the EL operated as a six-team loop, down from its customary eight-team format. Unlike the present-day boom in minor league expansion, few cities then possessed the resources, or willingness, to construct new baseball facilities to attract a team.

To Johnson's credit, he kept the league intact and balanced finances in spite of a shoestring budget. His undoing, ironically, stemmed from his former mentor. Tommy Richardson recaptured his old EL post in late 1967 at a league meeting. Though Johnson opposed Richardson, he bore little enmity toward him. In an interview Johnson stated, "Tommy Richardson always treated me well . . . he was like a father to me." Moreover, Richardson's deteriorating health forced Johnson into the role of de facto president of the league, as he assumed many of the responsibilities associated with the office.

When Williamsport joined the short-season Class A New York–Penn League (NY-PENN) in 1968, Erie businessman and club owner Joe Romano asked Johnson to be the general manager of the Williamsport Astros. Just as he had done in all his previous front-office stints, Johnson performed his duties in a professional and efficient manner. It was not an easy job because Williamsport fans had grown accustomed to Class AA ball and a full season of 140 games. The quiet Texan earned the respect of his colleagues in both the NY-PENN and Eastern Leagues. After the 1969 season, Johnson finally retired, ending thirty-four years in professional baseball.

Johnson's distinguished baseball career earned him enshrinement in the West Branch Valley chapter of the Pennsylvania Sports Hall of Fame, and the Bowman Field Hall of Fame. The latter honor was especially fitting as Bowman Field had been enriched by Johnson's accomplishments as a player and baseball executive. The Johnson legacy continues down to this day. One of Rankin Johnson's sons played professional minor league baseball. His grandson, Jason, pitched for Auburn University and later signed with the Colorado Rockies. He advanced to the Class AA level with the New Haven Ravens of the Eastern League before he sustained a career-ending injury to his pitching shoulder.

Promotions

Promotions have always been vital to the economic well-being of minor league franchises and Williamsport was no exception. Historically, the city has only averaged at best, modest season attendance figures at the gate. Always at a disadvantage due to its small market size (notwithstanding the financial clout of its benefactors), promotions took on even greater significance in attracting fans to Bowman Field. While not all of Williamsport's baseball promotions were unique (indeed, many minor league executives and clubs pooled their promotional ideas), some were novel enough to garner attention and emulation. Even the savvy Connie Mack learned a promotional trick or two from baseball's "Good Humor Man," Tommy Richardson.

Though the early efforts to market Grays baseball were modest by today's standards, they were evident from the beginning of baseball's modern era. When the city resumed professional baseball in 1923, club directors drew inspiration from the traditions and promotions associated with the old Tri-State League. On Opening Day of that year, the Williamsport club and visiting team rode in open cars in a downtown parade and cavalcade to the uptown ballpark. The baseball parades, led by marching bands such as the Imperial Teteques, Elks Repasz, and Williamsport High School, were very popular and served as excellent promotions to boost ticket sales and generate fan interest.

One of the most successful and long-lasting promotions was "Booster Day," or "Booster Night," when night baseball was played in Williamsport. Introduced in 1925, this promotion entailed reduced ticket rates for fans on certain designated dates. The booster dates often featured "giveaway" promotions, such as automobiles, bicycles, major appliances, and on rare occasions, a pony. Some of the best single-game attendance figures were achieved on booster nights, the success of which could financially carry a club for the season.

Exhibition games involving the Grays and Major League teams at Bowman Field always did well at the gate, generating enough revenue to buffer the club through tough financial times. The best example occurred in August 1932 when the Grays played the Cleveland Indians and Philadelphia A's within a two-week span. Revenue gained from these two contests saved the season and baseball for city. Later, many other Major League teams came to Williamsport in search of a hefty paycheck: the Pittsburgh Pirates, Boston Red Sox, St. Louis Browns, Cincinnati Reds, Philadelphia Phillies, and New York Mets. Connie Mack's Philadelphia A's played thirteen games in Williamsport between 1931 and 1953—the most appearances by any Major League team.

Promotions took on a special urgency during the bleak years of the Depression. Reduced ticket prices for women on Ladies Day were intended to attract female fans to the ballpark. A slight variation involved free admission for women accompanied by a paying adult male. In 1933 a new federal tax on admissions forced Williamsport club officials to charge women ten cents on these special days to cover the tax.

In 1933, Williamsport's management initiated several new promotions that later became staples of the game. The first of the automobile giveaways—by far the most popular promotional event—took place on August 17, 1933, following a game between the Grays and Binghamton Triplets. Over three thousand fans attended the drawing. In addition to the car, the lucky winner received 150 gallons of gasoline. A New York advertising executive won a 1933 Pontiac (donated by Richardson's dealership) valued at $825. The initial success of the car giveaway prompted club officials to make it the promotional anchor of the baseball season—with Richardson's assistance. The automobile giveaway was often linked to one of the special Booster Nights, or sponsored by a community's service organizations such as B'nai B'rith.

Fig. 16 Members of the 1931 Philadelphia Athletics pose with Williamsport fans and the Camp Davitt Bus prior to an exhibition against the Grays at Bowman Field. Exhibition games against Major League teams permitted fans to have easy access to their baseball heroes. (*Grit*)

Recognizing that the future of professional baseball in Williamsport depended on the club's ability to attract families and cultivate long-term fan loyalty, many Grays promoters focused on the young. Introduction of the Knot-Hole Gang program in July 1933 proved to be a prudent investment in the city's baseball future. Many of today's older fans fell in love with the game through their participation in the program. Knot-Holers had their own special seating area in the temporary bleachers (donated by Williamsport High School) erected along the left-field line. Members also received special membership cards. John H. Bower, Williamsport's YMCA secretary, ran the program for many years and his efforts resulted in the establishment of a loyal fan base for the Grays over several decades.

In the 1930s the Grays introduced another popular promotion geared toward youngsters—"Bicycle Night." Many Williamsport parents were cajoled by their children to

Fig. 17 Special promotions by the Williamsport Grays drew large crowds to Bowman Field during the 1930s. One of the most popular giveaways was a raffle for a new automobile, donated by Tommy Richardson's Buick dealership. One of these fans was the lucky winner. (*Grit*)

attend this event in hopes of being the lucky raffle winner of a brand new bike. One sure-fire promotion was the sponsorship of a night honoring a player or official associated with baseball, whether from the hometown Grays or the opposing team. For example, there were honorary nights for the Grays legendary radio broadcaster, Sol "Woody" Wolf, manager Spencer "Spence" Abbott, local ballplayer Don Manno, and Williamsport Tigers manager, Jack Tighe.

During the World War II era, ballpark promotions revolved around patriotism and the domestic home front. One example was "Rubber Collection Night" held on June 27, 1942. Any boy or girl, fourteen and younger, was admitted free to the game if they brought two pounds or more of scrap rubber to the ballpark. The Grays also sponsored popular war bond promotions, setting aside a portion of the gate receipts for the purchase of bonds. One unique variation, "Bomber Bond Night," entailed the auctioning of Grays manager Ray Kolp and several popular players to the highest bidding fans between innings. The bids defrayed the cost of the bonds used for the manufacturing of bombers, and obligated the manager and players to attend a dinner or luncheon hosted by the winning bidders.

Promotions also served as a fundraising vehicle for a variety of worthy causes and civic enhancement. In 1938, the Grays sponsored "American Legion Night," using part of the gate receipts toward costs associated with the statewide American Legion convention held in Williamsport in 1939. Following the May 1946 flood that caused extensive structural damage to Bowman Field, proceeds from a "Flood Repair Night" helped to offset the $15,000 repair costs. On "Olympic Day," held on July 11, 1948, fans were asked to make a financial contribution to support the 1948 U.S. Olympic team, headed for the summer Olympic Games in London. When teacher and former athlete Ron Blackburn had been seriously injured in a car accident, the Grays held "Ron Blackburn Night" to assist with his medical bills. Revenues generated by one game were even used to purchase new uniforms for the Williamsport Police Department.

The above examples illustrate the value of the Grays public relations work, and how thoroughly Williamsport's minor league ballclub was interwoven into the community's social fabric. Public-spirited promotions centered at the ballpark unified the community, with greater good arising from the shared passion of baseball.

When minor league baseball experienced declining attendance during the 1950s, Williamsport felt the fiscal pinch as well. Promotions took on greater urgency as owners tried novel and quirky ways to attract crowds to the ballpark. Some ideas, given initial runs during the previous two decades, were resurrected during the 1950s. One such promotion was "Baseball Field Days," an event pitting of Grays players against an opposing team in a variety of contests—fungo hitting, throwing the ball the farthest, and foot races. Winners of these events received prizes provided by local merchants.

Baseball comedy promotions featuring Al Schacht (a former player for Binghamton), baseball trickster Jackie Price, and the "Clown Prince of Baseball," Max Patkin, proved immensely popular with local fans from the late 1940s to the 1970s. (Patkin died in 1999.) Large crowds were drawn to these baseball "clowns," just as present-day Williamsport baseball fans flock to Bowman Field to witness the antics of the Phillie Phanatic and Myron Noodleman.

Area merchants, industries, and businesses, whether as participants in a general "Merchants' Night" or as individual sponsors, provided the backbone for baseball promotions. "Stroehmann's Cake Night," dating from the 1950s through the early 1970s, was one of the more successful corporate-sponsored promotions in Williamsport. This event involved the drawing of numbers (from game ticket stubs) for a variety of Stroehmann's bakery products, such as cakes and pastries, and annually drew some of Bowman Field's largest crowds. Rankin Johnson Jr., promotions director for the Grays during the early 1960s, recalled that umpires frequently complained that the announcer disrupted the flow of the game by constantly reading out the winning ticket numbers over the public address system.

Cow-milking contests were among the most humorous promotions staged at Bowman Field. Often, area dairies sponsored these contests during June, "National Dairy Month." One event, held on June 20, 1959, pitted Williamsport's irascible manager Frank Lucchesi against his Albany counterpart, Al Evans. In line with the agricultural theme for 1959, Bowman Field fans witnessed greased pig and chicken-catching contests. During one Family Night promotion held in that same season, Lucchesi was again at the center of high jinx as he and Reading manager Al Hollingsworth participated in a wheel barrow race—won by Lucchesi.

As noted previously, local community service clubs played an important promotional role for Williamsport baseball. While the B'nai B'rith, Chamber of Commerce, and Kiwanis Club organizations were in forefront, other service and civic entities also participated. One example was "Zafar Grotto Night," held on June 8, 1959, which drew 5,100 fans. The Williamsport Jaycees promotion on May 31, 1962, attracted 5,117 fans to the ballpark. And 6,845 fans attended a game on the evening of August 30, 1969, sponsored by the Lycoming County Central Labor Council, comprising the county's AFL-CIO affiliated labor unions. These promotions demonstrated the important partnership that service clubs, organized labor, and civic organizations had with Williamsport baseball.

One of the most unusual promotions in recent years was tied to a memorable (and bizarre) incident known in the annals of Williamsport baseball lore as the "Great Potato Caper" of August 31, 1987. Former Williamsport Bills catcher Dave Bresnahan was honored on May 31, 1988, for the recognition and publicity he brought to Williamsport and its baseball team. On "Dave Bresnahan Night," the admission price for fans entering the ballpark with a potato was $1, with the edible proceeds donated to the city food bank. As part of the festivities a "Dave Bresnahan Award" was established to honor the Williamsport player having the most fun playing baseball. Bresnahan also received a key to the city and had his jersey, number 59, officially retired and painted in a circle upon Bowman Field's center-field fence.

Booster Associations and Ownership Groups

As important as season promotions were to Williamsport baseball, off-the-field efforts to maintain and promote minor league baseball actually may have played a more decisive role in keeping the game alive in the city. Well into the 1940s, a small group of business leaders and self-described "sportsmen" administered the affairs of the Grays. This changed with the formation of the Williamsport Area Community Baseball Association, also known as the "Boosters." The Booster Association expanded the financial and administrative base of the ballclub by reaching out to a broad group of business, community, and professional leaders. Moreover, the Association planned preseason ticket sales, solicited corporate and community service organizations to sponsor promotions, and acted as a liaison with the parent clubs (the Tigers, A's, Pirates, and Phillies).

The Association even held a novel radio-thon to spur preseason ticket sales. Radio station WWPA held such a preseason promotion on April 5, 1961. Ticket booths were conspicuously placed in the lobbies of downtown hotels, banks, and businesses in order to generate ticket sales and enthusiasm for the Williamsport ballclub. The most successful promotional ticket package plan devised by the Booster Association revolved around the slogan, "Cheaper By The Dozen." Introduced as part of the 1958 preseason ticket drive, this plan enabled fans to purchase twelve grandstand seats for $10, six general admission tickets for $5, and ten bleacher seat tickets for $5.

When the Eastern League and New York–Penn League expanded to larger cities and market areas, Williamsport adapted. To give the city ballclub more regional appeal and expand its demographic base of fan support, the Association reorganized under the banner of "The Nine-County Baseball Booster Club." Expansion of Williamsport's regional fan base enabled the city to maintain professional baseball (with a few intermittent lapses) when larger cities lost their teams during the 1960s and 1970s.

Not all of Williamsport's administrative efforts on behalf of baseball achieved success. During the 1970s when minor league baseball again experienced one of its cyclical downturns, the game attracted a new breed of absentee owners who purchased teams at bargain-basement prices and then proceeded to shop them around to communities ripe for the fleecing. One such "carpetbagger" or buccaneer owner was Mal Fichman, who brought to Williamsport one of the worst minor league franchises in the history of the game—the Williamsport Tomahawks ("Tommies") of 1976.

Fichman headed an ownership group that included just one Williamsporter, Frank Luppachino. Aside from Luppachino, this group made little attempt to form a booster organization, or establish a coalition with business and community leaders. The results were disastrous. The Tommies inept play paled in comparison to the front office debacle at the end of the season. Vacating his temporary office in the dead of night, Fichman left the city with a debt totaling thousands of dollars, including a huge unpaid electric and utilities bill for the season. His deceitfulness and unscrupulous business methods dealt a severe blow to professional baseball in Williamsport. Local baseball fans were forced to wait over a decade before the city's gun-shy community leaders campaigned for the return of baseball and a minor league franchise.

Since 1987 the city's experience with outside owners and administrators has ebbed and flowed. General manager William (Bill) Terleckey and the ownership group of Northeast Baseball, Inc., worked hard at building bridges to the community and business leaders when the Class AA Bills (an Indians affiliate) played in Williamsport. Their departure to Scranton-Wilkes-Barre of the Class AAA, International League after the

1988 season deprived Williamsport of a talented front-office team, keen on aggressive marketing, promotions, and goodwill.

Their successors, Stuart and Larry Revo, were less successful. Following the 1988 season, Northeast Baseball, Inc. sold the Bills franchise to the Revo brothers. They had operated the Pittsfield Cubs franchise the previous year and then obtained a new working agreement, this time with the Seattle Mariners. Their one-year stint as owners was marred by several unpleasant off-the-field developments.

Immediately after acquiring the franchise, the Revos campaigned for the adoption of a local option ordinance that would permit the sale of beer at Bowman Field. The proposed beer license generated much friction within the community as churches and antibeer groups raised strenuous objections. Williamsport's state legislator, Tom Dempsey, had to sponsor special legislation allowing beer licenses for public facilities that held less than seven thousand people. Nearly one-half of the season elapsed before beer was sold at the ballpark, resulting in a substantial loss of revenue and a high-profile dispute with city officials.

The ugly dispute erupted on to the front page of the *WS-G* on July 24, 1989. City officials accused the Revo brothers of defaulting on their rent and utility payments for Bowman Field. The following day, Larry Revo countercharged that the city had failed to live up to its side of the agreement. Citing the costly delay in obtaining their beer license, the Revos argued that their loss of beer revenue should be applied against the money owed to the city. After several days of wrangling both sides reached a compromise. The Revos agreed to pay the city $4,250 in rent for the season, $6,500 in utility bills, and $458 to change the locks at Bowman Field. Larry Revo opined, "I really believe the Bills compromised when we really didn't have to."

The Revo brothers' outside and collateral baseball interests took up so much energy that they neglected the administration of the Williamsport franchise. They planned few promotions and made little effort to establish a working relationship with community leaders, merchants, and area businessmen. By 1989 Williamsport had become a forlorn minor league outpost, last in attendance among all Class AA teams and playing in a dilapidated stadium.

Bowman Field became an option of last resort for absentee owners, a temporary home until a larger market and stadium-package was secured as part of the relocation process. This was the situation at the end of the 1990 season when Marvin Goldklang purchased the Williamsport Bills and hired Skip Weisman to manage his baseball operations in Williamsport. Weisman restored a measure of fan support for the team and reached out to the business community and service organizations to plan promotions. Moreover, he introduced a new telemarketing campaign to boost pre-season ticket sales.

By late 1990 it became apparent that Williamsport no longer fit the demographic profile of the burgeoning Eastern League. While per capita attendance figures were respectable, the city's population base was simply too small to support Class AA baseball. The Mets shift of its AA farm club from Jackson, Mississippi, to Williamsport in early

1991 was tempered by the organization's public statements and preference for eventual relocation to Binghamton, New York, once the financial package for a new stadium was resolved. When Goldklang sold the franchise to the Mets, the move to Binghamton was essentially sealed. Following the announced franchise shift, Weisman initiated a fan survey to test the viability of short-season Class A baseball in Williamsport. Though the survey yielded positive feedback, especially among local business and civic groups, Goldklang decided against moving his short-season Class A Erie franchise to Williamsport. Bowman Field lay idle in 1992 and 1993.

With relocation of the short-season Class A Geneva Cubs franchise (New York–Penn League) to Williamsport in 1994, the city received, perhaps, its last remaining chance to support professional minor league baseball. Negotiation of a five-year lease agreement between the city and the new ownership group—consisting of Paul Velte, Mike Roulan, and Ed Smaldone—alleviated many fans' concerns about the possible intent of the owners to pull up stakes after one season. A new five-year lease agreement was signed in 1999, ensuring Williamsport fans a minor league team (and new affiliation with the Pittsburgh Pirates) into the new millennium.

From the outset, the Cubs front office management team—consisting of general manager Doug Estes, business and public relations director Gabe Sinicropi, and Susan Estes (telemarketing)—faced the daunting task of marketing short-season baseball to a community historically rooted in Class AA baseball. Moreover, they confronted a somewhat apathetic fan base, accustomed to losing seasons and franchise shifts over the years. Their hard work and savvy marketing campaigns reaped dividends as evidenced by three straight seasons of increased attendance at the gates—including Williamsport's highest short-season total ever, over 67,000, in 2000. While recent season attendance figures have failed to reach this high-water mark, attendance has been for the most part steady—averaging from 57,000 to 60,000 per year. The respectable attendance figures (putting Williamsport in about the middle of the fourteen-team NY-PENN League) are even more impressive when factoring in the following: competition from larger cities with new stadiums, unbalanced schedules, and the vagaries of the weather.

Corporate and civic support for the team, as evidenced by the successful "Pack the Park Nights" during the season, has remained solid since the Cubs arrival in 1994. Novel promotions such as "Diamond Dig Night," "Instant Vacation," and "Bark in the Park Night" are attracting more fans to the ballpark each year. The creation of a grass-roots Williamsport Boosters Club, and the popular "Adopt-a-Cub" program, have been important in establishing a family orientation at the ball park. The front office has also cultivated a younger fan base through its revival of the popular Knot-Hole Gang program and promotion of an official team mascot, "Rusty Roughcut."

Perhaps no front office group of the recent era has had such a high profile within the community. The Cubs and Crosscutters have actively assisted many charitable organizations with their fund-raising activities, and each season donates a portion of pre-season ticket revenue to a designated charity group.

The future of professional baseball in Williamsport, as in the past, will depend upon the community's ability and will to provide the requisite financial resources and fan support needed to maintain the game. Though the reality of a local ownership group emerging to purchase a minor league franchise seems remote, area boosters and promoters can continue to chart the future course of professional baseball in Williamsport. It is hoped that the city's current civic leaders, businesses, and local merchants, working collectively with the Williamsport Bowman Field Commission, the Crosscutters front office, and local government, will uphold the long-standing tradition of patronage to the game.

3

Bowman Field: Gateway to the Majors

Bowman Field has served as Williamsport's only venue for professional minor league baseball since 1926. Historically, it is the second-oldest operating minor league ballpark in the country, predated only by Centennial Field in Burlington, Vermont, which was constructed in 1923. In contrast to the retro-architectural aesthetic that typifies many of the newly constructed minor league facilities, Bowman Field has stood out as a cherished anachronism. It is an original. The ballpark's distinctive grandstand is one of only a handful of first-generation concrete and steel minor league structures still intact from the 1920s. Though significant renovations were made to the ballpark's exterior façade for the 2000 season, these changes have not compromised Bowman's Field's old-time charm. On July 29, 2000, the Pennsylvania Historical and Museum Commission formally dedicated Bowman Field as a state historic site. A historical marker located outside Bowman Field notes that the ballpark is Pennsylvania's oldest minor league stadium and the second-oldest operating minor league facility in the country.

Entering the portals of Bowman Field, one is transported back to an earlier era when baseball reigned supreme in the hearts and minds of sports fans and ball-parks reflected a community's booster spirit. When summer afternoon shadows creep over Bowman Field on rare Sunday afternoon games, old-timers delight in retelling stories of long-departed players, pennant races, and bean-ball wars witnessed over the years. Once considered the crown jewel of all minor league stadiums, the uptown ballpark has lost some of its luster over the years. But Bowman Field's quaintness (the close proximity of its grandstand to the ball diamond) offers the fan a unique and plea-surable spectator experience often lacking in larger minor league venues. Above all, Bowman Field has been a valuable community institution and asset throughout its sev-enty-year existence. As in the past, the venerable ballpark continues to be used for a variety of purposes, hosting other sporting events, exhibitions, civic celebrations, pag-eants, and concerts.

Through seven decades, Bowman Field has symbolized Williamsport's ever-chang-ing relationship with professional baseball. Early on, civic-minded businessmen estab-lished and operated the ballpark as a philanthropic endeavor. In later years, Bowman Field became a ward of the City of Williamsport, maintained by the Department of Streets and Parks and dependent upon private foundation funds and state government grants for its survival. As costs mounted to operate minor league franchises, municipali-ties relied more upon absentee owners and ownership groups to underwrite the game. But many absentee owners demanded the construction of new public-financed ball-parks, or state-funded renovations to meet the stadium guidelines mandated by the National Association of Professional Baseball Leagues (NAPBL). Communities had little desire to fund exorbitant stadium projects only to see owners and franchises pull up stakes for new opportunities elsewhere. Minor league ballparks thus became contested arenas, pitting absentee owners against the communities they served. Part private enter-prise and part municipal stepchild, the maintenance of Bowman Field and minor league baseball in Williamsport has never been an easy task. But the city has adapted to the changing economic dynamics of today's game and managed to keep professional base-ball alive.

Bowman Field: The Formative Years

The origin of Bowman Field can be traced to a meeting between city officials and officers of the Williamsport Grays held at the Ross Club during the late summer of 1924. The point of discussion concerned the construction and leasing of a new ballpark for the Grays on a parcel of acreage (situated in the northwest corner of Memorial Park) owned by the Williamsport Water Company. Well into their second year of affiliation with the New York–Pennsylvania League (NYPL)—and enjoying success at the gates—the Grays had simply outgrown the Williamsport High School Athletic Field. Because

Fig. 18 The erection of Memorial (Bowman) Field's steel and concrete foundation took place during the winter months of 1926. Constructed at a cost of $75,000, Memorial Field was one of the crown jewels of minor league baseball. (*Grit*)

the team was involved in a tight pennant race that year, further discussions and proposals for a new ballpark were tabled until the end of the 1924 season.

Construction of a new playing facility gained greater urgency the following year when the club and school district officials disagreed over the scheduling and use of Athletic Field. In July 1925, the Grays reached an agreement with the city to construct a new ballpark on the proposed Memorial Park site. The stadium was to be completed and fully operational by opening day of the 1926 season. J. Walton Bowman formed an eleven-man holding company to finance and manage the construction of a $75,000 baseball stadium for the Grays. Many prominent businessmen, civic leaders, and corporate sponsors contributed to the stadium fund campaign. Among the influential investors

Fig. 19 View of Memorial Field prior to Opening Day in April 1926. Note the ballpark's distinctive left-field terrace and the outfield billboards taking shape. The original dimensions were cavernous—400 feet to left field, 450 feet to center field, and 367 feet to right field. (*Grit*)

were James and Irving Gleason, the Reese-Sheriff Lumber Company, the Grit Publishing Company, J. Roman Way, Max Jaffe, Harder's Sporting Goods Store, and Ralph "Pat" Thorne. In all, twenty-three investors contributed $1,000 or more, and ten others gave at least $500.

These investors later drafted a statement of principle that appeared in local newspapers at the time of the christening of Bowman Field in May 1926. It read in part: "While the primary object of this movement is to provide the Williamsport Baseball Club with a suitable playing field, the ultimate and more important aim is to give eventually to our home city a modern public ballpark for the benefit and use of all its people."

Ground was broken for the stadium in the fall of 1925. The James V. Bennett Construction Company of Williamsport, Drennen Brothers Construction Company of Philadelphia, and the J. C. Dressler Construction Company of Cleveland, Ohio, were retained as contractors for erecting Memorial Field's grandstand and laying out the playing field. Favorable weather conditions in early 1926 enabled the contractors to meet their construction deadline, though the local press reported that the newly sodded field still needed several months to attain a lush green look. The *Williamsport Gazette & Bulletin* (*WG&B*) of May 4, 1926, noted that the original dimensions of Memorial Field were quite cavernous, even by the current standards of the era. Home plate to right field measured 367 feet, home to center field 450 feet, and home to right field 400 feet.

Though Memorial Field's formal Opening Day was scheduled for May, the first recorded game of baseball played in the new stadium took place on April 22, 1926, when the Grays defeated the Bucknell University nine 5-3, in an exhibition game. On April 27 and April 29, the Grays hosted the Harrisburg Colored Giants in the first professional competitions at Memorial Field, dropping both games. In the first game, Harrisburg's manager and first-baseman, Oscar Charleston, hit the first home run recorded at the new uptown park. Charleston became one of the established stars of Negro League Baseball, and was later elected into the Baseball Hall of Fame.

Memorial Field formally opened on May 4, 1926, with much fanfare and pageantry. Over two thousand fans attended the Grays inaugural game, a 5-1 win over the visiting Shamokin Indians. The small turnout (less than half the capacity of Memorial Field) was largely attributed to the unseasonably cold weather. Visiting observers and reporters opined that the newly opened ballpark was "one of the finest baseball plants in the land."

From 1926 to 1929 Williamsport's stadium was known simply as Memorial Field. On June 26, 1929, the Grays officially re-christened the ballpark "Bowman Field" in honor of Grays president, J. Walton Bowman, who had done so much for baseball in Williamsport. A crowd of 2,214 was on hand to celebrate, serenaded by the Imperial Teteques, the community band that Bowman had founded. Grays players presented Bowman with a Swiss watch, and his granddaughter, Mary Louise Lentz, raised the American flag and a blue-and-white banner that read "Bowman Field." The ubiquitous Tommy Richardson, who later participated in so many notable occasions at Bowman Field, served as master of ceremonies.

Over the years, Bowman Field has undergone numerous structural changes and renovations. The first notable alteration took place in 1932 with the erection of stadium light towers for night baseball. The Williamsport School District and the directors of the Williamsport Grays jointly funded the project. Irv Gleason, one of the Grays leading proponents of night baseball, donated $4,750 of his own money for the illumination of Bowman Field. Bowman Field was one of the earliest ballparks in the NYPL to have lights, though the Binghamton, New York, team had been playing night games since 1930. Night baseball gained greater popularity during the depths of the Great Depression when minor league teams adopted the measure to increase attendance at games.

Fig. 20 D. Vincent Smith, Williamsport's most famous photographer, captured this stunning shot of Bowman Field on July 4, 1930, from the vantage of Wildwood Cemetery Ridge. Memorial Park's roller coaster can be seen in the background. (D. Vincent Smith Collection, Lycoming County Historical Society)

Local sportswriters noted the positive correlation between night games and larger gate receipts, and attributed the survival of game during the lean financial times to the novelty of baseball played under the lights.

On the evening of June 6, 1932, the Grays and York White Roses played the first night game at Bowman Field before two thousand curious spectators. Among those on hand was the NYPL president, Percy Farrell. Irv Gleason even cut short his Pacific Northwest visit to attend the event. Officials from General Electric and Lycoming Edison boasted that Bowman Field was "the best lighted field east of Des Moines, Iowa." One hundred and fifty-two lamps—each with 1,500 watts of power, the equivalent of 400,000 units of candle power—illuminated Bowman Field. Unfortunately, the Grays disappointed fans by losing a 9-5 decision to the White Roses.

The next major change to Bowman Field's configuration involved the ballpark's outfield dimensions. From 1926 to 1933 only ten home runs had been hit out of the ballpark—by both home and away teams. With attendance languishing during the Depression, Grays directors hoped to attract more fans by adding offensive punch to the game. Williamsport fans, no doubt enamored with the prodigious home-run feats of legendary sluggers Babe Ruth, Lou Gehrig, and Jimmy Foxx, thirsted for their own local home run heroes.

Bowman Field's original outfield dimensions were as great, if not greater, than many of the era's Major League ballparks. When the Philadelphia A's and other Major League clubs appeared in Williamsport for exhibition games, their sluggers considered it a challenge to breach the outfield walls with circuit clouts; very few actually did. Pre-game home-run hitting contests, featuring such stars and fan-favorites as Jimmy Foxx and "Mule" Haas, highlighted these exhibition games. Lacking a Williamsport version of the "Sultan of Swat," ownership did the next best thing—they built a bandbox. In 1934 Grays directors authorized the construction of a new inner fence that reduced the distance to all fields by fifty to sixty feet. This inner fence roughly corresponds to the present-day dimensions of Bowman Field. The ballpark's original wood-buttressed outer wall (resembling a frontier fortress) was not razed until 1961.

This reconfiguration of field dimensions had an immediate impact upon the Grays offensive performance. In addition to winning the 1934 NYPL championship, the Grays batted a collective .291, one of the highest team averages of the twentieth century. Moreover, Horace "Red" McBride's twenty-six homers in 1934 nearly equaled the previous seven-year total of home runs hit by both visitors and the Grays.

In 1936 Bowman Field survived its first major brush with a natural disaster when the catastrophic flood of March 1936 devastated the city and the entire Susquehanna Valley. The crown jewel of the NYPL suffered over $2,000 in flood damage—a sizable amount of money for repairs in the midst of the Depression. The damage to Bowman Field included bleachers moved off their foundations, box seats removed from the base of the grandstands and splintered, and the left-field fence toppled by the surge of Lycoming Creek waters. Club secretary J. Roy Clunk and NYPL president P. B. Farrell

---

Fig. 21 The 1936 flood engulfed Memorial Park and Bowman Field, causing extensive structural damage to the ballpark. Repairs to the box seats and the stadium grandstand were funded by the Works Progress Administration. (*Grit*)

inspected the flood damage on April 1, about one month before the baseball season opened in early May. Clunk announced that the Williamsport Baseball Club could not afford the repair costs to Bowman Field outlined by President Farrell. There existed the real possibility that the Grays franchise might be moved to another community if city officials failed to find a way to defray the renovation expenses. Mifflinburg, in neighboring Union County, was mentioned prominently as the new site for the franchise.

The additional disaster of Williamsport losing its team was averted when Clarence "Harry" Kempf (city councilman and superintendent of parks and public property) announced on April 2, that the New Deal's Works Progress Administration (WPA) would take on the task of repairing Bowman Field. WPA workers installed new box seats, strengthened the bleachers, and erected a new left-field fence. The work was inspected and approved by the Pennsylvania Department of Labor and Industry in early May, just in time for the opening of the season.

An enduring feature that marks the environs of Bowman Field first appeared in May 1936, the signboard placed at the West Fourth Street entrance to Memorial Park. For decades, this sign has proclaimed the team and league affiliation of the Williamsport clubs for each season. During the years that the city did not have a team, the billboard served to remind fans of a by-gone baseball era and offered the possibility of new tenants for Bowman Field. The original 1936 sign simply stated: "New York–Pennsylvania League, Bowman Field, Home of the Grays." Over the years the sign has marked numerous name and team affiliation changes. Perhaps the most memorable sign inscription appeared during the late 1940s and early 1950s: "Bowman Field: Gateway to the Majors." The current sign reads: "Bowman Field: Home of the Williamsport Crosscutters, Class A Affiliate of the Pittsburgh Pirates."

Bowman Field had several idiosyncratic features in its formative era. In 1939 the Grays adorned the grandstand roof with baseball's Centennial Emblem and pennants with the name of each Eastern League affiliate. The alignment of the pennants varied from day to day, reflecting the current league standings. New reflective foul poles (resembling the striped barber's pole) also added a quirky touch to Bowman Field. A long pipe-chute was constructed under the grandstand that enabled the return of foul balls hit outside the ballpark.

In 1939 the Grays erected a bleacher area along the left-field side of Bowman Field. This structural alteration increased the ballpark's seating capacity from 4,200 to 5,400 and instantly transformed Bowman Field into one of the largest ballparks in the Eastern League. The left-field bleachers remained intact until 1988 when the city and the management of the Williamsport Bills finally demolished them.

Not all the alterations to Bowman were by design. "The Days of Pompeii" game on August 28, 1931, may have been the most unusual and wildest game in the annals of Williamsport baseball. The game with Elmira was played at Bowman Field, resplendent with backdrops and scenery from the Last Days of Pompeii pageant that was held during the last week of August. Many of the elaborate props, including large columns and fountains, remained in the outfield. Choosing not to reschedule the game, club officials re-configured the ballpark and improvised ground rules—reducing the game to an absurd burlesque. Williamsport won the game by the outlandish score of 31-18, with the contest marred by several cheap home runs and ground-rule extra-base hits.

One of the most memorable alterations to Bowman Field transpired on August 17, 1955, in a game with the Reading Indians. Roger Maris (the future Yankee star), playing left field for the Indians, crashed into the left-field fence attempting a catch a drive off the bat of the Grays Johnny Powers. He plowed through the Hurr's Dairy sign, knocking the nose and tail off the cow. Maris left the game but returned to play the second game of a doubleheader. He was later thrown out of that game after a heated argument with the home-plate umpire after being called out on a play at the plate.

Fig. 22 Putsee Vannucci, a commercial photographer, captured this stunning panorama of the interior of Bowman Field in 1947. Bowman Field's buttressed outer wall was not removed until 1957. (Putsee Vannucci Collection, Courtesy of Lycoming County Historical Society)

Postwar Bowman Field Renovations

Bowman Field underwent several structural and grounds changes in the immediate post–World War II era. Recurrent floods were a problem as the ballpark was located in the flood plain of Lycoming Creek. After the flood of 1946, the Detroit Tigers (Williamsport's new parent club) allotted $40,000 to pay for stadium repairs and upgrades. Major improvements included the laying of a structural concrete base, new box seats, and the transfer and installation of grandstand seats from Detroit's Briggs Stadium to Bowman Field's grandstand area. In addition, the Tigers installed Bowman Field's first sprinkler system to irrigate the outfield and infield turf.

Fig. 23 In 1947 the parent Detroit Tigers made several structural changes to Bowman Field, including the construction of new box seating area and the installation of seats from Detroit's Briggs Stadium to replace the old grandstand benches. (*Grit*, Courtesy of the *Williamsport Sun-Gazette*)

By the late 1950s, however, Bowman Field had deteriorated due to the lack of funding and proper maintenance. Conditions became so bad that in 1957 the Pennsylvania Department of Labor and Industry condemned portions of the bleacher and grandstand areas as "unsafe and unfit for use." This occurred during a year when no pro ball was played in Williamsport, and uncertainty as to its future return. City leaders were reluctant to undertake a major stadium overhaul under such circumstances. Rather than a cherished community asset, Bowman Field became a financial liability to the city. In fact, the city offered the stadium to the Little League Baseball, Inc., as a site for its annual Little League World Series. However, Little League officials rejected the offer because the estimated field and stadium renovations carried a hefty price tag of $100,000.

In an era when many communities razed old ballparks (and spurned minor league

Fig. 24 In 1955 Putsee Vannucci photographed this aerial view of Bowman Field from a Piper Cub plane. It was one of the last images remaining documenting Bowman Field's original outer fence and the ballpark's retro look of the 1940s. (Putsee Vannucci Collection, Lycoming County Historical Society)

baseball), Williamsport took a more prudent course. In 1957 the city established the Bowman Field Commission to oversee the maintenance of the ballpark and administer its future use. Long-time baseball booster Joe Mosser was named as the commission's first chairman. Bill Pickelner, the present-day chair of the Bowman Field Commission, was one of the original members of the first commission. In 1958, the commission secured the return of professional baseball, shored-up the grandstand, and replaced Bowman Field's rotting bleachers to meet state safety specifications.

Other changes were afoot. The dirt path between the pitcher's mound and home plate—a vestige of baseball's early era—was finally removed in 1958. Bowman Field had been one of the few remaining ballparks that retained the "catcher's walk" well into the 1950s. That same year, the Robert M. Sides Music Company donated an organ for use at Bowman Field, one of only a handful of minor league ballparks to have one. Mrs. Evelyn Strang, the ballpark organist, entertained and delighted Bowman Field fans and contributed much to the ballpark's ambiance.

When the New York Mets became affiliated with Williamsport in 1964 they added another historic feature to Bowman Field. The Mets transported their old light towers from the recently vacated Polo Grounds to Bowman Field. These lights illuminated Bowman Field for the next twenty-three years. In addition to the lights, New York mandated the layout of a ten-foot warning track as a buffer between the outfield grass and the thirteen-foot outfield fence.

Reconstruction for the Modern Era

With the loss of minor league baseball between 1973 and 1986, Bowman Field again fell into disrepair. The surprise announcement of the return of Class AA baseball in 1987 prompted the city and Bowman Field Commission to initiate one of the most extensive and costly stadium renovation projects up until then. Over $1 million were poured into the facelift of Bowman Field. The ballpark's structural steel girders were sandblasted and painted, repairs were made to the grandstand roof, and new weather-resistant aluminum seating replaced the old wooden grandstand seats. Plastic-molded auditorium seats (donated by the Montgomery High School) were installed in the box-seat area to replace the old folding chairs that formerly occupied this space. In 1988 the city removed the ballpark's rotting left-field bleachers, bringing Bowman Field's seating capacity back to 4,200. A concession and picnic area, rented out to groups during games, now occupies that space, offering a unique view of the ballgame.

In 1987 new light towers were erected to replace the old Polo Grounds lights. This upgrade in lighting actually met the more stringent standards of Class AAA baseball due to the anticipated use of Bowman Field as a short-term AAA franchise of the Philadelphia Phillies. Though legal complications thwarted the relocation of AAA baseball in

Williamsport, future occupants of Bowman Field possessed one of the best illuminated fields at the Class AA level.

The final era of renovations coincided with the return of professional minor league baseball to Williamsport in 1994. As a pre-condition for the Chicago Cubs to move their short-season Class A New York–Penn League team from Geneva, New York, to Williamsport, the franchise owners required that new locker and training room facilities be constructed. This was done along with other upgrades prescribed by the National Association of Professional Baseball Leagues. Though Williamsport dropped down in classification from AA to short-season A baseball, the new stadium guidelines required a greater financial commitment to retaining professional minor league baseball.

Among the stadium renovations that were completed between 1994 and 2000 were the construction of one thousand new box seats, a new press box, a new public address and sound system, padding and a new chain link fence around the perimeter of the field, exterior painting of the park, and a new sanitary sewer hook-up. These improvements amounted to $400,000 (funded by federal urban and state community block grants and the Williamsport-Lycoming Foundation), bringing the cumulative price tag for renovations over the decade to nearly $1,500,000.

The playing surface of Bowman Field required extensive work if Williamsport was to keep its minor league team. Major League organizations feared the possibility of career-ending injuries to talented minor league prospects due to poor field conditions. Bowman Field's outfield was not level and drained poorly after rain. Various turf problems (particularly fungi that caused unsightly barren patches in the infield and outfield grass) were directly attributable to the lack of an in-ground sprinkler and irrigation system. During long stretches without rain, the infield became rock-hard. Jimmy Piersall, the Cubs roving instructor for their farm system, compared the modern field conditions at Bowman Field to those of the 1940s when he played here with the Scranton Miners: "Bowman Field was beautiful when I played here forty years ago, but now it's become a rock pile."

The whole field required leveling, grading, resodding and the installation of a new drainage and irrigation system. The cost for the project totaled over $192,000 and was completed in time for the beginning of the Cubs 1997 season. Funded entirely by the Williamsport-Lycoming Foundation, an organization pooling monies from various local philanthropic trusts, the field renovations secured Williamsport's immediate future as a member of the New York–Penn League. Without the estimated $1 million that the Foundation has generously donated since 1987, Bowman Field probably would have degenerated into a rusting hulk of a stadium. Professional baseball would have died an ignominious death in Williamsport.

In 1998 the city and the owners of the Williamsport Crosscutters franchise signed a new five-year lease agreement that extended minor league baseball into the next millennium. Shortly thereafter, they announced a bold funding initiative to undertake the most extensive stadium reconstruction project since Bowman Field was built in 1926.

In July 1998 Pennsylvania's Lt. Governor, Mark S. Schweiker, visited Williamsport and announced the state's commitment of $750,000 in matching funds toward the renovation of Bowman Field. In 1999, the city raised its portion of the state grant and awarded bids for the renovation work. Construction commenced in early January 2000 and was completed in May, one month before the Williamport Crosscutters had their home opener in the New York–Penn League.

Bowman Field's $1.5 million facelift retained the best features of the old ballpark that appealed to baseball purists, while adding new features that catered to casual baseball fans. Victorian-style dormers now adorned the grandstand roof. The construction of a turreted ticket office (part of the Crosscutters' new front-office complex) paid homage to the Victorian-era mansions dotting West Fourth Street's "Millionaire's Row." Beyond these ornamental touches, the Bowman Field renovation project completed many upgrades and improvements (long overdue) geared specifically for the fans. These included refurbishing the stadium concourse and grandstand to accommodate the needs of the handicapped, constructing larger restroom facilities for men and women, building a walk-in souvenir shop, and expanding Bowman Field's concessions area.

Bowman Field Personalities

A fan's psychological attachment to the hometown ballpark is one of the more enduring and unique relationships in all of sports. Beyond its wooden, steel, or concrete edifice, a ballpark comprises more than the sum of the space it occupies. It is the cumulative spirit and experiences shared by fans that breathe life and vitality into the structure. Bowman Field has had many remarkable people associated with it over the past seventy years. Perhaps the most memorable figure to leave an indelible mark upon the uptown park was not a ballplayer or club executive but a humble groundskeeper, Alfred (Al) Bellandi.

Born in Pisa, Italy, in 1886, Bellandi immigrated to Williamsport in 1927. Equipped with a borrowed shovel and an unparalleled energy and dedication, he began his groundskeeping career at Bowman Field. In a *Williamsport Sun-Gazette* (*WS-G*) column written by sportswriter Mike Bernardi in 1959, Bellandi reminisced about his start at Bowman Field:

> I had been doing odd jobs for Mike Orso [concessionaire and part-time groundskeeper at Bowman Field in 1935] when I learned that Mr. Lundy [Dick Lundy, Grays' Director] needed a couple of men to dig holes for the construction of the inner fence. I asked him for a job and he gave it to me but asked if I had a shovel. When I said no, he said that he couldn't use me so I asked Mike Orso if I could borrow one. When I reported for work and saw two other men

Fig. 25 From 1936 to 1961, head groundskeeper Al Bellandi transformed Bowman Field into the "garden spot of the Eastern League." Though offered positions by the Detroit Tigers and Baltimore Orioles, Bellandi never strayed from Williamsport and his beloved Bowman Field. (*Grit*)

> . . . I started and dug seventy-six holes at twenty cents a hole. Then I found out that I had dug two more holes than the other two men had dug together.

Lundy found out about this, fired the other two men, and urged Grays business manager Roy Clunk to hire Bellandi as an assistant to the groundskeeper for the remainder of the 1935 season. In the following year, Clunk promoted Bellandi to head groundskeeper and arranged off-season employment for him at Avco, an aircraft engine manufacturer. In 1946 Bellandi quit Avco to work full-time at Bowman Field.

During his tenure, Bellandi gained a reputation as one of the best groundskeepers in organized baseball. George Trautman, president of the National Association of Professional Baseball Leagues at the time of his visit to the city in 1951, paid Bellandi a high compliment by remarking, "You sure make a fine ballpark, one of the most beautiful in the country." According to reports and club-insiders, the Baltimore Orioles and

Detroit Tigers had courted Bellandi to become their respective groundskeepers; but he refused turn his back on his beloved Bowman Field.

Bellandi's resourcefulness, mechanical ability, and dedication made Bowman Field "the garden spot of the minor leagues" according to Williamsport sport scribes Ray Keyes and Mike Bernardi. It was not unusual for Bellandi to work eighteen-hour days manicuring, sprucing, and doing the odd jobs vital to the maintenance of the ballpark. He arrived at Bowman Field around 6:00 A.M. and often worked past midnight, only taking time out for meals. On numerous occasions, he returned to the park in the middle of the night to turn off sprinklers or cover the field if rain threatened. Bellandi did most of the groundskeeping work himself well into his seventies, until he finally hired his grandson, Dennis, as an assistant.

Though not a college-educated turf specialist, Bellandi possessed an intuitive landscaping ability and Yankee ingenuity. His talent as a handyman and jack-of-all-trades saved the ball club thousands of dollars, allowing the Grays to remain financially solvent in lean times. Bernardi noted that "among his odd jobs at the ballpark [were] painting, plumbing, carpentry and mechanical work." A gifted mechanic, Bellandi designed and fabricated his own grounds and landscaping tools. Perhaps the most prized possession among Bellandi's jerry-rigged mechanical devices was the motor scooter that he equipped with a rake and infield drag, spreader roller, and mower. Bellandi reduced scientific turf management to its essential elements: "Hard work, plenty of water and sunshine, plus the right kind of grass seed will do the trick."

Bellandi retired as Bowman Field's head groundskeeper in June 1961. He was honored with a special night at the ballpark on July 15, 1961, co-sponsored by the Grays and the Sons of Italy. In appreciation of his life's work and dedication to Bowman Field, Bellandi received congratulatory telegrams from many friends and associates affiliated with the Grays and Tigers. Among the telegrams were those from former Williamsport Tigers general manager Bob Steinhilper, and ballplayers Jim Bunning and Paul Foytack. Frank Lucchesi, who managed the Grays to their first championship in twenty-six years, also offered his congratulations. Dick Carter, the 1958 Grays manager, humorously stated to Bellandi in his telegram, "You're the greatest. But before you leave, smooth out the dip by the third base coaching box."

A poignant footnote to Bellandi's retirement appeared in a special Ray Keyes column during the winter of 1962. Keyes recalled how Bellandi visited the Grays office at Bowman Field and remarked to general manager Otto Stradley, "I'd like to sweep out Roy's cigar butts for the last time." This was in reference to the passing of his longtime friend, former Grays business manager Roy Clunk, who died the previous November. "His volunteer task completed," Keyes reported, "Bellandi turned, said, 'Well, I guess that's it,' and walked out." Bellandi continued to attend games at Bowman Field and even served as a consultant to the groundskeepers who succeeded him. He passed away on March 20, 1972.

Most baseball teams have had their share of "super fans," those charismatic personalities and fixtures at ballparks who are part of the memorable spectator experience. The Brooklyn Dodgers had Hilda Chester, with her famous cowbell. Williamsport had its own locally nurtured talent in Jimmy Mileto, one of the most colorful and unforgettable fans to appear on the Bowman Field scene.

Like Bellandi, Mileto had been a native of Italy. Following the destruction of his village by an earthquake, he left Italy at the age of fourteen and immigrated to the coal fields of West Virginia to work as a miner. He later settled in Williamsport, gaining employment as a lumber cutter. In 1927 Mileto opened a shoeshine and magazine stand on West Fourth Street across from the old Capital Theater (the present-day Community Arts Center), where he became a downtown fixture for the next thirty years. Mileto's love for baseball had been whetted by the Grays championship season of 1934. From that point on the local ball club became his passion. Around 1938 he opened a small grocery store on the site of his former newsstand. Mileto's store served as a "hot-stove league," where heated discussions took place around Grays baseball. Mayor Leo Williamson and Tommy Richardson often dropped by to exchange their opinions and promote minor league baseball in Williamsport.

Mileto attended Grays games religiously and earned a reputation as Williamsport's number-one fan and cheerleader. His trademark was a cowbell that he rang throughout the game, and a white towel that he waved at opposing pitchers to distract them. He exhorted hometown fans to root for the Grays and led the grandstand cheers himself. Mileto was very popular with the Grays players, particularly the 1939 team. He frequently hosted spaghetti dinners for outfielders Larry Bettencourt, Como Cotelle, and infielder Hank Camelli. In recognition of his devotion to the ballclub, Mileto earned the singular honor of throwing out the first ball to usher in the 1942 season. Normally, that honor had been exclusively reserved for mayors, club officials, and distinguished civic leaders.

That same year, business manager Roy Clunk asked Mileto to refrain from his towel and cow bell-ringing antics. Clunk thought that Mileto's behavior was undignified and an embarrassment to Williamsport's reputation within the Eastern League. Hurt by Clunk's ban on his demonstrative cheering, Mileto refused to attend any Grays games for several weeks that season. But his love for the game and the Grays ultimately pulled him back to Bowman Field. Mileto remained Williamsport's most vocal and energetic baseball fan until a near-fatal heart attack slowed him down in the mid-1950s. When he died on December 31, 1957, a colorful era of Williamsport baseball had passed away, adding another chapter to the lore of the Grays.

Bowman Field: Special Events and Baseball Memories

Over the years, Bowman Field has functioned as an important community venue for many special events (sporting and nonsporting) beyond the realm of minor league baseball. It was in fact a multipurpose stadium long before the concept came in vogue during the 1960s. Countless district and state high school baseball tournaments were held at Bowman Field over the past half century. Moreover, local and area college baseball teams (Lock Haven, Mansfield, and Penn College) also enjoyed access to the ballpark. Exhibition softball games featuring barnstorming teams and players (including the legendary pitching ace Eddie Feighner of "The King and His Court") became an annual event at Bowman Field during the 1960s and early 1970s. Williamsport High School scheduled its 1932 and 1962 home football games there, as did Lycoming College in 1958. Moreover, many city fans packed Bowman Field to watch professional and amateur boxing cards during the 1930s and 1940s.

Bowman Field also served as a convenient venue for many civic-related activities, pageants, regional entertainment events, circuses, and music concerts. In conjunction with the Pennsylvania State American Legion Convention of 1939, the ballpark hosted one of the state's largest Drum and Bugle Corps competitions. The popular city-sponsored Kids Day (later "Joel Garrison Day") found a frequent home in the ballpark as well. Bowman Field was the site of many war-bond rallies held during the World War II era.

Bowman Field was retained on numerous occasions to showcase and celebrate the city's history and milestones: Williamsport's Sesquicentennial Pageant in 1956; the Bicentennial Pageant of 1976; and the Woodsman's Rally, held in conjunction with the Susquehanna Boom Festival (Boomfest) during the early and mid-1980s. Bowman Field also hosted rock concerts (Three Dog Night, Badfinger, the Beach Boys, and the Four Tops), country music performances (Randy Travis), and the ever-popular "Battle of the Bands" featuring local musical talent.

Over the span of seven decades, Bowman Field has had its share of baseball history and lore. Several memories stand out: the first night baseball game played in the area (1932); the no-hitters tossed by Williamsport pitchers in 1933, 1948, and 1967; Williamsport's pennant-winning teams (1934, 1960, and 1962); future Yankee great Roger Maris crashing through the left-field fence in pursuit of a fly ball; and Dave Bresnahan's infamous Great Potato Caper. Add to this, the sparkling play of hundreds of players who eventually earned their way to the Major Leagues, and the talented few—Ralph Kiner, Leon Day, Richie Ashburn, Juan Marichal, Bob Lemon, "Big" Johnny Mize, Whitey Ford, Larry Doby, Jim Bunning, and Nolan Ryan—enshrined in Baseball's Hall of Fame.

Bowman Field also hosted some of the finest baseball talent ever seen in the old Negro Leagues when teams such as the Homestead Grays, the Newark Eagles, the Baltimore Elite Giants, the Harrisburg Colored Giants, and the Philadelphia Stars barnstormed here. Their ranks included many baseball stars—Satchel Paige, Josh Gibson, Oscar Charleston, Leon Day, and Buck Leonard—who shined brightly in their exhibition appearances at Bowman Field.

As minor league baseball heads into the next millennium, Williamsport's future is

Fig. 26 Satchel Paige, the legendary Negro League pitching star, brought his Philadelphia Stars to Bowman Field in 1950 to play an exhibition game. Paige is pictured here with Frank Delycure, a local businessman who sponsored the game. (Putsee Vannucci Collection, Lycoming County Historical Society)

looking more secure. Bowman Field has been given a new lease on life with the most recent stadium renovation. Communities have spent lavish sums to duplicate what Williamsport already has in place—an authentic old-fashion ballpark that hearkens back to an earlier era of baseball. But what can't be purchased or fabricated is the unique history and shared experiences that shapes the ambiance of a ballpark. New chapters will undoubtedly be added to Williamsport's grand baseball story.

4

The New York–Pennsylvania League Era to Wartime Baseball, 1923–1945

On March 23, 1923, the modern era of Williamsport's professional baseball history was ushered in at the Arlington Hotel in downtown Binghamton, New York. There, a meeting of prominent baseball and civic leaders (including Williamsport's most prominent baseball booster, Thomas Gray) convened to establish the fledgling Class B New York–Pennsylvania League (NYPL). Also attending the meeting were John Farrell (secretary of the National Association of Professional Baseball Leagues (NAPBL) and former president of the New York State League) and other baseball supporters representing prospective league members Wilkes-Barre, Scranton, and Elmira. Little did Gray envision the success enjoyed during the first three seasons of the NYPL. During this period (1923–25), Williamsport won two championships, tied for a third, and won 246 games, the most of any period in Williamsport's baseball history.

Gray contributed to that success by prudently arranging working agreements with both the Pittsburgh Pirates and Philadelphia Phillies to procure player talent such as George "Mule" Haas and Walter French, both of whom

Fig. 27 Team portrait of the 1923 Williamsport team that won the first New York–Pennsylvania League (NYPL) championship that season. The team included George "Mule" Haas, who was a prominent of the Philadelphia A's championship teams of 1929–31. (*Grit*)

were key members of Connie Mack's great Philadelphia A's teams of the late 1920s. The Pirates also made available such Grays mainstays as Roy Leavitt, Harold Fulweiler, Charlie Stell, and Dudley Foulk. He leavened these acquisitions with local talent such as Arnold "Bucky" Poole and "Punch" Miller.

A fine managing job by Harry Hinchman contributed to the early success of the team. He had been recommended to the directors of the Williamsport Baseball Club by his own brother, Bill Hinchman, chief scout of the Pittsburgh Pirates. Bill Hinchman had been a member of Williamsport's Tri-State championship team of 1905 and, later, the formidable Lycoming Foundry team of Williamsport's Industrial League of the World War I era.

Prior to joining Williamsport, Hinchman had managed Toledo in the American Association and had stints in the Virginia, Southern, and Blue Grass Leagues. He was a wizened veteran of the baseball wars of a by-gone era and played briefly for the Cleveland Indians in 1907.

Williamsport defeated Wilkes-Barre 10-4 in the 1923 season opener—the NYPL's first game ever—and never looked back. The Grays clinched the league's inaugural pennant over their chief rival, the York White Roses, with a 82-42 record and a .862 winning percentage, the finest record ever compiled by Williamsport in minor league play.

The Billtowners were keyed by effective pitching, led by twenty-game winner Dudley Foulk and fifteen-game winners Jim Bishop and Harold Fulweiler. The batters led the league with a franchise record .318 team batting average led by "Bucky" Poole's .372 and Walter French's .352 averages. Stanley "Rabbit" Benton scored a franchise record 133 runs.

In 1924, Williamsport gained not only a second consecutive pennant but also a team nickname. During the previous season, local sportswriters used numerous monikers in lieu of an official team name. Such names as the "Bald Eagles," the "Hinchmanites," and the "Billies" or "Bills" were predominant in written accounts of the team's exploits. Though club directors were ambivalent about the name situation, the *Williamsport Gazette and Bulletin* (*WG&B*) took a different tack, hoping to sell more newspapers by fostering civic loyalty to the team. The newspaper conducted a contest to name the local team. The prize was a season ticket to all Williamsport home games, worth $45. There were 197 different team-names submitted by local fans. The winning entry was submitted by Jess Gilbert who suggested the "Grays" in honor of the late Sheriff Thomas Gray. Williamsport adopted the new team name on May 10, 1924, on the eve of the start of the NYPL season.

York again was Williamsport's major rival for league honors. The White Roses race with the Grays was much closer in 1924 than the previous season, climaxing in a crucial five-game series in late August at the Williamsport High School Athletic Field. The series coincided with a statewide Elks convention hosted by the city, resulting in raucous crowd scenes as many Elks members attended the games. According to accounts in the *WG&B*, "The games were played amid the wildest scenes imaginable with umpires frequently halting play to have the field cleared of seat cushions, score cards and pop bottles."

One of the memorable moments of this critical series occurred in the ninth inning of the third game when the Grays "Bucky" Poole leaned far out over the plate to slap the game-winning hit. Crafty veteran pitcher Thomas "Lefty" George attempted to give Poole an intentional pass but Poole crossed him up and swatted at the pitch.

In 1924, the Grays again had an efficient blend of timely hitting and consistent pitching. Bill Hunnefield took the league batting crown with a .346 average and Roy Leavitt led the league in homers with eighteen. The pitching staff got nineteen wins from Bobby Burns and eighteen wins each from Carlton Demarest and Henry "Lefty" Huffman. They beat York again for the pennant with an 80-48 record.

Fig. 28 This image of a Williamsport Grays game played at the Williamsport High School Athletic Field was captured from the roof of the Culler furniture factory. (*Grit*)

Following the 1924 season, the Grays were feted with a celebratory dinner at the Ross Club. A gold watch was presented to Grays manager Harry Hinchman. Lycoming County Judge Max Mitchell said at the gathering, "A good baseball team is one of the greatest assets that a city could have. It advertises Williamsport and spreads abroad its reputation as a wide awake place."

The Grays battled York for the pennant for the third straight year in 1925, ending the season deadlocked with like records of 77-55, setting up an exciting, hard-fought play-off series to decide the pennant. York won the first game 5-2 behind the clutch pitching of "Lefty" George. Williamsport clinched the second game 3-2. York won the third game in a 10-4 romp. The pennant was decided in exciting fashion in the fourth game 5-3 on a dramatic home run by York's Del Bissonette. Though heartbreaking for local fans, the loss epitomized the torrid rivalry between the two teams that dominated the NYPL's first three seasons.

The 1925 season also marked the beginning of the pitching career of nearby Montoursville's Tracey "Kewpie Dick" Barrett, one of the all-time prolific minor league pitchers. Signed as a nineteen-year-old under the assumed name of "Dick Oliver" to protect his collegiate eligibility, Barrett went on to win 325 minor league games, ranking him the eighth winningest pitcher in league history. He recorded eight twenty-win seasons while pitching in the storied Pacific Coast League (PCL) and still holds the league's all-time strikeout mark with 1,866. Barrett (Oliver) was 8-6 in his debut season with the Grays.

Another all-time pitching standout on the Grays staff that year was Walter Tauscher. This iron-armed wonder pitched in 856 games (seventh on the all-time minor league list) including 527 games (an all-time record) in the American Association.

The only thing notable about the following season was that it marked both a beginning and an ending. On May 4, 1926, the Grays played their first regular season game in their new home-grounds, Memorial Field (later renamed Bowman Field). They won this inaugural game 5-1 over the Shamokin Indians.

This season also marked the end of Harry Hinchman's tenure as Grays manager. From 1923 to 1926, Hinchman compiled a record of 310-215 during a four-season stint. He later resurfaced briefly as the Grays skipper during the turmoil-filled 1932 season. Hinchman has the distinction of being Williamsport's all-time winningest manager.

The Grays dropped to the unaccustomed depths of last place in the forgettable 1927 season, despite having former New York Giants standout player George J. Burns, as player-manager. In the following season, the Grays disappointments continued, though fortunately they escaped last place. This was not enough for Burns, however. He resigned as manager on August 9, after a series of crippling injuries sidelined key players. Business manager J. Roy Clunk, who had previous managerial experience in the Piedmont and Blue Ridge Leagues, finished out the 1928 season as manager.

After three seasons in the doldrums, the Williamsport Grays enjoyed their best season since 1925 in 1929. They were in the thick of the NYPL pennant chase to the very end and flourished under new player-manager Glenn Killinger, a former member of the 1925 Grays. Killinger was a former standout football player at Penn State, he later served as head football coach at West Chester State College and was enshrined in the College Football Hall of Fame.

During the 1929 season, Grays moundsmen spun four consecutive shutouts between May 21 and May 25, compiling a string of sixty-two consecutive scoreless innings. Pitching like this made the Grays solid contenders. Their inability to beat the Binghamton Triplets crippled their pennant chances, however, losing ten of thirteen games with them.

But they still had a chance to redeem their dim play-off hopes with Binghamton in early September 1929. To publicize these important games to local fans the *WG&B* erected a Play-o-Graph board on the side of the newspaper's building at the corner of West Fourth and Hepburn streets. The board gave a pitch-by-pitch account of the games as information came off the wire from Binghamton. Alas, the Grays lost consecutive games 10-6 and 5-4, dashing their play-off hopes. Following the devastating 5-4 loss, Grays bat-boy, Dick Spotts, wept in the locker room. It was still a fine season nevertheless, for the Grays compiled a 79-60 record. Six weeks following the end of the season the stock market crashed, ushering in hard times for the nation, the Williamsport Grays, and the rest of professional baseball.

The Grays entered the 1930s and the first season of the Depression years as a pennant contender, battling throughout the whole season but coming up short, finishing in third place. One important milestone in 1930 had important consequences for the Grays. The WRAK radio station broadcast of Opening Day against Hazleton at Bowman Field marked the first live baseball Williamsport broadcast ever. Grays'officials originally had fears that radio broadcasts would have negative consequences at the gate, particularly with the tightened economic circumstances of the Depression. They restricted the broadcasts of Grays games to just Monday and Friday. Later, team directors would become more solicitous and cooperative of the electronic media when they learned that broadcasts actually increased attendance.

The Grays were involved in another milestone on July 22, 1930, when they played in the first NYPL night game at Binghamton. Binghamton's use of lights came only two months after Des Moines of the Western League became the first team in organized baseball to play under artificial lighting. The use of lights became a necessity to spur attendance during the lean economic times of the Depression and may have saved minor league baseball from extinction.

As the Depression deepened, the Williamsport Grays entered some lean years in which their lack of a stable financial base threatened the very existence of the team. This perilous state was not helped, when on February 14, 1931, club president and long-time benefactor J. Walton Bowman died suddenly of a heart attack.

The Grays financial woes coincided with a decline in the on-field fortunes of the team. Despite the team's disappointing third-place finish, fans enjoyed the fine play of stars Bucky Walters, who led the team in hitting with a .316 average, and pitcher Chant Parkes, who won twenty-two games—the most by a Williamsport pitcher since Jack Warhop's twenty-nine wins in 1907. Walters later excelled as pitcher for the Cincinnati Reds and Phillies and won the National League's Most Valuable Player Award in 1939 and 1940.

The 1932 Grays lacked both talent and depth, factors that contributed to a turbulent and unsuccessful year. During the 1932 season the Grays employed three different managers and teetered on the brink of extinction. Herb Moran started the season as the Grays manager, but when they got off to a bad start he was fired on May 13. Harry Hinchman suceeded Moran as manager from May 14 to the end of June, hoping he could weave his old managerial magic. Finally, Glenn Killinger finished the season as skipper. Unfortunately, the Grays just didn't have the talent.

Lack of success on the field aggravated the Grays money woes because fans didn't want to come out to see a floundering team. More important, the number of fans with disposable income to spend on baseball games greatly declined as the Depression worsened. Not only did this imperil the Grays franchise but it also threatened the existence of other teams in the league, as well as the league itself.

Everyone's financial problems were compounded in June when the federal government imposed a surcharge of eight cents and five cents, respectively, on all seventy-five-cent and fifty-cent tickets. The Grays management absorbed the cost of this newly imposed tax, although they were the only NYPL team to do so. However, by mid-July the Grays' financial crisis deepened to such an extent that the team faced the real possibility of insolvency. Other teams were in similar dire straits, but fate intervened.

The demise of the old Eastern League (EL), due to its own financial crisis, resuscitated the teetering New York–Pennsylvania League. The EL's collapse forced the Boston Braves to relocate their defunct Hartford club to Harrisburg. The New York Yankees took over the Binghamton Triplets (the Yanks earlier considered buying the Grays but bought Binghamton instead). This restructuring stabilized the league in its darkest hour.

The Grays economic crisis was averted when club president Ralph "Pat" Thorne dipped into his own pockets to meet the team's pressing financial obligations, thereby saving the franchise. At the same time he worked out an informal agreement with the Cleveland Indians to cut costs associated with player development. The final step that stabilized the traumatic season was the hiring of Glenn Killinger as manager. Killinger, a popular figure with local fans, became available with the demise of the Allentown team during the collapse of the old Eastern League.

Some explanation is in order here about the structure of the minor leagues during this period. Beginning in 1921, the minor league's governing body, the National Association of Professional Baseball Leagues (NAPBL) allowed minor league teams to be owned by Major League clubs. The St. Louis Cardinals, led by general manager Branch Rickey, started buying minor league teams to develop talent for the club. Before this time Major League teams signed players and optioned them to unaffiliated minor league teams for further seasoning. This is the type of informal agreement that the Williamsport Grays had with the Pittsburgh Pirates in the period from 1923 to 1926, and with the New York Giants in 1926 and 1928. The arrangement that Thorne worked out with the Cleveland Indians was an extension of these earlier agreements.

In 1933 the Grays entered into a formal player development agreement with Connie Mack's Philadelphia A's. The A's stocked the Williamsport team with new players for development and optioned veteran players for rehabilitation assignment after injuries. In return, the Grays received money when the players were sold back to the A's for advancement to the Major League team.

———

The introduction of night baseball at Bowman Field in 1932 helped to stabilize the club's financial situation and ensure the continuance of the Grays. On June 6, 1932, the Grays played their first game under the lights at Bowman Field, falling to York 9-5 as a curious throng of over two thousand fans looked on. The new light towers became a permanent fixture at Bowman Field. The Grays finished this very trying season with a lackluster 63-76 record. Chant Parkes was again one of the bright spots for the Grays, compiling his second consecutive twenty-win season, with twenty-one wins.

In 1933 the NYPL's owners' decision to move the league to a higher classification level—from Class B to Class A status—further compounded the tenuous financial condition of the Grays. This upgrade placed Williamsport one level below the highest minor league classification of the time, Class AA, and such premier circuits as the International League, the American Association, and the Pacific Coast League. Though the move enhanced the status of the NYPL, it was a financial hardship for the team due to higher players salaries associated with the new classification. Under the NAPBL rules the team payroll limit was $3,600 in Class A as opposed to $2,600 in Class B. Elmira and Harrisburg joined Williamsport in opposing the classification change, fearing the imposition of the new salary structure during the throes of Depression spelled financial ruin for professional baseball in their respective cities.

A mass meeting (covered live by WRAK radio) convened on March 28, 1933, at the Lycoming County Courthouse to gauge whether sufficient financial and fan support existed to sustain professional baseball in Williamsport. Philadelphia A's coach Ira Thomas gave an inspirational speech about the value of professional baseball to a community. The *WG&B*'s Boy's Band gave a rousing concert in front of the courthouse before the meeting. Grays vice-president Tommy Richardson reported club expenses in 1932 were $48,000 with losses of $8,300. The projected expenses for the club would be a minimum of $36,000. Numerous fans pledged support for the continuation of baseball in Williamsport by buying season tickets for the upcoming season. As a result of the overwhelming support for baseball expressed at the meeting, professional baseball's future in Williamsport seemed secure.

The 1933 season was a rebuilding year for the Grays. Their new manager, Mike McNally, was a proven winner, having piloted pennant clubs in Binghamton, Scranton, and Wilkes-Barre. He started to build a club that gained ultimate success the following year.

That season also marked the beginning of the distinguished baseball career of Williamsport's own Don Manno. Manno played briefly for the Boston Braves in 1940 and had an outstanding minor league career that lasted until 1951. His career began inauspiciously, playing in a Grays exhibition game at York on April 29 as a high school senior. When this was reported to the Pennsylvania Interscholastic Athletic Association (the governing body for high school sports in the state), Manno was banned from competing in a track meet at Williamsport High School on May 16. While the PIAA vacillated on a ruling regarding Manno's amateur status, he continued to skirt eligibility

Fig. 29 The 1934 NYPL champion Williamsport Grays featured such stalwarts as Horace "Red" McBride, who won the league's first MVP award, and twenty-game winner "Bunny" Hearn. (*Grit*)

rules. During the last two weeks of the 1933 season, Manno played under the assumed name of "Don Dixon" in order to protect his collegiate sports eligibility at West Chester State Teachers College.

After a ten-year hiatus, the Williamsport Grays returned to the NYPL's winner's circle, capturing the 1934 pennant. They were beneficiaries of the league's experimental split-season format, which consisted of a season made up of two halves, with the two winners meeting in a play-off series to determine the overall champion. The new format was largely adopted to spur attendance and give those clubs that played poorly in the early part of the season a chance of redemption. The Grays finished the first half in third place. They won the second half, largely by starting it off with an eight-game wining streak, and then beating off strong challenges from Scranton and Binghamton.

Another notable feature to this season was the playing of legal Sunday professional games in Williamsport for the first time. Previously, baseball was banned on Sundays due to the strict Blue Laws in Pennsylvania. The Grays lost their first ever legal Sunday game, April 15, 1934, in a 6-5 exhibition game against the International League's Montreal Royals. The ability to play legal Sunday games also spurred attendance and produced much needed revenue.

The 1934 Williamsport Grays were an awesome hitting team. A model of consistency, they used the same starting line-up for much of the season and batted a collective .295. Zach Smith was in center field, Joe Bonowitz in right, and Horace "Red" Mc-Bride in left. McBride had what was arguably the greatest offensive season any Williamsport player has ever had. He batted .368, led the NYPL in hits with 197, homers with 26, and RBIs with 129. He was named the league's Most Valuable Player in the first year the award was given, and received a gold watch. The infield consisted of Ollie Marquart at second, Bobby Hipps and Jake Plummer sharing first, Bernie Snyder at shortstop, and Fred Myers at third. Bill Baker caught and Jack Ernst served as a reserve backstop. Williamsport area sandlotter and former batboy, Dick Spotts, filled in as a utilityman toward the end of the season.

The Grays had a solid pitching staff consisting of "Bunny" Hearn (who led the league with a 21-8 mark), Luther "Bud" Thomas, Art "Jockey" Mills, and Bill Thomas, who later became the minor league's all-time leader in number of games pitched with 1,015, and all-time game winner with a 383-346 record. Another notable hurler for the Grays that season (however, one who did not figure prominently that season) was Claude Passeau, who later became one of the National League's best pitchers of the 1940s with the Phillies and Cubs. He started for the National League in the 1946 All-Star Game and anchored the 1945 Cubs pennant-winning pitching staff.

The Grays finished the season with a 78-60 record, two games in front of Binghamton. The major highlight of the season was the scintillating play-off series with Binghamton to determine the NYPL champion. The Grays won Game One at Bowman Field 5-4. Joe Bonowitz was the hitting star of that first game, while Bernie Snyder went 4 for 4. Art Mills pitched well for the win.

The Grays lost Game Two 7-4. A near-riot ensued in the sixth inning when the umpire called Binghamton's Jack Shipley safe at third. Grays second-baseman and future manager Marquart objected strenuously to the call and was ejected from the game. Following Marquart's ejection, some of the Bowman Field faithful left the right-field stands and swarmed onto the field. Police escorted the fans back into their seats and finally restored order.

The improbable happened in Game Three when Binghamton's Hormidas Aube tossed a no-hitter, winning 3-1. Ollie Marquart scored the Grays only run on a ground-out. This marked the first time that Williamsport went hitless in a game since the league's inception in 1923. The Grays won Game Four 5-1, as Bill Baker, Ollie Marquart, and Bill Thomas keyed the win. The Triplets won Game Five at Bowman Field 3-1, averting elimination.

The Grays faced a crisis on the eve of Game Six, as the contest coincided with Yom Kippur, the holiest of Jewish holidays. Joe Bonowitz, Williamsport's hottest hitter, was a devout Jew and decided to sit out the game in observance of this holy day. Fortunately, for the Grays, George Miner filled in admirably for Bonowitz in the outfield. He drove in three runs as the Grays won the game and the NYPL pennant 7-2. Bunny Hearn pitched a good game in the clincher but needed late-inning relief help from Luther

"Bud" Thomas. Each Grays player received a $94.50 share of the pennant-winner's jackpot. Additionally, Grays club president James B. Gleason gave each player a personal gift.

After the heady taste of championship vintage in 1934, the Grays sampled the bitter dregs of the second division in 1935. They lost the services of slugger "Red" McBride, who opted to play for the Goodyear Tire Company team in Akron, Ohio. His offensive presence was sorely missed by the Grays and a major factor in their plunge to the second division.

The Grays had two notable players on their team that year, Tony Kubek Sr., father of future Yankee standout shortstop Tony Kubek Jr., batted .307 and knocked in forty-eight runs. The second player was jack-of-all-trades, utilityman Johnny Reder. He won the NYPL's MVP Award, batting .332.

The 1936 Grays are remembered by many old-time fans as one of the most exciting teams ever. Even though they failed to capture the NYPL pennant, they were one of the best hitting teams ever seen in Billtown, leading the league in team batting with a .312 average.

The adoption of a split-season format kept the Grays in the pennant race throughout the season. They barely missed the play-offs, finishing only one game in back of Elmira for the second-half title. The Grays overall record was 78-62.

Henry Peploski paced this hard-hitting team with a .356 average and led the league in hits with a franchise record 210. "Red" McBride was lured back to the Grays, batting .335, tying for the league-lead in homers with 19, and driving in 102 runs. Scrappy catcher Bill Steinecke slapped the ball at .339 and led the league in RBIs with 110. Shortstop Art Funk hit .335 and Woody Wheaton hit .309. Two Grays pitchers even got in on the act, hitting .250 or above. Staff ace Edgar Smith, who went 20-8, batted .257, and George Turbeville sported a .250 average.

Following the 1937 season, the NYPL elected a new president, none other than Williamsport's own Tommy Richardson. The league offices were moved to Williamsport, where they remained until 1970. One of Richardson's first moves as president was to formally change the name of the NYPL to the "Eastern League." The change was suggested by Trenton Senators manager Spencer Abbott, who thought a new league name better reflected the league's expanded regional base and the larger cities it now encompassed: Hartford, Connecticut, Trenton, New Jersey, and (later) Springfield, Massachusetts.

The 1938 Williamsport Grays served as the inspiration for a worldwide youth sports phenomenon, Little League Baseball. Although Little League was not established until the next year, the seed for the idea was firmly planted within its founder, Carl Stotz. He saw how hard his nephews Carl, Dutch, and Jimmy Gehron tried to emulate the feats of those 1938 Grays as they played simulated games in his backyard and improvised sandlots. The lads also imitated WRAK radio broadcaster Sol "Woody" Wolf and his accounts of Grays games. In the vernacular of the golden-tongued Wolf, they tried not

---

Fig. 30   Members of the 1937 Grays warm up at a practice session at Bowman Field. (*Grit*)

to become victims of the "whiffer pill," or strikeout, when they batted against one another. They also had the sometime treat of attending Grays games, further whetting their appetite to play "real games with real uniforms." Stotz resolved to have his nephews to play in an organized league, on teams outfitted with those sought after "real uniforms," youth-sized equipment, and brand new bats and balls—just like their idols at Bowman Field. His was a promise made and a promise kept.

Stotz's nephews' idols included Babe Barna, who led the Grays in hitting that year with a .304 average, Irv Bartling, who batted .301; Larry Bettencourt, who averaged .276; and "Big Bill" Nicholson, who supplied the power, leading the Grays and the newly christened Eastern League with twenty-two circuit clouts. Randy Gumpert was the Grays leading dispenser of the whiffer pill, piling up 147 strikeouts, good enough for second in the league. Ralph Buxton and Glenn Spencer each compiled 12-11 slates, while Pete Blumette was 9-7. While the 1938 Grays finished a disappointing sixth with a 65-74 mark, they can always be remembered for their role in the start of Little League Baseball.

The Williamsport Grays closed out the 1930s as a contender, having climbed to second place as late as July 20, but fading due to threadbare pitching. By mid-August the pitching situation became so acute that outfielder Como Cotelle and manager Marty

McManus were forced to hurl for the Grays on consecutive nights. The Grays faced no such shortages on offense as they led the Eastern League with a .279 team average. George McQuinn led the team with a .325 average. Al Brancato led the league in RBIs with ninety-eight, and Ken Richardson batted .309 and led the team in homers with twenty-two.

When Carl Stotz's Little League started its initial season on June 6, 1939, in the very shadows of Bowman Field, Williamsport Grays officials helped to nurture and promote the fledgling league. They gave the boys their first widespread exposure when two of the first Little League teams played between games of a Grays doubleheader on "Community and Suburban Night." Little Leaguers also participated in a pageant commemorating the first seventy-five years of baseball in Williamsport. Grays players also held clinics for Little Leaguers, giving them tips on the finer points of pitching, hitting, and fielding.

After a forgettable 1940 season in which the Grays finished in seventh place, the Grays' directors made several changes to try to bring them back to respectability. Chief among these was the hiring of legendary minor league skipper Spencer Abbott to pilot the Grays. His managerial career spanned forty-three years, from 1903 to 1947. During that time he won two thousand games and managed four pennant winners. Writers dubbed him the "John McGraw" of the minor leagues, after the legendary manager of the New York Giants.

Abbott followed McGraw's hard-nosed, aggressive, and shrewd managerial style. He was brought in to shake-up and rebuild a mediocre team, and turn them into contenders. Abbott succeeded brilliantly. He fired-up the holdovers from 1940 and brought in several players who played for him at Springfield the previous season. Among them was veteran shortstop Hal Quick. Quick became the Grays captain and formed an efficient double-play duo with second-baseman Irv Hall. The rest of the infield was composed of consistent hitting and fielding third-baseman Don Richmond from nearby Wyalusing, in Bradford County, and hard-hitting first-baseman Irv Kolberg.

The outer gardens were patrolled by left-fielder Dave Goodman, center-fielder Ken Richardson, and right-fielder Ron Northey. The catching chores were handled ably by Harry Chozen and Dewey Williams. Roger Wolff, a roly-poly knuckleballer, led the pitching staff. He was joined by Johnny Cordell, Alex Mustaikis, and the versatile Art Jones, who was acquired from Hartford in a trade.

The 1941 Grays were one of the most interesting and exciting teams in Williamsport's baseball history. They participated in one of the most sizzling pennant races in the history of the EL. Fifteen members of the '41 team graduated to the Major League ranks. The excitement generated by the club was reflected at the turnstiles. In 1941, Williamsport passed the 100,000 mark in attendance for the first time, drawing 111,734 fans for an all-time franchise record.

The Grays charged out of the gate, capturing first place by mid-May. By early June, they had slumped somewhat and dropped out of the lead. Williamsport became locked

Fig. 31 The 1941 Grays pose at Elmira's Dunn Field prior to a play-off game against the Pioneers. Fifteen members of '41 Grays made it to the Major Leagues, including Roger Wolff, Irv Hall, and Don Richmond. (*Grit*)

in a tight race with three other teams: the Wilkes-Barre Barons, the Elmira Pioneers, and the Scranton Miners. Wilkes-Barre's outstanding pitching staff was led by Charles "Red" Embree. Embree won the EL's pitching triple crown that season, leading the league in wins, strikeouts, and earned run average. They got good hitting from that year's league home-run champ Larry Barton, and third-baseman Bob Lemon, a future Hall-of-Fame pitcher.

Elmira was paced by EL batting-titlist Frank Madura, and the pitching staff by future Major League standout Sal "The Barber" Maglie. Scranton got timely hitting from hard-hitting outfielder Pat Colgan, shortstop Danny Carnevale, and outfielder Len Kensecke.

The most memorable game of this epic pennant race was the dramatic August 24 "brawl" between Williamsport and Wilkes-Barre at Bowman Field. The Barons had been in relentless pursuit of the Grays and first place when they entered the confines of

Fig. 32 Scene from a baseball brawl at Bowman Field between the Grays and the Wilkes-Barre Barons, August 24, 1944. Williamsport police were called to the stadium to help break up the brawl. (Tommy Richardson Collection, Courtesy of Louis Hunsinger Jr.)

the uptown ballpark. Trouble arose in the first game of a doubleheader, when Grays pitcher Art Jones was thrown out of the game for arguing balls and strikes by umpire John Showalter. Grays manager Spence Abbott asked if Jones's replacement could have more time to warm up. Barons' manager Earl Wolgamot objected to this and started arguing with Abbott. In the heat of the argument, Wolgamot took a swing at Abbott and was subsequently decked by Art Jones, precipitating a wild free-for-all. Both dugouts emptied.

Players threw punches at one another and fans poured in from the bleachers and joined the fray. Soda bottles flew in all directions. Williamsport police arrived at the ballpark and eventually restored order. Alex Mustaikis replaced the combative Jones and won the game in dramatic fashion 4-1 by hitting a home run in the bottom of the thirteenth inning. The Grays won the second game as well. Unfortunately, Mustaikis's heroics were not enough to overtake Wilkes-Barre for the regular season pennant. The Grays finished with a fine 82-55 record, four games back of the Barons.

The Grays hoped to meet Wilkes-Barre in the Governor's Cup play-offs but the Barons were upset in the opening round by a surprising Elmira team. The Grays disposed of Scranton in three straight, setting up a very exciting final play-off series with the Elmira Pioneers. Roger Wolff pitched a four-hitter to defeat Elmira 4-1 in Game One at Bowman Field. Wolff benefitted from the good hitting support of Ken Richardson, who drove in two runs with a triple.

In Game Two, Sal Maglie out-pitched Art Jones 2-1. The Grays lost Game Three 4-3 in thirteen innings. Elmira's Andy Cohen saved the game for his team when he robbed the Grays Don Richmond of a sure double to halt a Williamsport rally in the tenth inning.

The Grays lost Game Four, as ex-Gray Ray Roche won a 3-2 decision over ace Roger Wolff. The Grays clobbered the Pioneers 13-2 in Game Five at Bowman Field. Alex Mustaikis pitched a two-hit gem. Ron Northey was the hitting star for the Grays with a homer and a triple. The Grays defeat of Sal Maglie 2-1 in Game Six set up the climatic seventh game.

Elmira's Willie Duke ended the Grays fine season in Game Seven with a dramatic and monstrous homer to center field in the eighth inning, giving the Pioneers a 3-1 win and the Eastern League pennant. The disappointing play-off did nothing to diminish old-time Williamsport fans' fond recollection of this memorable team, one that is still remembered with great warmth.

Wartime baseball was ushered in with the 1942 season. For the Grays and the country it could not be business as usual, a point brought home all too dramatically when, shortly after the start of the Eastern League season, Corregidor in the Phillipines fell to the Japanese. Some of the league's best players were called to the colors, depleting the rosters of many EL clubs; Williamsport was no exception. Pitcher Art Jones and catcher Bill Peterman, two players that the Grays were counting on heavily during the 1942 season, were snatched by Uncle Sam.

As the shadow of the draft hung over the Grays players, team officials feared the loss of even more team members. Perhaps more threatening than the draft was the transportation crisis that the Grays and other EL teams experienced. Gas rationing had been instituted, making it difficult for ball clubs to procure adequate fuel for their team buses. On June 1, 1942, the Office of Defense Transportation ordered a ban on all charter-bus use, including baseball team buses. This dealt a crippling financial blow to the Grays. It forced them to rely on more expensive and troublesome rail transportation. The transportation mandate contributed to the temporary demise of the Williamsport Grays in 1943.

Despite transportation problems, Williamsport baseball did its utmost to support the war effort during the 1942 season. Special promotions were tied to the patriotic home-front effort and typified the community's commitment to winning the war. Some pro-motions involved war-bond sales and giveaways. Youngsters were given free admissions to games for bringing in a certain amount of scrap rubber. The Grays also followed organized baseball's practice of asking fans to return foul balls for donation to service-men on duty throughout the far-flung battlefronts of the world.

Despite the drain of key players to the draft and other teams, the Grays were still able to field a respectable and contending ball club. These key player departures ultimately doomed the Grays pennant chances, however. Despite a working agreement with the Philadelphia A's, the Grays received little or no impact players from them. Admittedly, the A's had trouble keeping their own team stocked with talent; still local sports scribes believed the A's could have made a greater effort to shift some talent within their minor league chain to help the Grays in their pennant drive.

This produced some strain within the Grays and may have been another aggravating factor prompting Grays officials to fold the team after the 1942 season. Despite these travails, the Grays were still in the play-off hunt until the waning days of the season. They just missed a play-off berth by two games, edged out by Wilkes-Barre. They finished fifth with a 76-63 mark, the last record above .500 a Williamsport team achieved until 1948.

Irv Hall, who batted .297 and led the league in hits with 158, and Ken Richardson, who led the team in homers with eight, helped to key the Grays offense in 1942. Alex Mustaikis was the Grays leading pitcher with a 15-8 mark. Sam Zoldak, who later pitched for the 1944 American League champion St. Louis Browns, was 11-10.

Following the 1942 season, the directors of the Williamsport Grays left the Eastern League because of money woes. Economic constraints caused by the war, including the high cost of transportation and an uncertain player pool, led to their painful decision. The Philadelphia A's transferred their working agreement to Elmira, where several of the Grays 1942 standouts—such as Alex Mustaikis, Barney Lutz, and Nate Pelter—played in 1943.

Williamsport's baseball fans felt an aching void without baseball. It had been a good diversion for them during these difficult wartime years and helped to maintain morale.

Baseball's return to Williamsport in 1944 was made possible when Baltimore laun-dryman Joe Cambria, owner and operator of the Springfield, Massachusetts, franchise in the Eastern League, relocated his franchise to Williamsport in early 1944 because of lagging attendance. This was the first time that baseball came to Williamsport as the result of another city's inability to support its team. In subsequent years this became the norm rather than the exception.

Cambria, a scout for the Washington Senators, enjoyed a close working relationship with Senators owner Clark Griffith. Griffith had earned the reputation as a notorious skinflint and always appreciated an opportunity to obtain ballplayers on the cheap. Cam-bria obliged Griffith by tapping Cuba to supply ballplayers to the Senators and stock the

Fig. 33 Cuban players, who dominated the roster of the Williamsport Grays between 1944 and 1945, receive their uniforms from manager Ray Kolp in May 1945. (*Grit*)

rosters of the club's farm system. In the words of Roberto Gonzalez Echevarria in his excellent history of Cuban baseball, *The Pride of Havana,* "Cambria was a cagey man . . . he started a network of bird dogs who scouted the bushes and Havana. By the forties he boasted quite a system." Unfortunately, a good number of players Cambria signed failed to meet expectations. This stemmed in part because many of the best Cuban ballplayers were on the "wrong" side of the color line and were denied a chance to compete in the states. Cambria signed so many Cuban players that Griffith and the Senators, in the words of Washington baseball historian Morris Beale, "had to find a special farm for them in Williamsport, Pa." Thus began one of the most interesting and unusual eras in Williamsport's baseball history—dubbed by older fans as the "Cuban Years."

The 1944 Williamsport Grays consisted mostly of Cambria's Cubans and are remembered for their colorful, hustling approach to the game and their speed on the basepaths. In a time before Williamsport and Central Pennsylvania became more multicultural, the

Cubans' Spanish chatter during the games was regarded as an amusing curiosity. In the words of *WG&B* sportswriter Lou Pickelner, "It was undoubtedly the club's daring, dash, and sheer love of the game that made an indelible impression. . . . It was, most fans would agree, an entertaining season." Sportswriters in other Eastern League cities soon tabbed the Cubans the "Laughing Latins" and the "Rhumba Rascals." The Cubans made Williamsport one of the leading road attraction in the EL. The Grays were in the thick of the 1944 pennant race through most of the season. Several of the Cubans were outstanding players, particularly the double-play combination of Frankie Gallardo, Chino Hidalgo, and catcher Rogelio Valdes.

One of the interesting side effects of the baseball manpower crisis resulted in a treat for local fans in 1944, when sixteen-year-old sandlot sensation Dick Welteroth saw some action with the Grays, most notably pitching against the Philadelphia A's in an exhibition game at Bowman Field. The next year, he saw further action with the Grays after his high school year ended.

The Grays were managed by veteran baseball hand Ray Kolp. Kolp pitched in the Majors with the St. Louis Browns and the Cincinnati Reds in the 1920s and 1930s. He also served as the pitching coach of the Minneapolis Millers of the American Association. The team often tried Kolp's patience as a manager. In mid-August Gallardo and Valdes became homesick and returned to Cuba. As every baseball fan knows, a team has to be strong up the middle to win consistently, and the departure of Gallardo and Valedes greatly weakened the Grays stretch-drive for a play-off spot. They battled gamely, but the key departures proved too much and the Grays finished fifth with a 64-75 record.

Despite the Grays being known as a "Cuban team," it was American-born Jim Langley who was voted the team's Most Valuable Player, batting .320 and driving in seventy runs. Langley had the odd superstition of having the public-address announcer at Bowman Field play "Memphis Blues" before each game.

Danny Parra, who at one time was one of Cuba's outstanding amateur pitchers, led the Grays staff with a 14-9 slate, striking out sixty-seven. Johnny Krall went a respectable 13-12. The season was marred by the wartime tragedy suffered by Krall, who lost two brothers aboard the USS *Juneau*, along with the five Sullivan brothers.

The last of the Cuban years (1945) was tarnished by several ugly incidents with other EL teams, particularly the Utica Blue Sox who were led by the racist firebrand first-baseman Cecil "Turkey" Tyson. Tyson made no bones about showing his dislike and hatred for Williamsport's "Rhumba Rascals" on the field.

Tyson's race-baiting escalated throughout the season, culminating in several ugly confrontations in July 1945. The first occurred during the July 8 game at Bowman Field. Tyson went after Grays pitcher Leonard Goicochea with a bat after taking exception to one of Goicochea's high, hard ones. Players from both sides intervened before any real harm was done. *WG&B* sportswriter Lou Pickelner wrote that "Umpire-in-chief Dick Kuzma went soliciting for trouble when he permitted the incident to pass without penalty." Things only settled down briefly. Goicochea finally struck out Tyson to end the inning; but instead of heading back to the dugout, Tyson rushed the mound toward Goicochea. Blows were exchanged, precipitating a benches-clearing brawl that had to be broken up by Williamsport police. The Grays Hector Arrago and Bill Schaedler then got into a fight in front of the team dugout. Several days later, Schaedler again got into a fight with another of his Cuban teammates before a game with Bing-hamton. Grays club officials, tired of Schaedler's hotheaded intolerance, suspended him indefinitely.

Bad blood between the Grays and Blue Sox continued throughout the season, espe-cially during the July 16 game at Utica. Grays pitching ace Danny Parra and the com-bustible "Turkey" Tyson got into a fight at first base. Again, both dugouts emptied. Utica won the game on a late RBI by a young outfielder named Richie Ashburn. Ash-burn later returned to Utica in 1947 after a stint in the army and went on to a Hall-of-Fame career with Phillies, Cubs, and Mets.

The Grays were badly shaken by the hate-mongering and racially motivated inci-dents. Lou Pickelner opined, "The Grays haven't been the same since their contact with 'Turkey' Tyson, and their July debacle can be traced directly to his Cuban baiting." The Grays suffered twenty one-run defeats out of forty-six losses by July 28, 1945.

Other sportswriters throughout the league also chronicled the unwarranted Cuban-baiting as well. *Scranton Tribune* sportswriter Chic Feldman wrote, "It grieves me to report that some Eastern League players and even some managers, went out of their way to abuse the Cuban kids." He continued, "This blind hate may have been responsi-ble for Williamsport's failure to crash the first division in 1944. It would be a hard allegation to prove, yet there was talk in reliable circles that the other clubs 'ganged up' on Williamsport. Yes, even saving their best pitchers to toss at the once-laughing Latins."

All of the turmoil and hatred displayed toward the Cubans may have taken the heart from the Grays. In 1945 they nose-dived to last place, finishing with a 52-85 record. The Cubans were among the Grays most productive players in 1945. Aurelio Fernandez led the league in RBIs with eighty-two and doubles with thirty-nine, hitting .315. Chino Hidalgo batted .307 and Hector Arrago hit .298. Danny Parra led the pitching staff with a 16-14 mark.

5

Postwar Boom to Short-Season Bust:
Williamsport Baseball in Transition 1946–1972

 The Williamsport Grays experienced many changes in the immediate postwar era. Gone were Joe Cambria and his colorful cast of Cubans. Earle E. Halstead, a Dearborn, Michigan, businessman and former American Association umpire, gained controlling interest in the Williamsport ballclub. In giving up his lucrative electroplating business to run the Grays, Halstead explained, "I don't like business; I like athletics. I'm the kind of fellow who would sooner make less doing something I like than doing a job I don't have my heart in."

Among the many changes initiated by Halstead, none proved more important than Williamsport's new working agreement with baseball's reigning World Champion, the Detroit Tigers, an affiliation that continued through 1952. Under Williamsport's arrangement with Detroit, the Grays drew talent from several Tiger farm clubs, chiefly Rome, New York, of the Canadian-American League, and Jamestown, New York, of the Pennsylvania–Ontario–New York (PONY) League. Moreover, the excess talent from Detroit's top farm club at Buffalo was made available.

Veteran minor league manger Gerald "Nig" Lipscomb was named the Grays skipper.

The 1946 season ended up a disappointing reflection of all of the teams Williamsport fielded during their relationship with the Tigers. The Grays got off to a dreadful start, losing twenty of their first twenty-seven games. To make matters worse, the waters of Lycoming Creek ravaged Bowman Field in late May, producing more than $15,000 in damage. Adding insult to injury, "Nig" Lipscomb bailed out as manager, replaced by former Tigers and St. Louis Browns first sacker, Harry Davis. The Grays finished tied for sixth place with Utica, with a 59-80 record.

The Eastern League's silver anniversary season of 1947 marked several changes for the Williamsport baseball club. For the first time since 1923, the Williamsport team was known by a name other than the "Grays." At the behest of the parent club, the Detroit Tigers, the directors of the Williamsport ball club changed the team name to the "Williamsport Tigers." The team also hired a new general manager. On May 21, 1947, former Williamsport newspaper man Robert J. Steinhilper replaced general manager and chief stockholder Earle Halstead as the club's chief administrative officer. Steinhilper transcended the stormy circumstances surrounding his appointment as general manager, becoming one of the EL's most respected executives.

It appears that some intrigue surrounded the dumping of Halstead. *Scranton Tribune* sportswriter Chic Feldman reported in a column that Halstead's ouster had stemmed from his on-going feud with Detroit's front office. Feldman further speculated that EL president Tommy Richardson "may have helped to engineer" this move because of disagreements he had with Halstead about the internal administrative affairs of the Williamsport ball club. Despite Richardson's lofty status as EL president, he still maintained a keen interest in the day-to-day administration of the team. It was a dreary season for the Williamsport Tigers as they finished fifth, with a 67-74 record. But the losing 1947 season gave several players—who later contributed to an exciting 1948 season—a chance to cut their baseball teeth. They included Frank Heller, Bruce Blanchard, and Ken Humphreys.

The Williamsport Tigers 1948 campaign marked the best season for a Williamsport baseball team since 1942. The Tigers played well, staying in contention throughout the season. They trailed off down the stretch, however, as their pitching and hitting lapsed. The outstanding pitching the Tigers enjoyed from Lou Kretlow, Ed March, and Charlie Giddens offset this bad stretch. In yet another whirl on the Tigers managerial merry-go-round, Gene Desautels replaced George Detore as manager.

Pitcher Lou Kretlow was the Tigers premiere player in 1948, enjoying one of the best seasons ever by a Williamsport pitcher. He tossed a no-hitter at Binghamton May 24, a feat that came in the midst of an outstanding streak from mid-May to mid-June in which he won eight straight decisions and hurled thirty-five scoreless innings. He racked up 219 strikeouts—still a franchise record—and piled up a 21-12 record, becoming the last Williamsport pitcher ever to win twenty games in a season.

Fig. 34 Williamsport Tigers first-baseman Frank Heller takes a throw in game action from 1948. Heller led the Eastern League in RBIs in 1947 with ninety-eight. (*Grit*)

Fig. 35 This view from centerfield captures a game in progress between the Williamsport Tigers and the Scranton Red Sox. An overflow crowd of 7,265—one of the largest ever to attend a Tigers game—watched the action from the comfort of the shaded grandstand. (*Grit*)

Fig. 36 Two local natives, Ollie Byers (left) and Don Manno (right), returned to Bowman Field in 1946 in the opposing uniforms of the Hartford Chiefs. Manno had a distinguished minor league career that lasted eighteen years. (*Grit*)

The Tigers drew 102,714 fans to Bowman Field that season, for their best attendance since 1941. It was also the first time a Williamsport team finished above the .500 mark since 1942. Had the Tigers not slipped down the stretch they might have qualified easily for the play-offs. Their fourth-place finish resulted in a tie with Hartford, forcing a one-game play-off to advance to the Governor's Cup play-offs. Unfortunately, the Tigers lost to Hartford 5-2 in ten innings when the Chiefs scored two runs on an error by third-baseman Bruce Blanchard. The highlight for the Tigers was Ken Humphrey's inside-the-park home run.

The Tigers had other notable performances that year. Bruce Blanchard was the EL's batting champ, becoming the first Williamsport player to win a batting title since Cy Anderson hit .382 in 1929. Lou Kretlow's outstanding season garnered him the league's Most Valuable Player award.

During their final four seasons, the Tigers returned to their pre-1948 mediocrity. However, in 1950 and 1951 they had two interesting and notable managers: in 1950 it was Jack Tighe, who in 1957 piloted the Detroit Tigers; 1951's skipper was Lynwood

Fig. 37 Lynwood "Schoolboy" Rowe, the Williamsport Tigers manager, looks on from the Tigers' dugout in 1951. (*Grit*)

"Schoolboy" Rowe, backbone of Detroit's pennant-winning pitching staffs in 1934 and 1935. The Williamsport Tigers sorry situation even produced a few pitching outings for this old-time ace.

In 1951 Williamsport's Don Manno ended his eighteen-year career by finishing out the season in a Tigers uniform. Manno was named to the second team of the EL's all-star team, the only Tiger to garner league honors. He batted .249 with nine homers and forty-eight RBIs.

The 1952 Tigers crashed to last place in their final season in Williamsport. The only bright note was that five players from this sad-sack team made it to the Majors, the most notable being Hall-of-Fame pitcher Jim Bunning, who compiled an unremarkable 5-9 mark with eighty-five strikeouts, a feat not reflective of his future greatness.

Five anonymous businessmen signed their name to a $7,500 note to buy the Williamsport franchise from the Detroit Tigers following the end of the 1952 season, and in 1953 the Williamsport Tigers became the Williamsport A's. Tommy Richardson's close relationship with the venerable Connie Mack and Richardson's membership on the A's board of directors (at Mack's behest) were key factors enabling Williamsport to obtain a new working agreement with the Philadelphia A's.

Another historic milestone for Williamsport baseball occurred in 1953. The first African Americans to ever play for a Williamsport professional baseball team entered the Williamsport A's line-up. They were Joe Taylor, an outstanding slugging outfielder and a former veteran of the Negro Leagues; and Hector Lopez, who achieved prominence with the Kansas City A's and the great Yankee teams of the late 1950s and early 1960s. In actuality, Johnny Braithwaite was the first African American to play in a Williamsport uniform, in an exhibition game against Savannah on March 29, 1953. However, Braithwaite was cut from the Williamsport team following spring training.

Unfortunately for Williamsport fans, the affiliation change failed to reverse the team's on-field fortunes. The Philadelphia A's simply did not have enough talent to stock two Class A teams—the second being Savannah of the South Atlantic or "Sally" League. The A's belatedly recognized this and they declined to renew their working agreement with Williamsport following the 1953 season. The Williamsport A's also suffered from poor pitching and little or no timely hitting. In the opinion of *Williamsport Sun-Gazette* (*WS-G*) Ray Keyes, the "A's would have been a much better team, except for inconsistent pitching."

The A's lost fifteen of seventeen games from late May to mid-June. By the last part of June they plunged to the EL cellar, where they remained until mid-July. The A's finished sixth with a 65-85 record, thirty games behind that year's EL pennant winner, the Reading Indians, and their future Major League slugger Rocky Colavito. The trailblazing Joe Taylor led the A's in hitting with a .324 average in just seventy-eight games. Hector Lopez batted .270.

Keystone Partners: Williamsport and the Pittsburgh Pirates, 1954–1956

For the first time since 1942 the Williamsport baseball club became a community-owned, independent operation. Until 1954, a combination of outside businessmen and representatives of the Detroit Tigers and the Philadelphia A's either owned or operated the team. One of the advantages of the new independent status was that the team re-adopted its traditional nickname, the Williamsport Grays.

The Grays then entered into a working agreement with the Pittsburgh Pirates. The Pirates allowed the Grays to coordinate some of their roster moves in conjunction with the Pirates Southern Association affiliate, the New Orleans Pelicans. The Pelicans could select any player under contract to Williamsport, in turn, the Grays had first crack at any of the Pelicans' excess talent. Moreover, as the Pirates began to sign promising

Fig. 38   The 1955 Williamsport Grays, a Pirate farm club, featured future standout second-baseman Bill Mazeroski (second row, second player from left) (*Grit*)

African American prospects to their farm chain, the only other Class A franchise able to absorb such talent—Charleston, South Carolina—was deep within the grips of Jim Crow. Given the tenuous state of race relations in the South, and in baseball for that matter (still only seven years removed from Jackie Robinson's epic integration struggle), Pittsburgh's willingness to accommodate Williamsport had both sociological and economic ramifications. The Pirates believed that this gifted young talent might develop and flourish in a more racially tolerant community, like Williamsport.

Despite the Pirates best efforts to stock Williamsport with good talent, they were only able to send the Grays young, inexperienced players who required further seasoning in the crucible of a long Eastern League (EL) season. Several players exhibited potential for greatness, however, including a seventeen-year-old second-baseman, Bill Mazeroski, fresh out of high school. The Grays inexperience and inconsistency resulted in a 63-77 record and seventh place. Some players returned to Williamsport the next season with more proficiency and experience under their belts.

Professional baseball in Williamsport almost became extinct in 1955. Williamsport, like many other minor league teams in the mid-1950s, experienced declining attendance and revenue brought on by flagging fan interest. Among the contributing factors to fan apathy were the proliferation of TV and radio broadcasts of Major League games; an increase in disposable income that gave people more options of things to do with their leisure time; and the growth of Little League Baseball in Williamsport—and, with it, the desire of parents and grandparents to see their sons and grandsons play. As a result, the majority of America's minor league ballparks housed sparse crowds throughout the decade. Locally, the Grays seemingly perennial second-division finishes further eroded fan support.

Demographically, as the smallest city in the EL, Williamsport suffered proportionally more than its larger sister cities. In 1954 alone, the Grays lost $25,000. This set the stage for the bleak financial situation the Grays faced in the spring of 1955. The club directors announced in January 1955 that a pre-season goal of $50,000 in advanced ticket sales by March 1 would need to be reached in order to keep professional baseball in Williamsport in 1955. The slogan for this drive was "Keep Baseball Alive in '55."

But the ball club failed to reach this goal, and the continuation of baseball in Williamsport hung in the balance. On March 4, 1955, the directors decided to proceed with baseball despite the economic shortfall. A second pre-season ticket drive was launched on March 29 to raise additional pre-season revenue. A new slogan, "Take Care of the Indians Instead of the Chiefs," accompanied the initiative. In a major windfall, the Pirates helped ease the fiscal situation by contributing $6,000 to the operation of the Grays.

The 1955 Grays were a much better club than the previous year. Many of the young, inexperienced players of 1954 had matured sufficiently to produce a big year in 1955. The Grays started out very well, posting a brilliant 21-8 mark in May, and were in first place from mid-May to mid-July. Manager-pitcher Larry Shepard won eleven straight decisions to start out the season, most of them coming in relief. At thirty-six, Shepard was both the oldest pitcher in the EL and the Grays best pitcher that season.

Having Myron Hoffman from nearby Watsontown as a member of the Grays pitching staff stimulated local interest in the team. Hoffman set an EL record that season by appearing in fifty-seven games as a pitcher, mostly in relief. He eclipsed the Grays old record for appearances, forty-nine, set by Sam Page in 1939. Another local standout played briefly for the Grays that season, infielder Bill Witmer, playing parts of six seasons in the Tigers and White Sox farm systems.

Witmer was working in his native Williamsport when an emergency summons from the Grays came during the season. Shortstop Dick Barone was injured and the Grays were short on competent infielders. Barone had played with Witmer at Great Falls in

Fig. 39 Williamsport's 1955 baseball season hinged upon a critical preseason ticket drive that guaranteed generated revenue of $50,000. Charles "Chet" Lucas (seated) and Paul Bailey (left) successfully coordinated the "Keep Ball Alive in '55" campaign. (*Grit*)

the Pioneer League in 1951, and he reminded skipper Larry Shepard that Witmer had gotten a double and single off Shepard when he had pitched for and piloted the Billings, Montana, team. Witmer's fill-in stint only lasted for a few weeks but it was, according to Witmer, a "worthwhile experience to play for the hometown team."

The Grays faded down the stretch. One of the primary reasons for the 1955 fadeout was the late-season call-up of the Grays best hitter, Dale Coogan, to New Orleans. Ray Keyes, stated in a column, "The Grays slipped after Coogan's call-up and even though their pitching dropped below par, many cited the loss of Coogan as the most severe blow." The Grays finished fifth, with a 71–66 record, edged out for fourth place and a play-off berth by Schenectady.

Milt Graff was the Grays MVP in 1955 with a .317 average and 55 RBIS. Emil Panko had twenty-four homers and 103 RBIS. Bill Mazeroski batted .295 before his call-up to New Orleans. A measure of the Grays pitching woes was that manager Larry Shepard was the Grays leading pitcher with a 16–9 mark.

The promise shown by the 1955 Grays never materialized in 1956, due in large part

Fig. 40 A Grays player is nipped at first base in game action against the Reading Indians at Bowman Field in 1955. (*Grit*)

to poor hitting and the lack of a reliable power hitter. Additionally, the Grays did not have good enough pitching to offset their poor hitting. The Grays finished seventh with a poor 60-78 record.

The bright spot for the Grays in 1956 was first-baseman Tony Bartirome, winning one of the most heated batting races in the history of the New York–Pennsylvania/ Eastern League by a single point, with a .305 average. Manager Jack Fitzpatrick, who replaced Larry Shepard as manager, offered Bartirome the option of sitting out the final game to ensure his batting title. Bartirome, perhaps inspired by Ted Williams's example in 1941, declined to take the backdoor to take the title. He went four for four to claim his crown and was voted Grays MVP for 1956.

Just like the previous year, the 1956 Grays were plagued with money problems. The club directors convened an emergency meeting on July 19 to decide whether to finish the 1956 season. Joe Mosser, Grays president, reported that $20,000 was urgently needed continue the season. The directors decided to continue the season and hoped that the needed operating revenue would materialize at some point. B'nai B'rith, which had already sponsored a Booster Night earlier in the season, stepped up to the plate to fund a second night on August 23.

The generosity of the B'nai B'rith epitomized why professional baseball survived in Williamsport for so many years when larger cities failed to sustain the game. The second Booster Night temporarily saved the endangered Williamsport franchise but the Grays poor record contributed to the bleak financial situation as fan interest waned. The Grays experienced a decline of twenty thousand fans at the turnstiles. Money problems, poor attendance, as well as the Pirates withdrawal of their working agreement after the 1956 season spelled the temporary demise of the Williamsport franchise. Pro baseball in Williamsport would lie dormant in 1957.

The Phillies Years

The 1958 season marked the beginning of one of the most glorious eras in Williamsport baseball history. Baseball returned to Bowman Field as the Grays became an affiliate of the Philadelphia Phillies. Under the Phillies, Williamsport earned EL play-off berths four out of five seasons. The Phillies shifted their EL farm club from Schenectady, New York, to Williamsport because of declining attendance. They provided the Grays with some of the best talent available in their organization, complemented by veteran talent from Schenectaday's 1956 EL championship season.

Away from the playing field, further changes for the better were afoot. Beginning in 1958, and for all subsequent seasons until 1967, the Grays were community-owned and operated by a group of businessmen known as the Nine-County Baseball Boosters, Inc. It was hoped that local ownership in tandem with the Phillies affiliation would restore the Grays regional appeal. Joseph Mosser stepped down as club president in favor of insurance executive B. C. "Red" Jones. The new affiliation with the Phillies, coupled with the one-year absence of baseball, heightened fan interest in the Grays. Pre-season ticket sales amounted to $35,000, the greatest in franchise history to that date.

The Eastern League tried a new two-division set-up in 1958. There would be a Northern and a Southern Division, with Williamsport in the Northern Division. It was hoped that this would enhance fan interest by giving more teams a chance at the play-offs. The two-division format was further expanded on July 1 when EL officials adopted a split-season format. Under the new play-off format the first- and second-half division leaders faced each other in the championship play-offs. The Grays took full advantage of this new arrangement by winning the second half of the Northern Division and clinching one of the available play-off spots. Dick Carter, who won the EL title with Schenectady in 1956, was the Grays' skipper that season.

The hot hitting of Dale Bennetch, Mack Burk, and Fred Van Dusen carried the Grays to the play-offs, but deserted them in the series with Binghamton. Williamsport lost Game One 3–0, as well as Game Two 7–6 after being down 6–0. Dale Bennetch and Mack Burk, in their only hitting spurt of the play-offs, each drove in two runs. The Grays were eliminated when they lost Game Three 5–1. The Grays had their second EL batting titlist in three years when John Easton did the trick with a .321 average.

The Nine-County Baseball Boosters launched an ambitious pre-season ticket drive in March 1959, adopting such innovative marketing techniques as setting up ticket booths in area banks and having area youth groups canvass the community for ticket sales. As an extra incentive, the youth groups received $20 on each $120 in tickets sold. The girl or boy who sold the most tickets won a bowling ball and the honor of throwing out the first pitch on Opening Day at Bowman Field.

The Grays opened the 1959 season well and stayed near the top of the standings throughout the season, remaining in first place from June 7 to August 26. By July 15, near the mid-point of the season, they were playing at a sizzling .617 pace. The Grays might have finished first but for the untimely call-up of three of their better players and an arm injury to one of their better pitchers. Art Mahaffey, who racked up an 8–0 record and a sparkling 1.67 ERA, was called up to Buffalo in late June. Ed Keegan, the Grays top pitcher that season, soon followed. Hard-hitting catcher Mack Burk also was ticketed to Buffalo in late August. Bob "Gunner" Gontkosky, one of the stalwarts of the Grays' pitching staff, suffered arm trouble in mid-July that further crippled the depleted rotation. This attrition occurred during the crucial stretch drive for the pennant.

The 1959 Grays were arguably the most power-laden team in Williamsport's history, clubbing 133 round-trippers. Three Grays hit twenty or more homers. This proved to be an expensive proposition to the Williamsport restaurant owner who promised a free steak to any Gray who hit a home run at Bowman Field. He also promised the same to any Grays pitcher who spun a shutout at the uptown ballpark. One barber offered free haircuts for any home-run hitting Gray. This aggregation of power prompted Frank Lucchesi (the successor to Dick Carter as Grays manager) to dub his charges the "Blitz Kids." The animated and popular Lucchesi later managed the Phillies and the Texas Rangers in the Majors.

The power generated by the 1959 team was one of the chief reasons why they were the best Williamsport team since Spence Abbott's fine 1941 team. Like that 1941 team, they too lost in the Governor's Cup finals—this time to a powerful Springfield Giants team that featured future Hall-of-Fame pitcher Juan Marichal and future Major League standout Mateo "Matty" Alou of the fabulous Alou brothers.

The Phillies tried to breach these losses by assigning a once-great pitcher, Curt Simmons, to Williamsport on a rehabilitation assignment. Simmons had badly injured his

Fig. 41 Veteran Philadelphia Phillies pitcher Curt Simmons (right) passes on tips to young Grays pitcher Bob "Gunner" Gontkosky. Simmons was on a rehabilitation assignment in Williamsport in 1959. (*Grit*)

foot in a lawn-mower accident, an injury that altered his pitching motion. Nevertheless, Simmons's maturity and presence on the mound proved to be a boon to both the pitching staff and attendance at Bowman Field. Over two thousand fans saw him in his first start on July 27 as he tossed a five-hitter, and as Tony Curry drove in seven runs in a 14–1 romp over Allentown. The Phillies offered to call up Simmons several weeks later but he decided to remain with the Grays until the end of the season. He compiled a 4–1 record in his short stay with the Grays. Besides providing an additional arm, Simmons became a de facto pitching coach, imparting his veteran knowledge and experience to the Grays' young prospects. His service in this capacity, during an era in which few minor league teams could afford the luxury of specialized coaches, made the Grays pitching staff a more cohesive unit.

The Grays finished third in 1959 with an 81-60 mark only four games behind first-place Springfield. In the play-offs, the Grays swept Allentown in the first round, three games to none. The highlight of that series was the Grays Al Neiger's fifteen-strikeout performance in Game Two, a 4-2 win. Williamsport's fine season came to a disappointing close in the second round of the play-offs as they lost to Springfield three games to one. The Grays entered that series with a sub-par line-up due to an injury to Gordy Figard, an excellent infielder and one of the Grays' most consistent players.

Fred Hopke led the Grays with a .316 average, clouted thirty homers, and drove in a franchise record 130 runs. Jacke Davis set another franchise record when clubbed thirty-three homers, and drove in 116 runs. Tony Curry led the EL in hits with 178 and runs scored with 108. Enroute to his Eastern League MVP season, he slugged twenty-one homers and drove in 90 runs. Amazingly, Curry (a native of Nassau in the Bahamas), had only started playing baseball five years before.

After knocking on the door to the EL honors the previous two seasons, the Grays finally kicked in the door and won the championship in 1960. Williamsport's accomplishment was somewhat bittersweet because they ended up sharing the title with the Springfield Giants. Torrential downpours unleashed by Hurricane Donna in September forced the cancellation of the championship series after just one game. In an unprecedented action, EL officials declared the Grays and Giants co-champions—the first and the last time in league history this was done. It was the Grays first pennant in twenty-six years.

Local sports scribes dubbed the 1960 team the "Go-Go Grays" because the team was blessed with excellent speed, good pitching, and timely hitting. Ray Keyes, sports editor of the *WS-G*, observed the success of the Grays was the product of "the take-charge play of Norm Gigon, the lusty hitting of John Hernstein, the base thievery of Ted Savage, and catcher Dick Harris's masterful handing of the pitchers. Not to be overlooked is Manager Frank Lucchesi's mastery of pulling the right switches at the right times." Keyes also expressed the opinion that the 1960 Grays "may have been the most exciting team ever to represent Williamsport."

The Grays didn't start out the season very excitingly. They opened the season with

Fig. 42 The "Go-Go Grays" were the co-champions of the Eastern League in 1960. Danny Cater (first row, third from left) was one of the more successful graduates of the team, playing for the Phils, A's, Yankees, and Red Sox. (*Grit*)

five straight losses, including an opening night one-hit, 10-0 loss to Allentown. The Grays soon righted themselves and by June 21 were in first place, where they remained for the rest of the season. From July 4 through August 28, they played at an impressive .607 clip. By late August, they had an insurmountable eleven-game lead over second place Binghamton.

The 1960 Grays featured ten future Major Leaguers, including John Hernstein, a key player on the ill-fated 1964 Phillies; Lee Elia, future manager of the Phillies and Cubs; and Danny Cater, who played eleven big-league seasons for several clubs, including the Yankees. Cater finished second to Boston's Carl Yasztremski in the 1968 American League batting race. Outfielder Ted Savage, perhaps the Grays most athletically gifted player, appeared briefly in the Majors but never achieved his full promise.

The Grays clinched the pennant on August 29 but, in a bit of let-down, they lost their next six games, reducing their pennant-winning margin from eleven games to six over Binghamton.

In the opening round of the Governor's Cup play-offs against Reading, the Grays won the first game 1-0 with masterful shutout pitching by Jerry Kettle. Ted Savage drove in the game's only run. The Grays won Game Two 5-4 in fourteen innings, as John Hernstein drove in the winning run and Ed Keegan pitching brilliant one-hit ball in seven innings of relief. This set up the final series with the Grays nemesis from the previous two years, the Springfield Giants. Williamsport won the first and, as it turned out, the only game of the series 6-1, as Charlie Fields and John Hernstein hit homers for the Grays. The fact that the Grays had to share their championship with Springfield does not diminish the accomplishment of the 1960 Grays. It marked the last time that a Williamsport team won a championship.

John Hernstein was the Grays leading hitter in 1960 with a .305 average, sixteen homers, and eighty-five RBIs. Ted Savage batted .288 and led the EL in stolen bases. Charlie Fields led the team in homers with seventeen and had seventy-six RBIs. Danny Cater hit .269, with twelve homers and sixty-nine RBIs. Bob Gill led a consistent mound corps with a 12-7 record and 86 strikeouts. Norm Camp was 12-8 with 103 strikeouts. Dave Baldwin was 9-5 with 85 punchouts. Dwight Seibler, the Grays leading reliever and spot starter, was 7-0 and led the staff in strike-outs with 136.

The 1961 Grays team was by every indication a success, despite the fact that the team failed to match the lofty championship perch they enjoyed the previous season. Nevertheless, several veterans from the 1960 championship club—among them, Danny Cater, Charlie Fields, Ed Lunsford and Ed Hughes—instilled a winning attitude in the clubhouse and mentored the younger players in coping with the pressure of a pennant race.

The 1961 season marked the retirement of two long-time familiar figures who were an important part of the Williamsport baseball scene for many years, business manager J. Roy Clunk and long-time groundskeeper Al Bellandi. Clunk had been associated with the Grays off and on since 1927; and Bellandi had given Bowman Field his loving care since the late 1930s.

Frank Lucchesi did not return to manage the Grays in 1961. Instead, he piloted the Chattanooga Lookouts of the Southern Association to a championship that year. Former "Whiz Kid" Andy Seminick, who had been a catcher for the memorable Phillies team of 1950, managed the Grays. Seminick previously managed at Elmira and Des Moines, and later piloted Chattanooga and Miami.

The Grays had an outstanding defensive team in 1961, highlighted by the fine play of catcher Larry Cutright. Mike Bernardi, a local sportswriter, rated Cutright as one of Williamsport's best all-time receivers and compared him favorably with such outstanding catchers as Bill Baker, Bill Conroy, Dewey Williams, and Joe Ginsburg.

The Grays contended throughout the season and would have made the play-offs easily—but the EL suspended play-offs for the 1961 season. The Williamsport team enjoyed a stretch in early to mid-June in which they won seventeen of twenty-four games. However, by late July, they cooled due to the bane of all minor league teams: the mid-season call-ups by the parent club. Two of the Grays best pitchers were called up in July. Henry Mason compiled a 5-1 mark and batted .482 before being sold by the Phillies to Honolulu on July 4. Paul Brown, who had a solid 8-5 record was called-up on July 20. These transactions probably dashed the Grays' pennant hopes.

One of the pitching highlights of the 1961 season occurred on August 28 when the Grays Jack McCraken tossed a seven-inning no-hitter in the first game of a double-header with Lancaster. The Grays finished second with a respectable 79-61 record. Danny Cater led all Grays hitters with a .342 average and the league in hits with 193. Marcelino Lopez led the pitching staff with a 10-5 record with 121 strikeouts.

The 1962 campaign marked the high-water mark of Williamsport professional base-ball, arguably the last great season enjoyed by a local ballclub. Fans witnessed one of the greatest Williamsport teams ever assembled. The 1962 season was also the last time that a Williamsport team carried the venerable name "Grays." The Grays enjoyed their best season record since the championship team of 1924 as Frank Lucchesi returned to Williamsport to weave his managerial magic. For the third consecutive year, he led a team to a first place finish. During his three-year tenure at Williamsport, he compiled the second-best record of any Williamsport manager, a record exceeded only by Harry Hinchman.

The Grays charged out of the gate and never looked back. By June 14 they had an eleven-game lead over Charleston, a team featuring such future standout hurlers as Luis Tiant, Tommy John, and Sonny Siebert. Williamsport rolled to a thirteen-game win-ning streak in June and a ten-game stretch from mid- to late July. The Grays also achieved a home-game winning streak of nineteen games, a franchise record. Part of the streak included an oddly scheduled ten-game series with Springfield. The Grays racked up a sizzling 49-22 record at Bowman Field that year. By early August they established a twenty-game lead over their nearest competitor.

The Grays blended all of the necessary elements for a successful team: consistent and timely hitting, slick fielding, excellent speed, and outstanding pitching. The hitting attack was led by slugger Dick "Richie" Allen, later a star with the Phillies and the White Sox, among other teams. Lucchesi is credited with moving Allen from second base (where his fielding was spotty) to the outfield, where he took the unusual measure of wearing a batting helmet for protection in the field. Allen's signature use of the batting helmet became part and parcel of his turbulent Major League career. Grays outfielder Bobby Sanders also turned in an outstanding offensive performance, leading the EL in runs scored. The Grays got great pitching from Gary Kroll, Ray Culp, and Harry Oliver.

There were, however, some ominous rumblings on the horizon concerning the fu-ture of Williamsport baseball. A report released by the club on August 9 noted the

Fig. 43 Dick "Richie" Allen was one of the offensive standouts for the 1962 Williamsport Grays. Though he struggled in the field, he led the team in batting average, homers and RBIs. (Legends of Bowman Field photo card, Courtesy of the Williamsport Crosscutters)

Grays had operated at a deficit estimated at between $6,500 and $10,000. Clearly, such losses thwarted efforts to sustain local ownership of the Williamsport team over the long term. In fact, 1962 was the final year a Williamsport team was locally owned and operated. Attendance had slipped since the Grays led the EL in attendance in 1960 with 100,298 fans. Williamsport again led the league in attendance in 1961, despite drawing a much reduced 79,123. In 1962, the team drew 77,595, good for third in the EL. This seemed inexplicable, given the fine team that the Grays fielded that year. Fearing a declining market, the Phillies severed their affiliation with Williamsport on October 1. Thus began the pattern of wholesale franchise shifts and absentee ownership that has charted Williamsport's course in professional baseball down to the present era.

The Nine-County Baseball Boosters felt badly hurt by the move, but *WS-G* sportswriter Mike Bernardi tried to put things in perspective, writing, "Twice the Phils saved the Grays from going thousands of dollars in debt by scheduling two exhibition games here. The Phils never took a nickel for expenses or anything else." He further observed that "they would go out of their way to find a player for the Grays when they needed one for a certain position, frequently going out of their organization to procure talent." The Grays closed out the "Phillies Era" with a stellar 83-57 record, the second-best in Williamsport history. They finished first, eleven games in front of Elmira.

The Grays opened the first round of the 1962 play-offs with a 7-2 loss to Springfield. The Grays took the second game 7-3 on homers by Dick Allen, Bill Sorrell, and Jerry Griffin. Bob "Gunner" Gontkosky struck out eight. The Grays moved to the second round with a 3-2 win in ten innings.

In the final round of the play-offs, Elmira won the first game 3-2, as John Miller struck out twelve, and the second game on a 2-0 shutout by wild flame-thrower Steve Dalkowski. The Grays won the third game 7-2, as Allen homered and "Gunner" Gontkosky scattered four hits. Elmira won the play-off series 10-4, raking four Grays pitchers for sixteen hits. Future Toronto Blue Jays and Baltimore Orioles general manager Pat Gillick pitched the clincher for Elmira. Still, the 1962 season is remembered fondly by those privileged to have witnessed and cheered the feats of this outstanding team, one of the greatest ever to played at storied Bowman Field.

Dick Allen led Grays batters with a .332 average and 109 RBIs, and tied Bobby Sanders for the team lead in homers with twenty. Sanders batted .310 and led the EL in runs scored with ninety-eight. Future Major League standout Ray Culp led the pitching staff with a 13-8 record and strikeouts with 185. Gary Kroll compiled a sparkling 12-2 mark before being called up by the Phillies. Future Hall-of-Fame pitcher Ferguson Jenkins was briefly on the Grays pitching staff but appeared in no games for them.

Meet the Mets, 1964–1967

Williamsport became a part of the wild and zany world of Casey Stengel's lovable losers, the New York Mets, as baseball returned to Williamsport after a one-year hiatus. The new team was named the "Williamsport Mets," and became the first New York Mets Class AA team in their young franchise history. Previously, the Mets had farm clubs at Buffalo in the Class AAA International League, and Salinas, Kansas, Raleigh, North Carolina, and Quincy, Illinois, in the lower classifications.

A little on the reorganization of the minor leagues by the Major Leagues is in order here. In 1963, the National Association of Professional Baseball Clubs, at the behest of the Majors, overhauled and reconstructed the minor league landscape. Class B, C, and D leagues were eliminated and upgraded to the Class A level, though the talent differential still existed within the broad Class A designation. The Eastern, South Atlantic

(Sally), and Texas Leagues, formerly Class A leagues, were reclassified as Class AA. The two Class AAA leagues, the International and Pacific Coast, remained intact.

The New York Mets owned the Williamsport Mets outright, but the Nine-County Baseball Boosters, Inc., operated the franchise as a community enterprise. The Nine-County group assumed responsibility for promoting the club, overseeing its daily operations, and raising $30,000 in pre-season ticket sales as per an agreement with the parent Mets. Bill Pickelner continued in his post as president of the Nine-County Baseball Boosters. In fact, he had negotiated with the New York Mets front office to bring the Mets to Williamsport shortly after the conclusion of the 1963 World Series

The New York Mets launched their new Class AA club in Williamsport with a fanfare seen rarely in Williamsport. Their publicity and marketing campaign included public appearances by players and members of the New York Mets hierarchy at the Baseball Boosters annual Winter Baseball Banquet in February 1964. Among those attending were farm-club director Johnny Murphy, Mets Club controller Joe DiGregorio, Mets players Ed Kranepool and Tracey Stallard, coaches Yogi Berra and Warren Spahn, and, last but not least, the inimitable Casey Stengel, who stole the show.

The Mets provided Williamsport a well-respected manager in Ernie White, a former standout pitcher for the Cardinals in the 1940s. The Mets even retrofitted Bowman Field with light towers from New York's fabled Polo Grounds. They stocked the new farm club with some familiar players—Bob "Gunner" Gontkosky, outfielder Bobby Sanders, and ex-Springfield Giant and nearby Montgomery, Pennsylvania, native Bob Farley.

During the Williamsport Mets first two seasons, they were not very competitive. Despite the energy and resources poured into the new farm club, success on the diamond was impeded by the New York Mets inexperience and growing pains as a young franchise. Roster instability was symptomatic of the Mets internal disorganization. This was also the era of the so-called Bonus Babies, highly regarded prospects—some just out of high school—who were signed for enormous sums for the time, such as $100,000. The Mets signed their share of prospects, and Williamsport fans saw some of these new men of wealth, pitchers such as Les Rohr and Jerry Hinsley, and infielder Kevin Collins. Unfortunately, not one had much of a Major League career.

One of the most bizarre examples of this disorganization came in July 1964 when the Williamsport Mets demoted five players to the Mets Auburn affiliate in the Class A New York–Penn League and Auburn promoted five of its players to Williamsport. These events represented a disaster for Williamsport. Williamsport lost two of its best pitchers, Malcolm "Bunky" Warren and Tom Belcher, in the deal. Most of the players that came from Auburn were not ready for the fast EL competition, which helped to seal the Mets place in the EL's second division that season.

The parent New York Mets stimulated area interest in baseball by playing their Williamsport farmhands three different years. These games were always well attended, but the most memorable was the 1964 exhibition contest. In that game, Williamsport's best hitter, Ron Swoboda (later a major cog for the "Miracle Mets"), launched a dramatic homer over the left-field fence in the bottom of the eleventh inning to lift the Williamsport Mets to an unforgettable 4-3 victory over the New York Mets. Bill Wakefield surrendered Swoboda's game-winning blast. Swoboda and pitcher "Bunky" Warren were named to the 1964 EL all-star team.

The Williamsport Mets experienced even more chaotic decision making by their parent club in 1965. Kerby Ferrell was the Little Mets skipper that season, but that changed when Ferrell became enmeshed in the a chain of events beyond his control. The New York Mets colorful and legendary skipper Casey Stengel was put out to pasture when he broke his hip in mid-July. Stengel's departure resulted in wholesale coaching changes throughout their whole farm system. Buffalo Bisons manager Sheriff Robinson was elevated to New York to serve as third-base coach after former third-base coach Wes Westrum became the New Yorkers' interim manager. Ferrell was shuffled up to Buffalo to take Robinson's place on July 29. Malcolm "Bunky" Warren replaced Ferrell as Williamsport's manager. Warren, a relief pitcher and spot starter, had been one of Williamsport's better pitchers. At age twenty-eight, he became the youngest manager in Williamsport history up to that time, even though it was in a custodial role.

The last two seasons of the Williamsport Mets were seasons of improvement. In 1966, Bill Virdon, who did an excellent job of nurturing young talent, skippered the Mets. He was given the brief opportunity to work with a future Hall-of-Famer in the dying embers of the 1966 season when Nolan Ryan came to Williamsport for further seasoning.

Like his famed fastball, the "Ryan Express," Nolan Ryan's time in Williamsport was all too fleeting. Ryan was on the Williamsport roster for a little less than two weeks; nevertheless, he showcased some of the talent that destined him for Major League greatness. He arrived in Williamsport, a nineteen-year-old, fresh-faced and wiry Texan from Greenville, South Carolina, where he had completely dominated the Western Carolinas League, leading the league in wins (17) and strikeouts (272). Williamsport fans fortunate enough to be at Bowman Field on September 1, 1966, saw one of Ryan's most extraordinary performances ever. In that game, against the Pawtucket Indians, he struck out twenty-one batters in ten innings, only to lose a heart wrenching 2-1 decision. Ryan's statistics at Williamsport were hardly eye-catching: an 0-2 record, nineteen innings pitched, nine hits yielded, twelve walks, and thirty-five strikeouts. He was still an unknown prospect and, like most young power pitchers, wild around the plate.

In 1967, the Williamsport Mets enjoyed the best season of their brief four-season existence. The Mets came tantalizingly close to making the EL play-offs. The EL divided into two divisions that season, Western and Eastern. Williamsport joined Elmira, York, and Reading in the Western Division. The Mets contended for first place in the division throughout the season and held the top spot well into August.

What should have been a happy season for Mets fans, focusing all of their energies

Fig. 44 The Williamsport Mets young pitching staff of 1966 included (left to right) Bill Denehy, Jay Carden, Terry Christman, Jerry Craft, and bonus-baby Les Rohr. (*Grit*)

on rooting their team to the play-offs, was short-circuited on July 27 when reports circulated that New York Mets officials had met with Memphis, Tennessee, city officials to explore the possibility of locating their Class AA franchise there in 1968. Memphis native Bing Devine, then general manager of the New York Mets, probably engineered these machinations.

Williamsport baseball fans' worst fears were realized on August 2 when the New York Mets officials made the stunning announcement that they would leave Williamsport following the 1967 season. This stuck like a dagger directed at the collective heart of Williamsport's fandom. The Nine-County Baseball Boosters, led by Bill Pickelner, felt especially betrayed. They thought that the announcement was very ill-timed. The Williamsport Mets still had a full month left in their season and were in the thick of the pennant race. The announcement cast a pall over the whole Williamsport baseball scene

Fig. 45 Future Hall-of-Famer Nolan Ryan had a brief stay in
Williamsport in 1966, going 0-2, with an ERA of 0.95 and thirty-five
strikeouts. He lost one game 2-1 despite striking out nineteen batters.
(Legends of Bowman Field photo card, Courtesy of the Williamsport
Crosscutters)

and had a detrimental effect on attendance for the final month. Still, Williamsport finished a respectable third in EL attendance with 55,704, trailing only Reading and Pawtucket.

There were several notable on-the-field happenings that season, including the Mets
Ron Locke firing a no-hitter at the Pawtucket Indians on May 23. He faced the mini-

mum twenty-seven batters, fanning eleven. He threw only 106 pitchers, 67 for strikes. In an incident more typical of both the New York and Williamsport Mets earlier, zany seasons, catcher Duffy Dyer hit what appeared to be a grand-slam homer against York on June 22. In his enthusiasm, however, Dyer passed the runner in front of him, Jon O'Dell. Dyer was called out but given credit for a three-run triple.

Jim McAndrew ended the era of the Williamsport Mets with a flourish, winning their last game 5-0, tossing a one-hitter. McAndrew was the Mets best pitcher that season compiling a 10-8 record. He also set a franchise record with a 1.47 ERA.

Bernie Smith gave Mets fans a lot to talk about. He won the Eastern League's MVP Award that year, capturing the batting title with a .306 average and driving in fifty runs. Smith was a fixture in the Mets outfield dating back to 1964. Unfortunately, the talent he displayed at Williamsport never materialized in the Major Leagues, when he played briefly for the Milwaukee Brewers in 1970.

The Williamsport Mets era of the mid-1960s was an exciting and entertaining chapter in Williamsport's baseball history. Moreover, Williamsport served as a good proving ground for some of the players associated with the Miracle Mets of 1969. These players included Duffy Dyer, Ken Boswell, Rod Gaspar, Ron Swoboda, Gary Gentry, Jerry Koosman, Jim McAndrew, and Nolan Ryan.

Short Seasons: The First New York–Penn League Era, 1968–1972

During the turbulent 1960s, Williamsport professional baseball experienced a period of change and upheaval. In 1968, for the first time since 1923, a Williamsport professional franchise operated in a league other than the old New York–Pennsylvania and Eastern leagues. Despite the best efforts of Bill Pickelner and the Nine County Baseball Boosters, they failed to secure affiliation with a Major League club willing to keep it in the EL.

Eastern League president Tommy Richardson and Pickelner then contacted Norristown fruit wholesaler Joe Romano (owner of the Erie franchise in the short-season Class A New York–Penn League) about relocating his franchise to Williamsport in 1968. The goal of Romano and Williamsport's baseball boosters was the acquisition of another EL franchise in the near future. Membership in the New York–Penn League was seen as a temporary stepping stone, keeping baseball interest alive in Williamsport until EL baseball returned. Unfortunately for Romano and Williamsport's baseball fans, this strategy did not yield immediate results. Eastern League baseball did not return to Williamsport until 1976.

The step down from Class AA to short-season Class A ball was viewed by the local sporting press as exactly that—a step down—and they treated it as such in their reportage. Beat coverage of the new team was nonexistent, with box scores, game accounts, and features on players severely curtailed. The Williamsport teams during this era (1968–72) were treated as poor relations compared to the status of their former EL counterparts. The situation grew worse as the teams performed poorly on the field and at the gate during the later years of this period.

For the first three seasons of this period, the team was christened the Williamsport Astros, initially because it was operated on a cooperative basis drawing talent from both the Phillies and Astros organizations. This arrangement was not uncommon in the lower rungs of the minors where stocking short-season teams was often problematical.

For the first two seasons, the Astros were run by A. Rankin Johnson Jr., formerly a Grays player, assistant general manager, and EL president. The Nine-County Baseball Boosters continued to operate the team on a community basis. Johnson drew on his extensive baseball experience and promotional wizardry to achieve good results at the turnstiles. In 1969 the Astros were second in league attendance, proving Johnson's winning ways.

During the Astros years, Johnson remembers providing frequent shuttle service to the Williamsport Airport to pick up and drop off players. The Vietnam War was at its height then, and many athletes of draft age fulfilled their military obligations by enlisting in either the National Guard or the Army Reserve. Many of these units held their summer camps during the baseball season. The 1968 Astros were the best of the teams during the New York–Penn years. They made the play-offs with a 40-35 record and were the last Williamsport team to have made the play-offs. They lost their only play-off game to Auburn 12-2.

The 1968–70 seasons featured some fine performances by Astros players. Lambert Ford took the league batting crown in 1970. Larry Mansfield captured the league's home-run crown with twenty-one circuit clouts in 1969, and pitcher Marty Cott was named to the league's all-star team in 1969. Future Major League standout pitcher Bob Forsch also pitched for the Astros.

The only excitement produced during the Astros cellar-dwelling campaign in 1970 came when nearby Muncy's Ed Ott was signed by the Pirates and assigned to their club in the New York–Penn League, Niagara Falls. His appearances at Bowman Field with Niagara Falls generated great local interest. This helped the Astros to their best attendance during the first New York–Penn League era, drawing 43,599 fans.

When the Astros crashed to the New York–Penn League's basement in 1970, Romano and the Nine-County Boosters started looking for another affiliation. This time the team would be a Boston Red Sox farm club. Local sportswriters quickly tabbed the team the "BillSox." They were managed by Dick Berardino, formerly manager of the Johnson City Yankees of the Appalachian League. He later managed Boston's entry in the New York–Penn League (the Elmira Pioneers) until 1985, and he returned to the league in 1997 as skipper of the Lowell Spinners.

The Boston Red Sox did their best to provide talent to Williamsport, assigning their 1971 first-round draft pick Jim Rice to the BillSox. Rice had a brilliant career with

Fig. 46 Williamsport Astros pitching coach Jim Walton gives mound tips to Pat Darcy in 1970. Darcy gave up Carlton Fisk's memorable home run in the epic 1975 World Series. (*Grit*)

Fig. 47 Future Boston Red Sox slugging star Jim Rice started his professional career in Williamsport as a member of the Billsox in 1971. Here, he poses with his bat and his teammates prior to a preseason workout at Bowman Field. (*Grit*)

Red Sox and remains a strong candidate for the Hall-of-Fame to this day. Rice was a green and unhoned talent during the '71 season. He was so raw-looking that the late *Grit* sports editor Al Decker observed that "Rice looked like he was in his first pair of shoes." During the season Rice displayed occasional flashes of the brilliance he later showed during his Major League career.

The Red Sox also made available in 1971 the best pitcher Williamsport had during this era, Steve Foran. He dominated the league's pitching statistics that year, going 10–4 with 138 strikeouts and an ERA of 2.38. Unfortunately, he failed to meet expectations and never made it to the big leagues.

The last year of the first New York–Penn era, the Williamsport Red Sox fought to lift themselves from the depths literally and figuratively. The floodwaters of Hurricane Agnes hit Williamsport with a vengeance from June 21 to 23, shortly before the home opener. It caused widespread damage to Bowman Field and ruined all of the BillSox equipment. It also forced postponement of the team's home opener on June 24. This delay prevented the Williamsport Red Sox from becoming a part of baseball history. Bernice Gera was supposed to have her debut in Williamsport as the first woman umpire in the history of professional baseball. She umpired the Auburn-Geneva game instead, and promptly quit after one game. Gera was treated shamefully by fans, players, coaches, and managers alike. Local fans can only speculate what would have transpired at Bowman Field had she umpired the Red Sox home opener.

Williamsport did not play a home game until July 10. Having to play on the road for an extended period with a young and inexperienced team, the Red Sox experienced a horrible season and finished last in the league. Interestingly, one of the members of this sad-sack pitching staff did go on to have a decent Major League career—Don Aase, who compiled a forgettable 0-10 mark for the Bill Sox.

The dislocations caused by flood-related schedule changes and the Red Sox terrible record combined to attract only 19,038 patrons to Bowman Field. Owner Joe Romano thought he saw the writing on the wall and decided to move the franchise to Elmira, New York, where it remained through 1995 before transferring to Lowell, Massachusetts.

6

Twilight of the Eastern League

The road to the return of Williamsport baseball was actually paved on July 6, 1975, when the West Haven Yankees and the Reading Phillies played a regular season game at Bowman Field to test fan support for the possible return of Eastern League (EL) baseball. When 3,296 fans showed up for this game, their impressive response caught the attention of Mal Fichman, who then decided to move his Thetford Mines, Quebec, team to Williamsport. Fichman was known widely in minor league circles, having owned and operated minor league teams for over twenty years. He decided to name the new Williamsport team the "Tomahawks," as a nod to their new affiliation with the Cleveland Indians. Local sportswriters referred to the team as the "Tommies" or "Toms."

Eager to include local residents in his ownership group, Fichmann recruited Williamsport's Frank Luppachino, who had recently retired from the U.S. Air Force. Luppachino later became Eastern regional director of Little League Baseball, Inc., and a member of the Bowman Field Commission.

The Tomahawks were managed by capable long-time minor league skipper John "Red" Davis." Davis had managed the Minneapolis Millers to the 1957 American Association play-offs, Dallas to the Texas League championship in 1955, and Tacoma to the Pacific Coast League championship in 1961. Despite his enviable baseball pedigree, he was unable to work his magic on the Tommies, the worst team in the history of Williamsport baseball.

Things started out auspiciously, as the Williamsport Tomahawks made their debut on a sun-splashed Easter Sunday, April 25, 1976. Nearly 1,600 fans saw the Tommies beat the Reading Phillies 8-4. Soon the Tomahawks got hit by the injury bug, losing such key players as slugger Wayne Cage and pitcher Tom McGough, which started them toward their crash to last place. They would lose thirty one-run games. One of the most notable things about this otherwise forgettable season was that the Williamsport team played a historic, first-ever game on Canadian soil against the Quebec City Metros at Quebec City.

There were few bright spots for the Tomahawks in 1976. One such spot was the stellar play of shortstop Alfredo Griffin, who later had an outstanding career with the Blue Jays, Dodgers, and Mets. Red Davis described Griffin as the best shortstop he had ever managed, possessing a greater range than other outstanding shortstops he had coached, such as Jose Pagan and Eddie Leon. The bright spot on the pitching staff was Larry Andersen, who led the staff with a 9-6 record, seventy-four strikeouts, and a 2.71 ERA. Andersen went on to have a long and distinguished career with the Phillies, Red Sox, Indians, and Astros. The often-quoted pitcher gained a reputation as a baseball humorist and is currently the color broadcaster for the Phillies announcing team. Attendance could also be regarded as a bright spot. Despite having such a dreadful team, 53,756 fans came out to see the Tomahawks, almost double the number that saw the pennant-winning West Haven Yankees.

Despite decent attendance figures, Mal Fichman was not satisfied. He frequently clashed with the city over rent and maintenance obligations for Bowman Field. Moreover, he chafed at the city's reluctance to grant a license for the sale of beer at Bowman Field. Fichman said he would not operate a team in Williamsport without a beer license. Thirteen more years passed before beer was served at Bowman Field. Williamsport fans should have known all was not well when Fichman received league permission to play an August 22 game at Jersey City, New Jersey. This ultimately became the Tomahawks new home in 1977 and Bowman Field would be without professional baseball for another decade.

After a ten-year absence, professional baseball returned to Williamsport in 1987. The return of baseball had been a long and convoluted process. At one point, Williamsport actually flirted with the possibility of hosting a Class AAA International League franchise for the first time in its history. This scenario occurred when Northeast Baseball, Inc., of Scranton acquired the Maine Guides of the International League for relocation to the Scranton-Wilkes-Barre area in the latter part of 1986. Northeast Baseball and the Lackawanna County Commissioners were then in the process of building the home of the new team, Lackawanna County Multi-Purpose Stadium. In the meantime, a place was needed to house the team until the completion of the stadium. Williamsport's Bowman Field fit the bill and was selected as the venue. A great deal of anticipation accompanied this move. Despite its small market size, Williamsport would only be one step removed from the Major Leagues. Billtown fans anticipated seeing the International League's outstanding prospects, many of whom were destined for the Major Leagues.

This delightful scenario for Williamsport fans came crashing down on February 20, 1987, when U.S. District Judge Gene Carter handed down a stunning ruling that voided the sale of the Maine Guides to Northeast Baseball, Inc. The decision brought to closure a lawsuit initiated by Maine Guides' owner Jordan Kobritz over the rights to the Waterbury, Connecticut, Eastern League team. Kobritz and Northeast Baseball, Inc., had entered into an agreement to move his Old Orchard, Maine, team to Williamsport in exchange for relocating the Waterbury team to Old Orchard to replace the Guides. However, the Eastern League blocked Kobritz's bid to acquire the Waterbury franchise, in effect preventing the proposed swapping of franchises. Kobritz asserted that this action was a breach of contract; Judge Carter agreed. Approximately, $182,000 in ticket, fence, and scoreboard advertising had anticipated a Class AAA team coming to Williamsport, an overwhelming response that was instrumental in Northeast Baseball's decision to purchase the Waterbury team and move it to Williamsport.

Eastern League officials gave their blessings to this revised move on March 5, 1987. It is unknown why they disapproved of the move of the team to Maine, although their decision was likely more a reflection of their hostility toward Kobritz than any feelings of tenderness for the directors of Northeast Baseball, Inc. This move gave Northeast Baseball officials a little over a month to make frantic preparations for the opener with Reading. The rennovation to Bowman Field for the opener has been detailed in Chapter 3.

The new Williamsport team was named the "Bills." The team's general manager, Bill Terlecky, chose the name partly as a nod to Williamsport's nickname of "Billtown" and partly as a fitting tribute to long-time baseball booster, Bill Pickelner. "Bills" had actually been used as far back as 1904, during Williamsport's tenure in the Tri-State League.

In a touch of irony befitting Williamsport's return to professional baseball, the local team became an affiliate of the Cleveland Indians, just as it had been in 1976. The Indians selected former Major League catcher Steve Swisher as Bills manager, a position he held for a little over a month. Swisher moved up to Buffalo in the International League and Buffalo's manager, Orlando Gomez, was reassigned to Williamsport. Bills general manager Bill Terlecky said the Indians "felt Swisher was better suited for a AAA club and Gomez was a good teacher of baseball."

The Bills provided some offensive fireworks that season with three players reaching double figures in homers: Bernardo Brito, Luis Medina, and Mark Higgins. They may have benefited from Bowman Field's smaller dimensions that season, 345 feet to left

Fig. 48 Hall of Fame pitching legend Bob Feller made a promotional appearance at Bowman Field in 1976 as part of his tour of the Cleveland Indians farm chain. Here, "Rapid Rob," discusses pitching with Williamsport Tomahawks prospect, Tom Brennan. (Tommy Richardson Collection, Courtesy of Louis Hunsinger Jr.)

field, 350 to right field and 365 feet to dead center. Unfortunately, the Bills pitching staff was not equally effective that season, a situation that the Bills artificial power could not offset. They finished in next to last place with a 60-79 record.

The most famous incident in Williamsport's baseball history occurred in 1987. Although not some Olympian feat, it nevertheless etched the name of Williamsport across the American baseball landscape. On the night of August 31, 1987, the Bills and Reading Phillies played a doubleheader at Bowman Field. The Bills were playing out the string, hoping to avert a last-place finish.

In the fifth inning of the first game, Reading catcher Rick Lundblade was on third base. When Lundblade took a few steps off of third, Bills catcher Dave Bresnahan uncorked a wild pick-off throw over the head of third-baseman Rob Swain into left field. Lundblade did what any runner would do and dashed home. However, when he reached home, Bresnahan tagged him with a baseball for an apparent out. The object Bresnahan had thrown into left field was a potato. Plate umpire Scott Potter called Lundblade safe and play was ruled as an error. Potter immediately ejected Bresnahan from the game.

Controversy and publicity followed in the wake of the incident. Initially, some fans considered the incident an appalling and unprofessional bush league stunt. Others relished Bresnahan's moxie and ingenuity, especially his attempt to provide some humor for a lackluster season. Few anticipated the national media attention the incident gained. In fact, the Great Potato Caper quickly entered the annals of baseball lore. Manager Orlando Gomez was obviously not amused by the incident because he promptly fined Bresnahan $50 and gained his immediate release from the Indians organization. Instead of paying his fine in the customary manner, Bresnahan left a bag of fifty potatoes in Gomez's office with the inscription "This Spud's For You." Bresnahan's teammates, in a show of solidarity, chipped in to pay his fine. Before his departure from the clubhouse, Bresnahan placed a potato in each locker as a fond farewell to his teammates.

The Great Potato Caper generated instant national attention. The Bills director of media relations, Scott Ziegler, received over thirty calls from various media outlets across the country, wanting to know more about the incident. CBS Sports contacted Ken Sawyer, who broadcast many of the games that season for local CBS Radio affiliate WWPA, for a tape of the incident; unfortunately, WWPA hadn't broadcast that game. In order to take full advantage of the incident, Bills general manager Bill Terlecky decided to sponsor a promotion on the last night of the season where fans were admitted to the game by presenting a potato and one dollar. Nearly two bushels of potatoes were collected for the local food bank.

Bresnahan, a distant relative of Hall-of-Fame catcher Roger Bresnahan, was surprised by all of the attention his stunt had generated. He said he had gotten the idea from hearing of the same thing being done in the low minors years before. Bresnahan's potato stunt was not unprecedented in the annals of Williamsport baseball, apparently. Lock Haven catcher Davy Dunkle had pulled the same stunt in the 1880s. But Bresnahan's quirky stunt managed to distinguish an otherwise undistinguished minor league career. He batted an anemic .159 in fifty-two games for the Bills in 1987, but he left a lasting impression on Williamsport fans.

Two nights after the potato incident another novelty of sorts happened when Oscar Mejia, with the blessing of manager Orlando Gomez, played all nine positions in the game, a feat accomplished for the first time since Johnny Reder's around-the-horn performance in 1935.

The Bills last season as an Indians affiliate was much less eventful. The 1988 season was mediocre despite the able leadership of new skipper, Mike Hargrove, who later managed both the Indians and the Orioles. Local fans were able to get a look at future Major League superstar Ken Griffey Jr. when he appeared at Bowman Field in mid-August with the Vermont Mariners. They also saw the first brother act on a Williams-

Fig. 49 Williamsport Bills catcher Dave
Bresnahan masterminded the famous "Great
Potato Caper" against the Reading Phillies on
August 31, 1987. His retired number hangs on
the centerfield wall of Bowman Field. (Courtesy
of the *Williamsport Sun-Gazette*)

port team, Andy and Tony Ghelfi, since the McRoberts brothers of the 1970 Astros.
Future star Major League reliever Jeff Shaw dropped seventeen consecutive decisions
while pitching for the Bills that season.

The 1989 season was characterized by several tumultuous off-the-field developments. In addition to the beer revenue debacle precipitated by the Revo brothers, the
Bills' public image was further tarnished when outfielder Patrick Lennon was arrested
for attempted homicide following a dispute in a downtown Williamsport bar. Lennon
and one of his teammates, Calvin Jones, got into a verbal dispute with one of the bar's
patrons. Lennon went to his car and got a 9-mm pistol and fired it toward the head of
his antagonist. Luckily for Lennon, the shot hit no one, but the damage was done.

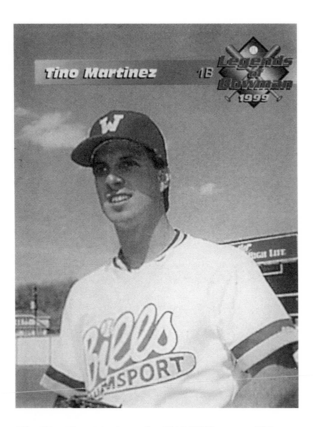

Fig. 50 Tino Martinez, the 1989 Williamsport Bills
first-baseman, later starred on the New York Yankees
World Championship teams of 1996 and 1998–2000.
(Legends of Bowman Field photo card, Courtesy of the
Williamsport Crosscutters)

Lennon's season was over. The Mariners suspended Lennon indefinitely. The incident
caused the Bills much embarrassment in the community and removed one of their
better hitters from the line-up. Lennon eventually received what amounted to a suspended sentence for the incident. Despite the dismal season, Williamsport fans saw Tino
Martinez on his way up to Major League stardom with the Mariners and Yankees, as
well as future Major League pitchers Jeff Nelson and Dave Burba.

The last Mariners season spelled no improvement for the Bills on the field, though
the off-the-field turbulence had subsided. New owner Marvin Goldklang, who owned
minor league teams at various levels and various leagues, provided a measure of stability
for the Williamsport franchse. The trademark of the Mariners years was poor hitting
and substandard pitching. The best pitcher the Bills had in 1990 was Mike Gardiner,

Fig. 51 The 1989 Williamsport Bills, a farm club of the Seattle Mariners, featured several future Major League players. Among the standouts were Tino Martinez, Jeff Nelson, Dave Burba, and Rich Delucia. (Courtesy of the Williamsport Bills)

who won twelve games and was the Eastern League leader in strikeouts (149) and ERA (1.90)

At the end of the 1990 season, it appeared that Eastern League baseball in Williamsport was doomed. But Williamsport fans enjoyed one more EL season in 1991. This was made possible by Binghamton's inability to put together a financial package to build a new stadium in time for the beginning of the 1991. The Bills franchise, still owned by Marvin Goldklang, was to have operated there in 1991. In fact, the New York Mets moved their Class AA Jackson, Mississipi, team of the Texas League to Binghamton in anticipation of playing in a newly constructed stadium. Unfortunately, financing and delays in construction short-circuited their plans for 1991 season. The Mets frantically sought an interim home for their team. On January 18, 1991, they announced the relocation of their farm club to Williamsport for one year until the stadium in Binghamton was ready.

Though the Mets stay was only temporary, the announcement stirred pleasant memories of the mid-1960s, the last time New York had a team in Williamsport. The climate of anticipation and excitement over the return of the Mets boosted the sagging spirits of local fans who feared Class AA ball had been lost forever. During the remaining winter months, speculation was rampant about the possibility of a new team affiliation for 1992. The team that was moving temporarily to Williamsport had finished first in the Eastern Division of the Texas League the previous season, but lost in the play-offs.

Williamsport fans looked forward to finally breaking the dreary cycle of noncontending clubs that plagued them for over twenty years. This air of expectancy was greatly reinforced by the cocky pronouncements of the Bills brash new skipper, Clint Hurdle, who boastfully proclaimed upon his arrival in Williamsport, "You [Williamsport] fans put up with the Indians and Mariners the last four seasons. They're dog meat compared to what the Mets have to offer." This optimistic air was reinforced when more than eight hundred fans turned out to watch the Bills work out shortly before their home opener. Unfortunately, the Bills underachieved and didn't reach the .500 mark until mid-June. They then dropped seven of their next nine decisions and never got close to the .500 mark that season, making Hurdle's boasts ring hollow.

The Bills drew a respectable amount of fans (96,711) for such a mediocre team. Many fans held out the vain hope that attendance figures might have been respectable enough to keep Eastern League baseball in Williamsport. These hopes were dashed in late June 1991. On a visit to Bowman Field to evaluate player talent, Mets farm director Gerry Hunsicker stated his opinion that "Williamsport was too small for AA baseball." Unfortunately, many other Eastern League owners concurred. Williamsport's days in the Eastern League were numbered. The league's emphasis on expansion to larger cities that were willing to finance new stadium projects rang the death knell for Class AA baseball in Williamsport.

Williamsport Mayor Jessie Bloom scrambled to keep minor league baseball in the city and worked closely (but perhaps unwisely) with Bills owner Marvin Goldklang to achieve this goal. A questionnaire was passed out to Bills fans coming to Bowman Field late in the 1991 season to gauge interest in Williamsport's possible membership in the short-season Class A New York–Penn League. Williamsport had been a member of that loop from 1968 to 1972. Approximately 60 percent of the fans polled indicated they would support a New York–Penn League franchise, so Goldklang promised to try to help Williamsport land a franchise in that league. Several local observers speculated that Goldklang planned to relocate his Erie franchise to Williamsport. But that didn't happen. Erie gave Goldklang a commitment to build a new stadium. Three more years passed before Williamsport gained membership in the New York–Penn League.

Several players stimulated fan interest in the Bills otherwise dreary season. D. J. Dozier, a major cog in Penn State's 1986 National Championship football team, was especially popular with local fans as an outfielder. He represented the Bills on the Eastern League all-star team before being called up to Tidewater and the parent New York Mets for a brief period. Tito Navarro, the Bills slick fielding second-baseman and leading hitter, had a promising Major League career cut short by a crippling knee injury in 1992. The slugging star for the Bills was outfielder Jeromy Burnitz, also a 1991 EL all-star. He led the league in homers with thirty-one, including three inside-the-park homers (two of them at Bowman Field)—a feat unequaled in Williamsport's baseball annals. He tied for the league lead in RBIs with eighty-five. He also accomplished an Eastern League first, stealing over thirty bases and hitting more than thirty homers. Burnitz

Fig. 52   Slugger Jeromy Burnitz, a member of the
1991 Williamsport Bills, became the first player to hit
more than thirty homers and steal more than thirty
bases in one season. He is currently an all-star player
with the Milwaukee Brewers. (Legends of Bowman
Field photo card, Courtesy of the Williamsport
Crosscutters)

threatened the Williamsport franchise record of thirty-three homers set by Jacke Davis,
falling two short. He established a Williamsport record drawing 104 walks that year.
The Bills pitching star was Dave Telgheder, who tied for the league lead in wins with
thirteen.

Eastern League baseball in Williamsport ended with a seeming whimper on Labor
Day, September 2, 1991. The Bills dropped a listless 11-0 decision to the play-off bound
Harrisburg Senators before approximately 1,300 mournful fans. Williamsport closed out
its last Eastern League season in seventh place with a disappointing 60-79 record.

With the passing of the 1991 season, a glorious chapter to Williamsport's baseball
history had ended. Williamsport had been a member of the Eastern League for forty-

eight seasons, the most of any EL city until Binghamton exceeded the mark in 1997. Williamsport had been the center of EL affairs from 1938 through 1970, when Williamsporters Tommy Richardson and Rankin Johnson served as league presidents. The Eastern League will always be remembered fondly by local fans as the heart and soul of Williamsport's baseball experience.

7

Welcome Back to the New York–Penn League

 The chain of events culminating in baseball's return to Billtown in 1994 began in the late spring and early summer of 1993. Bill Pickelner, Williamsport's long-time baseball booster, waged an intensive letter-writing and phone campaign to lure a New York–Penn League franchise to Williamsport. He struck pay dirt with Geneva Cubs owners Paul Velte, Mike Roulan, and Ed Smaldone. The men from Geneva, New York, came to the reluctant conclusion that they needed to relocate their franchise to a larger market with a broader fan base. Though other cities were considered, they deemed Williamsport as the best alternative.

After laborious negotiations with city officials in the fall of 1993, Velte, Roulan, and Smaldone decided to move the Geneva Cubs to Williamsport. The new team, known as the Williamsport Cubs, became a farm club of the Chicago Cubs. More important, the owners signed a five-year lease with the city, sending an important signal to local baseball fans that the team was here for the long-term. No longer would there be a yearly guessing game as to whether baseball would return in upcoming seasons. One other sign of the long-term commitment entailed the permanent presence of the Cubs' front-office staff at the ballpark. Cubs general manager Doug Estes and marketing director Gabe Sinicropi relocated to Williamsport that winter and established a permanent office at Bowman Field that stayed open year-round. Estes and Sinicropi circulated widely in the community to whip up interest in the Cubs. They planned many ambitious and successful promotions that yielded positive dividends at the box office. Their efforts amounted to the most aggressive and thoughtfully planned marketing campaign ever for Williamsport baseball. The Cubs ownership group—especially principal owner Paul Velte—also made frequent visits to Williamsport and the ballpark to oversee operations during the season.

An indication of the enthusiastic response to the return of baseball to Williamsport came on the "Meet the Cubs Night" held at the Sheraton Hotel two nights before the 1994 season opener. With approximately three hundred fans in attendance, the response was overwhelming, exceeding everyone's expectations and setting a fine tone to kickoff the season. This special night also marked the debut of a unique, furry friend, the Cubs new mascot, "Kid Cub." As the first mascot Williamsport ever had, Kid Cub was an immediate hit and became a fixture at Bowman Field for the next four seasons.

Another first was the establishment of a full-fledged Williamsport fan club to support the new team. The Williamsport Cubs Booster Club attracted the area's most loyal supporters of the Cubbies. Members provided emotional and material support to Cubs managers, coaches, and players and their respective wives and family members throughout the season. The Booster Club's "Adopt-A-Cub" program encouraged members to "adopt" players and act as their surrogate parents. These Booster families provided transportation for players—enabling them to navigate the city—and often invited team members to their homes for the occasional home-cooked meal. This program proved to be very popular with the players and their Booster Club "parents."

The euphoria of baseball's return to Williamsport was tempered by the poor performance of the 1994 Cubs on the diamond. The team spent most of its time in the Pinckney Division cellar, enduring ten-game and six-game losing streaks during the season. They finished with the league's worst record at 26-49. Despite this poor showing, they still drew 61,233 fans, almost doubling Geneva's attendance the previous season.

The major highlight of the season came on June 19, 1994, in Elmira, when the Cubs Joe Montelongo and Rob Rehkopf pitched a rare combined no-hitter. It was the first combined no-hitter ever pitched by a Williamsport team. Forty members of the Cubs Booster Club, who had traveled to Elmira on a chartered bus, cheered them on. Montelongo's father rode with the Boosters and witnessed his son's gem. That year also saw the pitching prowess of Geremi Gonzalez, who led the staff with four wins and later became the first Williamsport Cub to make the Majors.

The next year saw a marked improvement in the team as they finished on the threshold of the .500 mark with a 37-39 record. The Cubs also captured the first (and only)

Fig. 53 Kerry Wood, the Chicago Cubs
pitching sensation, pitched two games for the
1995 Williamsport Cubs, going 0-1 in his two
starts. (Legends of Bowman Field photo card,
Courtesy of the Williamsport Crosscutters)

"Challenge Cup" from the Elmira Pioneers by winning their 1995 season series. Fans
also got their first look at future star Kerry Wood, who pitched in two starts at the end
of the season for the locals.

The 1996 ballclub was the best team representing the Cubs years. Williamsport made
a legitimate run for a New York–Penn League play-off spot, the first Billtown team
since the 1968 Williamsport Astros. They were also the first team to finish above the
.500 mark since the 1969 Astros.

The Cubs were guided by one of the most distinguished coaching staffs that a Williamsport team ever had. At the helm was Ruben Amaro Sr., a former Major League
all-star shortstop. Amaro etched out a good career with the Phillies, Yankees, and
Angels, and was also a member of the coaching staff of the 1980 World Champion
Philadelphia Phillies. His hitting coach was former National League (Phillies, Cubs and

Expos) all-star second-baseman, Manny Trillo. Trillo had been a key player on the Phillies 1980 Championship team, and won the 1980 World Series Most Valuable Player trophy.

The youthful Cubs were the beneficiaries of Amaro's and Trillo's extensive knowledge and skills. It was a pleasure for anyone who arrived early at Bowman Field to watch Trillo conduct pre-game infield drills with the team. Trillo often fielded balls himself and still displayed the smooth hands that were his hallmarks as an infielder. A crowd favorite, he further showcased his talents by leading fans and Cub players in the "Macarena," the dance sensation that swept the nation in 1996. The Cubs contended right down the wire for a play-off slot, but unfortunately their bats went cold at an inopportune time and they barely missed the play-offs by two games.

Despite the disappointing finish to the season, Cubs fans still had much to celebrate during Bowman Field's seventieth-anniversary season. In addition to the team's winning record of 43-32, Cubs pitcher Courtney Duncan racked up one of the best seasons ever for a Williamsport hurler, earning a stellar 11-1 record and finishing with a team-high of ninety-one strikeouts. Nate Manning batted .317 and was named to the New York–Penn League's all-star team.

In 1997, the Cubs crashed to the depths again, finishing with a dreadful 29-46 mark, and averting last place by a mere game. The only positive note was the hitting of Ron Walker, who finished second in the league in batting with a lusty .349 average, clubbed nine homers, and drove in thirty-nine runs. Walker was also second in the league in slugging percentage with a .556 mark.

In 1998, the Williamsport Cubs had a highly competitive season. The Cubbies vied for a New York–Penn League play-off spot for almost the entire season. The team enjoyed fine pitching but were plagued by inconsistent hitting, despite having the two best offensive players—Eric Hinske and Chris Connally—the Cubs ever had. Both Hinske and Connally finished in the league's top ten in several offensive categories. They were an awesome one-two punch. The Cubs also had an excellent lead-off hitter in Mike Moreno. Despite these three, the rest of the line-up was unable to deliver runs when needed in close games.

There were two notable firsts in the 1998 season. The first player ever signed from the Pacific Rim by the Chicago Cubs was a member of the 1998 Williamsport Cubs, a Japan native, named Takkaki "Tiger" Kato. Kato spent most of his first year in professional baseball as a designated hitter. He hit .258 with nineteen RBIs in fifty-nine games. The other notable first was the employment of Taleen Noradukian as the first full-time woman trainer for a Williamsport baseball team.

The major highlight of the 1998 season occurred in the June 28 game at Bowman Field against the Watertown Indians, when the Cubs ripped six homers in a 13-3 romp. The Cubs turned in an historic feat when first-baseman Eric Hinske and catcher Marcel Longmire swatted back-to-back homers in consecutive innings. According to baseball

Fig. 54   The 1998 Williamsport Cubs had the historic distinction of having the first Japanese player to ever play on a Williamsport team, Takkaki "Tiger" Kato, and Williamsport's first female team trainer, Taleen Noradoukian. (Photo by Jon Smith, Courtesy of the Williamsport Crosscutters)

historian Bob McConnell, the feat had only been done one other time in minor league baseball history, on May 14, 1951, in a Texas League game between the Tulsa Drillers and the Houston Buffaloes. Hinske set a Williamsport Cub record by driving in fifty-seven runs in 1998. Connally finished second with fifty-five RBIs. Both were named to the New York–Penn League all-star team.

The Williamsport Cubs finished their farewell season with a respectable 39-36 record. At the end of the 1998 season the Chicago Cubs informed the owners of the Williamsport franchise that they had chosen to discontinue their affiliation with Williamsport. The owners did not have to wait long for another major club to show interest because the Pittsburgh Pirates contacted them and offered to strike an affiliation agreement. The Pirates were losing their previous New York–Penn League affiliation with Erie, since that city was moving up to the Class AA Eastern League.

Of course, with a new affiliation, a new team name was needed. Team officials decided that a team-neutral name would be best, and as a nod to Williamsport's prominent lumber heritage decided to call the team the "Crosscutters." The team name referred to the crosscut saw that nineteenth-century lumberman used as the tool of their trade. The Crosscutters front office decided that a new mascot was also needed and

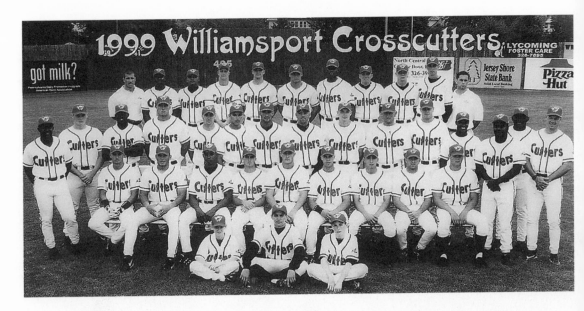

Fig. 55   The 1999 Williamsport Crosscutters, an affiliate of the Pittsburgh Pirates, featured the son of Pirates general manager Cam Bonifay, second-baseman Josh Bonifay (first row, sixth player from the left). (Photo by Jon Smith, Courtesy of the Williamsport Crosscutters)

launched a "Name the Mascot" promotion. The winning name was "Rusty Rough-cut," for the burly lumberjack character who would prowl the stands whipping up cheers for the hometown team.

The Crosscutters opened the 1999 season successfully, winning nine of the first eleven games. The team was in first place during twenty-one of the first twenty-five days of the season, and visions of a championship season danced in the heads of the Williamsport faithful. But the wheel started to come off in early July. B. J. Barnes and Diogenes Diaz, two of the Cutters better hitters were called up to Hickory in the Carolina League. After the call-up, Williamsport began a seven-game losing skid. Over-all, the Cutters dropped sixteen of nineteen games and plummeted to last place in the Pinckney Division. They never recovered from this horrid losing streak. Williamsport managed a feeble five-game winning streak in August, but finished in last past with a dismal 32-44 record.

Infielder Antonio Alvarez was the Crosscutters top player, finishing sixth in the league with a .321 batting average, hitting seven homers, and driving in forty-five runs. Alvarez won the Pinckney Division's MVP award—the first Williamsport player to win the award since Bernie Smith won the Eastern League's MVP in 1967. Jason Landreth also turned in a good season, batting .314 with six homers and thirty-seven RBIs. Juan Bazan led pitchers with a 4–3 record and a 3.02 ERA. Chris Rojas led the staff in strike-outs with eighty-five and Felix Montilla led the team in saves.

Fig. 56 The new Bowman Field, June 30, 2000. Following a $1.5 million renovation, Bowman Field combines the old with the new, offering the best in fan amenities, while paying tribute to Williamsport's lumbering heritage and historic Victorian mansions. (Photograph by Jon Smith, Courtesy of the Williamsport Crosscutters)

The Williamsport Crosscutters 2000 season opened with great optimism as the team celebrated the unveiling of newly renovated Bowman Field. More than three thousand fans turned out on opening night and were duly impressed by the $1.5 million renovations to the venerable ballpark. Unfortunately, the improvements to Bowman Field did nothing to enhance the on-field performance of the Cutters. They lost fourteen of their first nineteen games and quickly plunged to the cellar of the Pinckney Division. The Crosscutters righted themselves somewhat, putting together two six-game winning streaks during a 12-2 stretch midway through the season, which left them at 17-21, four games shy of the .500 mark. However, the team reverted to their losing ways and lost more ground in the Pinckney Division race. During the final two weeks of the season, the team had an excellent eight-day road trip during which they compiled a 6-3 record; but they lost the final five games of the season to finish with a 29-43 record, seventeen games back of the division-leading Mahoning Valley Scrappers.

All was not negative for the 2000 Williamsport Crosscutters. Two of their players were selected to the New York–Penn League All-Star Team. Catcher Ryan Doumit was the league's tenth leading hitter with a .313 average and led the team with forty RBIS. Pitcher Landon Jacobsen, another all-star, achieved a record of 3-2 and an outstanding 1.41 ERA. Jacobsen held opponents to a meager .188 average before being called up to Hickory, North Carolina, Pittsburgh's affiliate in the full-season Class A Carolina League. The Cutters also enjoyed workman-like relief pitching from Josh Higgins, who lead the team in saves with seven, going 3-1 and sporting a microscopic 1.04 ERA. Centerfielder Manny Revelo was among the league leaders in triples with seven, and batted .303. Jon Pagan led the Crosscutters with six home runs.

One of the most encouraging developments of the 2000 season was the level of support Williamsport fans gave a less-than-stellar team. The Cutters set a Williamsport short-season Class A attendance record, drawing 67,220 fans for the season and averaging 1,769 per game—the second highest per-game average in Williamsport baseball history.

As Williamsport baseball fans prepare to celebrate the seventy-fifth anniversary of Bowman Field in 2001, the immediate future for professional baseball in Williamsport appears stable for the moment. The Crosscutters have the benefit of a secure Bowman Field lease with the city, and recently inked a new five-year working agreement with the parent Pittsburgh Pirates. After the recent renovations and upgrades to the field, the uptown ballpark has been given a new lease on life. By all accounts, the Cutters owners and management have enjoyed their relationship with the Pirates front office. Even though the Pirates recent amateur drafts and roster moves have failed to produce a winner at Williamsport, attendance has not duly suffered. Should Williamsport ever field a pennant-contending team, or at least achieve a string of consecutive winning seasons, the Cutters envision annual attendance figures topping the 70,000 mark.

Williamsport's future in the professional game is still subject to the ever-changing dynamics of the economics and politics of administering minor league baseball operations. Even in the few short years since Williamsport embraced short-season Class A baseball, the costs associated with purchasing, owning, and operating a minor league franchise at this level have skyrocketed beyond the resources of many communities. Like Major League baseball, the New York–Penn League owners and administrators have sought larger regional markets for their product. This has contributed to franchise instability (with teams moving from one city to the next with little regard to the fans and cities that have made a substantial emotional and monetary investment in their respective teams) and created a chasm between large and small market clubs.

Much like the parent Pittsburgh Pirates, Williamsport remains a small-market team, finding itself at a disadvantage with respect to many of the top-tier New York–Penn League teams situated in larger cities and more advantageous regional markets. The political clout wielded by the bloc of large-market teams extends to such issues as season scheduling, division re-alignment, league expansion, and approval for franchise shifts.

Some of these clubs even have local or regional television contracts in place, guaranteeing a revenue stream denied to the small market clubs.

In the current minor league climate, every franchise is saleable for the right price—to the highest bidder. Unlike previous decades, new ownership groups and communities are willing to spend exorbitant sums to lure minor league teams and construct lavish stadiums to house them. The stakes have gotten higher because owners now operate minor league franchises as family entertainment enterprises and profit-driven businesses, tied to the economic redevelopment of the communities they serve.

Whether the present owners of the Williamsport franchise are content with these current conditions remains to be seen. In spite of its long association with the professional minor league game and grand baseball tradition, Williamsport's long-term future in the game is at best uncertain. The emergence of a local private ownership group or municipal purchase and operation of the Crosscutters (along the lines of the Harrisburg model in the Eastern League) would go a long way toward ensuring franchise stability in Williamsport for years to come. To date, no local parties have publicly expressed an interest in buying the team from the present owners; and few city council members would dare broach such a proposal given Williamsport's volatile fiscal and economic outlook.

The Cutters current ownership and management group have given every indication, by word and deed, they are here to stay. Their year-round presence in the community, and continuing commitment to provide an affordable family-oriented experience at Bowman Field, have been significant factors in breaking the long cycle of fan distrust and cynicism toward absentee owners. It is hopeful that Williamsport will have professional baseball to hand down to succeeding generations, and that minor league baseball will not go the way of the lumber and steel mills that vanished from the Susquehanna West Branch Valley decades ago.

In researching and writing this history of minor league baseball in Williamsport, the authors consulted a variety of sources for documentation. Our study incorporated primary source material (local newspapers, manuscripts and archives, and oral history interviews), secondary sources (books, articles, and reference literature), and nontextual material (photographic prints and images). Because of the breadth of the narrative and the immense amount of biographical and statistical information contained therein, we decided to dispense with citations so as not to burden the general reader. In lieu of footnotes and endnotes, this note on sources directs the reader to the most important sources we used as the basis for our research.

Among our primary sources, the Williamsport dailies and Sunday newspapers—the *Williamsport Gazette & Bulletin,* the *Williamsport Sun-Gazette,* and the *Grit*—provided an indispensable record of the ebb and flow of baseball seasons dating from 1865 to the present. Microfilmed copies of these newspapers are deposited in the James V. Brown Library, Williamsport, Pennsylvania. Although mid-nineteenth-century coverage of local baseball was sporadic at best, the *Gazette & Bulletin* provided a window to the formative amateur club era of baseball shortly before the emergence of the professional game. In addition to the daily coverage of baseball over successive eras, these newspapers contained insightful historical and retrospective articles and anecdotes that contributed to our community's collective baseball memory. Interested fans can learn much about Williamsport's baseball history by reading the articles of Major William P. Clarke (who wrote under the by-line of "Old Tymer"), Ray Keyes ("Sun Rays"), Michael Bernardi ("Sports Mike"), and Al Decker.

While newspaper research provided the main chronological and narrative framework for our book, oral history interviews offered an important personal and social context to our understanding of what minor league baseball meant to Williamsport. We interviewed club officers and front-office personnel, former players, sports reporters and journalists (print and radio), civic leaders, and a broad spectrum of fans. Our interviewees were chosen on the basis of their long association with Williamsport minor league

baseball and intimate knowledge of the business side of local baseball operations. All of the following individuals were interviewed for our book: Max and Alta Border, William "Buck" Byham, Al Decker, "Bud" Jaffe, Rankin Johnson, Frank Kitchen, Baney Levinson, Frank Luppachino, Don Manno, John Markley, Larry Maynard, Johnny Miller, Dorothy Parsons, Margarite Seiler, and Ev Rubendall.

The authors had access to rich primary source material held in public repositories and private collections. Our research on Williamsport's Tri-State championship teams, and Tommy Richardson's contributions to the administration of the Eastern League, benefited greatly by a visit to the National Baseball Hall of Fame Library and Archives at Cooperstown, New York. Though the Cooperstown Museum is more widely known, the Library and Archives constitute first-rate research facilities and house original documents, manuscript material, and periodicals every bit as essential to the preservation of the national pastime as its storied game memorabilia. The Hall of Fame Library's collection of *The Spalding Baseball Guides* yielded valuable season summaries and highlights covering Williamsport's golden era (1904–10) in the Tri-State League. A vertical file of press clippings and photographs devoted to Williamsport's Tommy Richardson, including his obituary printed in *The Sporting News* (November 18, 1970), is also deposited in the Hall of Fame Library.

Locally, we enjoyed unfettered access to a rich treasure trove of photographic prints, postcards, and other visual images documenting Williamsport's baseball past. The *Grit's* baseball photograph files (since donated to the James V. Brown Library) provided the bulk of the images reproduced here in this book. We uncovered several rare prints of old Athletic Park dating back to the early 1900s. The D. Vincent Smith and Putsee Vannucci Photograph Collections of the Lycoming County Historical Museum contained rich visual images of Bowman Field and the large crowds that attended ballgames during the 1930s and 1940s.

Tracing leads on sources, we contacted many boosters and fans who willingly shared documents, photographs, clippings, and memorabilia culled from their own private collections. Bill Pickelner and Ralph "Pat" Thorne Jr. allowed us to view an original charter agreement and stock certificates of the holding company formed by J. Walton Bowman to finance the construction of Bowman Field. Rankin Johnson Jr. shared with us his collection of correspondence, photo scrapbooks, and memorabilia documenting his playing days and tenure as a business manager for several Williamsport clubs.

Though unique in many aspects, Williamsport's baseball past cannot be divorced from the national minor league experience and the larger social and economic context in which professional baseball developed. The body of literature devoted to the history of minor league baseball has grown extensively over the past decade, in part a reflection of the resurgence of the game and renewed fan interest in local professional baseball. Though many fine histories of baseball have been published within the last two decades, Harold Seymour's three-volume work *Baseball* (New York: Oxford University Press, 1960) remains the definitive study of the national pastime. Seymour's history was espe-

cially insightful in tracing the rise of city sandlot, semipro, and corporate-sponsored industrial leagues that dotted the urban landscape around the turn of the century. The emergence of these leagues provided a crucial link between the amateur club era of baseball, and the rise of professional minor league baseball. Seymour's work also provided important background on the administrative history of the minor leagues, including the muddled period predating the formation of the National Association of Professional Baseball Clubs, the governing body of the minors.

David Quentin Voigt's excellent trilogy *American Baseball* (The Pennsylvania State University Press, 3d printing, 1992) is rapidly gaining ground as the standard scholarly text on the history of baseball. In addition to updating Seymour's work, Voigt's study provides a sharper focus on the rise of the professional game and the nineteenth-century battles among rising professional leagues to challenge the National League's ascendancy.

Neil Sullivan's *The Minors: The Struggle and the Triumph of Baseball's Poor Relation from 1876 to the Present* (New York: St. Martin's Press, 1990) provides a panoramic history of minor league baseball with a focus upon the dominant leagues, teams, and players. While his book is rich in the lore of minor league baseball, it gives only minimal attention to the history of the Eastern League. Indeed, the definitive history of the Eastern League and its predecessor, the New York-Pennsylvania League, has yet to be written. By contrast, the Class AA Southern and Texas Leagues, and the Class AAA International League, Pacific Coast League, and American Association have all had their chroniclers.

Consulted for the first chapter, Warren Jay Goldstein's *Playing for Keeps: A History of Early Baseball* (Ithaca: Cornell University, Press, 1989) and George B. Kirsch's *The Creation of American Team Sports: Baseball and Cricket, 1838–1872* (Urbana: University of Illinois Press, 1989) illuminate the lost era of amateur club baseball in the nineteenth century. These books offer interesting historical and sociological perspectives regarding the social norms and by-laws governing early baseball clubs as professionalism encroached upon the game. Several of their important chapters chronicle the changing relationship between players and fans as baseball evolved into a commercialized mass spectator sport.

Roberto Gonzalez Echevarria's *The Pride of Havana: A History of Cuban Baseball* (Oxford University Press, 1999), contains valuable information on several of the Cuban ballplayers who played for Williamsport during the years 1944–45. His work also provides some background on Joe Cambria, the Washington Senators super-scout and architect of that organization's recruitment of Cuban players.

Historical research on the topic of minor league baseball is best served by having access to accurate reference information. In compiling copious player and team statistics, and the accompanying appendices and lists that form part of this book, we used one of the best baseball reference sources available, Lloyd Johnson's and Miles Wolf's *Minor League Encyclopedia* (1992, 1997). Its contents include year-by-year minor league standings, the results of interleague championship series, batting and pitching leaders, and the all-time statistical records for each league—from the Class AAA down to rookie-level ball. Various publications by the Society for American Baseball Research (SABR), including the excellent series *SABR: Minor League Stars*, 3 vols., provide rich anecdotal information on many opposing teams and players who graced Bowman Field and contributed to Eastern League lore and legend.

Far from being a solitary endeavor, the writing of a book has been truly a collaborative effort, benefiting from and drawing upon the collective minds and research of others engaged in similar inquiry. National and regional meetings of SABR provided an excellent forum for exchanging and disseminating valuable information relating to Williamsport's minor league baseball experience. Follow-up correspondence with other minor league baseball historians, writing about their own locale, yielded important data and sources that were incorporated into the body of this work. Though not footnoted, they have contributed greatly to the writing of this book. Reed Howard, one of the acknowledged experts of nineteenth-century minor league baseball, shared the fruits of his extensive research on the various Pennsylvania state leagues and associations with which Williamsport was affiliated.

Major League Players Who Played For Williamsport
(1877–2000)

Don Aase	Bud Black	Ralph Buxton
Dick Allen	Ron Blackburn	Wayne Cage
Wayne Ambler	Walter Blair	Fred Caliguiri
Craig Anderson	Tim Bogar	Hank Camelli
John Anderson	Joe Boley	Joe Campbell
Larry Anderson	Jim Bolger	Paul Campbell
Fred Archer	Frank Bolling	Virgil "Rip" Cannell
Orrie Arntzen	Mark Bomback	Don Carlsen
Bob Asby (Asbjornsen)	Ken Boswell	Edgar Carroll
Jim Asbell	Al Brancato	Solly Carter
Bill Baker	Tom Brennan	Danny Cater
Dave Baldwin	Bernardo Brito	Bill Chamberlin
Babe Barna	Terry Bross	Jim "Tiny" Chaplin
Clyde Barnhart	Earl Brown	Chappy Charles
Dick Barone	Joe Brown	Walt Chipple
Tracey Barrett	Lloyd Brown	Harry Chozen
Tony Bartirome	Oscar Brown	Joe Christopher
Harry Barton	Paul Brown	Joe Cicero
Ed Bauta	Jim Bruske	Stuart Clarke
Bill Bayne	Clay Bryant	Gowell Claset
Chris Beasley	George Bullard	Otis Clymer
Al Benton	Jim Bunning	Alta Cohen
Bozey Berger	Dave Burba	Oren Collier
Jim Bethke	Bill Burich	Kevin Collins
Larry Bettencourt	Mack Burk	Adam Comorosky
Babe Birrer	Jeromy Burnitz	Bert Conn
Jim Bishop	George J. Burns	Bill Conroy
Max Bishop	Ed Butka	Dale Coogan

Pat Corrales
Bill Coughlin
Doc Cramer
Sam Crane
"Birdie" Cree
Pat Creeden
John Crowley
Ray Culp
Tony Curry
Pat Darcy
Hal Daugherty
Brandy Davis
Harry Davis
Jacke Davis
Bobby Del Greco
Joe Delahanty
Tom Delahanty
Rich Delucia
Gene Desautels
Frank Dessau
George Detore
Bo Diaz
Steve Dillon
Art Doll
Jerry Donovan
Whammy Douglas
Scott Downs
Carl Doyle
D.J. Dozier
Jacob Drauby
Davy Dunkle
Duffy Dyer
John Easton
Lee Elia
Luis Encarnacion
Roy Evans
Bob Farley
Al Federoff
Bill Ferazzi
Sid Fernandez
Dan Firova

Clarence Fisher
Harry Fisher
Ray Fitzgerald
Shaun Fitzmaurice
Ken Forsch
Eddie Foster
Paul Foytack
Walter French
Barney Friberg
Cy Fried
Danny Friend
Biznll Froats
Bob Garbark
Mike Gardiner
Rob Gardner
Rod Gaspar
Gary Gentry
Tony Ghelfi
Norm Gigon
Harry Gleason
"Kid" Gleason
Jerry Goff
Jose Gomez
Jeremy Gonzalez
Alex Grabowski
Milt Graff
Lou Grasmick
Sam Gray
Dallas Green
Fred Green
Julius Green
Alfredo Griffin
Ivy Griffith
Howdie Grosskloss
Johnny Groth
Harry Gumbert
Randy Gumpert
"Mule" Haas
Hinky Haines
Bill Hall
Irv Hall

Jack Hamilton
Lee Hancock
Todd Haney
Jim Hardin
Bob Harris
Ron Hassey
Gene Hasson
Bill Heath
Fritz Henrich
Frank Henry
Mark Higgins
Bill Hinchman
Jerry Hinsley
Tommy Hinzo
Cal Hogue
Joe Holden
Chris Howard
Pat Howell
Bill Hunnefield
Warren Huston
Ferguson Jenkins
A. Rankin Johnson
Bob Johnson
Jerry Johnson
John Johnstone
Baxter Jordan
Milt Jordan
Scott Jordan
Mike Joyce
Ed Keegan
Walt Kellner
Al Kenders
Russ Kerns
Joe Kiefer
Dennis Kinney
Bill Knowlton
Nick Koback
Jerry Koosman
Lou Kretlow
Gary Kroll
"Flip" Lafferty

Tom Lampkin
Norm Lehr
Patrick Lennon
George Lerchen
Glen Liebhart
Bob Lindemann
Carl Linhart
Pete Lister
Ron Locke
Dario Lodgiani
Dick Loftus
Dale Long
Hector Lopez
Marcelino Lopez
Del Lundgren
Johnny Lush
Jim Lyle
Jerry Lynn
Ed Madjeski
Jim Mahady
Art Mahaffey
Leo Mangnum
Rube Manning
Don Manno
Dick Marlowe
Ollie Marquart
Luis Marquez
Tino Martinez
Henry Mason
Walt Masters
Jon Matlack
Earl Mattingly
Bob Mavis
Bill Mazeroski
Jim McAndrew
Harold McClure
Les McCrabb
Frank McCue
Art McLarney
Marty McManus
Bob McNamara

Brian McNichol
Gerald McQuaig
Glenn McQuillen
Luis Medina
Jose Melendez
John Merena
Ralph Michaels
Bob Miller
Art Mills
Ed Montague
Joe Moock
Bob Moorehead
Charlie Moss
Mike Mowery
Ron Mrozinski
William Mullen
Joe Murray
Dennis Musgraves
Alex Mustaikis
Chad Myers
Tito Navarro
Al Neiger
Tom Neill
Jeff Nelson
Rod Nichols
Bill Nicholson
Jose Nieves
Ron Northey
Tom O'Hara
Jim Owen
Sam Page
Vernon Parkes
Leroy Parmalee
Len Parme
Claude Passeau
Tom Patton
Jack Peerson
Henry Peploski
Jon Perlman
Bill Peterman
Harding Peterson

Bubba Phillips
Tom Poorman
Ned Porter
Grover Powell
Johnny Powers
Tom Qualters
Hal Quick
Joe Rabbitt
Drew Rader
Jack Radtke
Earl Rapp
Charlie Reddock
Johnny Reder
Glenn Redmon
Jim Reninger
Steve Renko
Jim Rice
Pat Rice
Duane Richards
Ken Richarson
Don Richmond
Curt Roberts
Saul Rogovin
Les Rohr
Johnny Roser
Schoolboy Rowe
Emil Roy
Dutch Rudolph
Dick Rusteck
Nolan Ryan
"Slim" Sallee
Amado Samuel
John Sanders
Jack Sanford
Ted Savage
Don Savidge
Dutch Scheesler
Jay Schleuter
Al Schmelz
Bob Schmidt
Jerry Schpynski

Ossie Schreckengost
Jimmy Sebring
Dwight Seibler
Don Shaw
Jeff Shaw
John Sherlock
John Shockley
Ron Shoop
John Shovlin
Harry Shuman
Curt Simmons
Joe Skalski
Jack Slattery
Joe Smaza
Bernie Smith
Carr Smith
Edgar Smith
Bill Sorrell
Denny Sothern
Justin Speier
Glenn Spencer
Bob Spicer
George Staller
Eddie Stanky
Bill Steinecke
Bobby Stevens
Bill Stewart
Harry Stovey

Gabby Street
Ralph Stroud
John L. Sullivan
Russ Sullivan
Bill Swift
Ron Swoboda
Doug Tait
Wally Tauscher
Joe Taylor
Scott Taylor
Dick Teed
Dave Telgheder
Jim Tennant
"Bud" Thomas
Otis Thornton
Mike Tiernan
George Turbeville
Bill Tuttle
Johnny Tyler
Bob Unglaub
Rogelio Valdes
Ossie Van Brabant
Fred Van Dusen
Hy Vandenberg
Bill Virdon
Phil Voyles
Bill Wakefield
Mike Walker

Bucky Walters
John "Monte" Ward
Jack Warhop
Jim Waugh
Dick Welteroth
Tony Welzer
Buzz Wetzel
Woody Wheaton
Ernie Whitt
Kevin Wickander
Dewey Williams
Mike Wilson
Bobby Wine
Andy Woehrs
Harry Wolfe
Roger Wolff
Harry Wolverton
Kerry Wood
John Wyckoff
Al Yates
Rich Yett
Pep Young
Russ Young
Eddie Yount
Joe Zapustas
Jose Zardon
Sam Zoldak
Julio Zuleta

INDEX

Aase, Don, 145
Abbott, Spencer "Spence," 59, 69, 107, 109, 111
absentee owners, 72, 73, 78, 135
Addington, L. H., 58
admission prices, 27, 67, 72, 103
"Adopt-a-Cub" program, 74, 160
African Americans. *See* black teams and players
All Cubans, 27
Allen, Dick "Richie," 134, 135, 136
Allentown, 131
Alou, Mateo "Matty," 129
Altoona, 17, 37, 42
Alvarez, Antonio, 164
Amaro, Ruben, Sr., 161
American Association of Professional Clubs (American
    League), 18, 25–26
"American Legion Night," 70
Americans, St. Louis, 27, 28
Anderson, Cy, 121
Anderson, Larry, 148
Applegate, Fred "Snitz," 21, 26, 30, 37
Armour Leather Company, 50
Arrago, Hector, 116
A's, Philadelphia. *See* Philadelphia Athletics
A's, Williamsport, 122–23
Ashburn, Richie, 95, 116
Astros, Williamsport, 142
Aten, "Cannonball," 14
Athletic Park, 26, 31, 32
Athletics, Philadelphia. *See* Philadelphia Athletics
Athletics, Vallamont, 41
Athletics baseball club, Williamsport, 8, 9, 12, 13
Aube, Hormidas, 106
automobile giveaways, 67, 69
Autters, Micky, 21
Avco, 92

Badfinger, 95
Bailey, Paul, 126

Baker, Bill, 106, 133
Baker, Lewis, 18
"Bald Eagles," 99
Baldwin, Dave, 133
Baldwin, William, 14
Baltimore Elite Giants, 95
Baltimore Orioles, 92
Bankers, 22
"Bark in the Park Night," 74
Barna, Babe, 108
Barnes, B. J., 164
Barnhart, Clyde, 42, 56
Barone, Dick, 125
Barons, Wilkes-Barre, 110–12
Barrett, Tracey "Kewpie Dick," 101
Bartirome, Tony, 127
Bartling, Irv, 108
Barton, Harry, 30
Barton, Larry, 110
baseball
    in acculturation of immigrants, 2
    admission prices, 27, 67, 72, 103 (*see also* ticket sales)
    catchers, 9
    church-sponsored, 41
    classification guidelines for minor league teams, 25
    drinking associated with, 11
    evolution of professional, 1–2, 12–13
    fans of (*see* kranks [fans])
    first-basemen, 10
    gloves, 10
    impact of economic conditions on, 15
    injuries and, 40, 129, 131, 148
    leagues (*see specific leagues*)
    lumber barons and evolution of, 1–2, 15
    Major League-American League agreement, 25–26,
        36
    "Massachusetts game," 9

baseball (*continued*)
  "New York rules" for, 9
  organization of early, 8–12
  overhand pitching, 9
  press coverage of early, 13
  racism in, 2, 115, 116, 124 (*see also* black teams and
    players)
  recruitment of players, 14, 16
  restructuring of minor leagues, 24–28
  rules, 9–10, 25
  semipro periods, 13–17, 41–43
  social role of, 2
  stadium guidelines in, 4
  women involved with, 67, 89, 94, 145, 162, 163
"Baseball Field Days," 70
"Battle of the Bands," 95
Bazan, Juan, 164
Beach Boys, 95
Beale, Morris, 114
beer licenses, 73, 148, 152
Belcher, Tom, 137
Bellandi, Alfred (Al), 91–93, 133
Bellefonte, 15, 22
Bengough, Benny, 64
Bennetch, Dale, 129
Benton, Stanley "Rabbit," 99
Berardino, Dick, 142
Bernardi, Mike, 54, 91, 93, 133, 136
Berra, Yogi, 137
Bettencourt, Larry, 94, 108
Bevier, Frank, 28
Bicentennial Pageant, 95
"Bicycle and Suburban Night," 61
Bicycle Night, 68–69
Billies, Williamsport
  1902 season, 26
  1903 season, 27–28
  1904 season, 30
  1905 season, 30–31, 33, 34
  1924 season, 99
"Bills," Williamsport, 52, 72, 99, 149–57
BillSox, 142–45
Billtowners, Williamsport
  1884 season, 17
  1885 season, 17
  1886 season, 18
  1887 season, 19–20
Binghamton, 102, 154
Binghamton Triplets, 67, 101–2, 103, 133
Bishop, Jim, 99
Bishop, Max, 42, 56
Bissonette, Del, 100
Blackburn, Ron, 70
Black Sox scandal, 42
black teams and players, 27–28, 81, 95, 123, 135
Blair, Walter, 30, 36

Blanchard, Bruce, 118, 121
"Blitz Kids," 129
Bloom, Jessie, 155
Bloomsburg, 24
Blue Sox, Utica, 115
Blumette, Pete, 108
B'nai B'rith Night, 52, 54, 128
Boley, Joe, 42, 56
"Bomber Bond Night," 69–70
Bonowitz, Joe, 106
Bonus Babies, 137
Boomer Baseball, 41–43
Boomfest, 95
"Booster Day," 67
Booster Nights, 54, 67, 128
boosters
  Grays, 46–53, 71–72
  Nine-County Baseball Booster Association, 52, 72
  Nine-County Baseball Boosters, Inc., 128, 129, 135,
    137, 139, 141, 142
  Williamsport Booster Club, 54, 74
  Williamsport Cubs Booster Club, 160
Booth, Charles "Mother," 21, 24, 26
Boston Braves, 103
Boston Red Sox, 67, 142, 144
Boswell, Ken, 141
Bower, John H., 68
Bowman, Frank C., 26, 37, 45, 48
Bowman, J. Walton
  Bowman Field named after, 81
  construction of Bowman Field and, 79
  death of, 102
  on end of Millionaires, 40
  Max Jaffe and, 50
  NYPL and, 46
  recruitment of Sebring and, 30
  support for franchises, 45
  support for Railroad League, 41
  support for Williamsport baseball, 47–48, 49
  Williamsport Athletic Club and, 26
Bowman Field, 82
  absentee owners and, 73
  beer sales at, 73, 148, 152
  construction of, 3, 79–81
  "Days of Pompeii" game in, 85
  financing of, 2, 79–80
  first game in, 81, 101
  flooding of, 83–84, 118
  formal opening of, 81
  formative years of, 78–85
  foul poles, 85
  groundskeeper profile, 91–93
  idiosyncratic features of, 85
  modern era reconstruction of, 89–91
  modern renovations of, 165

naming of, 81
night games, 81, 83, 89, 104, 137
origin of, 78–79
outfield dimension changes in, 83
postwar field renovations of, 86–89
repair of 1936 flooding of, 84–85
return of professional baseball in 1987, 149
signboard, 85
special events and memories surrounding, 94–96
Bowman Field Commission, 89
Bowman Field Hall of Fame, 66
Boy's Band, 104
Braithwaite, Johnny, 123
Brancato, Al, 109
Brandons, 21, 41
Braves, Boston, 103
Brennan, Tom, 150
Breon, George, 26
Bresnahan, Dave, 71, 150–51, 152
Bresnahan, Roger, 151
Bressler, "Rube," 28, 30, 33
Brewery Colts, 22
Briel, Jack, 18
Brito, Bernardo, 149
Britton, Ollie, 36, 37, 40
Brooklyn, 27
Brown, Joe E., 58
Brown, Paul, 134
Brownies, 22
Browns, St. Louis, 67
Bubb, N. Burrows, 26, 33, 36, 45, 48
Bucknell University, 81
Bullock, Edward, 51
Bunning, Jim, 93, 95, 122
Burba, Dave, 153, 154
Burk, Mack, 129
Burnitz, Jeromy, 155–56
Burns, Bobby, 99
Burns, George J., 101
Buxton, Ralph, 108
Byers, Ollie, 121

Cage, Wayne, 148
Cambria, Joe, 113–14, 117
Camelli, Hank, 94
Camp, Norm, 133
Cannell, Virgil "Rip," 37, 40
Carden, Jay, 139
Cardinals, St. Louis, 103
Carnevale, Danny, 110
Carpenter, Charles F., 36, 39
Carpenter, Jim, 4
Carter, Dick, 93, 129
Carter, Gene, 149

Cartwright, Alexander, 9
Case, "Pop," 22
Cater, Danny, 132, 133, 134
"Cavalcade of Baseball," 62
Central Grand Division Railroad title, 42
Central Pennsylvania League, 16, 24
Centrals, Jersey Shore, 42
"Challenge Cup," 161
championships
    Central Grand Division Railroad title, 42
    "Challenge Cup," 161
    Farnsworth Cup, 29, 30, 31, 36
    Governor's Cup, 133
    Grays, 99–100, 105–7, 112
    NYPL, 83
    "President's Cup," 42, 61
    Tri-State League, 31, 34, 35–36, 37, 38
Charles, "Kid," 33
Charleston, Oscar, 81, 95
Chester, Hilda, 94
Chicago Cubs, 90, 159–63. *See also* Cubs, Williamsport
Chicago teams, of National League, 27
Chozen, Harry, 109
Christman, Terry, 139
Church-sponsored baseball, 41
Cincinnati Reds, 67
Cincinnati Red Stockings, 12
City Hotel team, 22
City Industrial League, 56
City League, 21–22, 56
Clarke, William P., 16, 18, 36, 37
Clayton, Harry "Hack," 21
Cleveland Indians, 103, 147–48
Clover Leaves, 22
"Clown Prince of Baseball," 70
Clunk, J. Roy, 42, 49
    as business manager of Williamsport Grays, 56–57
    as a director of Williamsport Grays, 51
    on flood damage to Bowman Field, 83–84
    hiring of Bellandi as Bowman Field groundskeeper, 92
    on James Gleason, 50
    Johnson as assistant to, 65
    as manager of Grays, 101
    retirement of, 133
    super fan Mileto and, 94
Clymer, "Dutch," 28
Cochran Elementary School, 26
Cockill, George, 36, 37
Cohen, Andy, 112
Colavito, Rocky, 123
Colgan, Pat, 110
Collins, Kevin, 137
Colored Giants, Harrisburg, 81, 95
"Community and Suburban Night," 109
Connally, Chris, 162, 163

Conroy, Bill, 133
Coogan, Dale, 126
Cordell, Johnny, 109
Corridon, Frank " Fiddler," 33
Cotelle, Como, 94, 108
Cott, Marty, 142
Coughlin, Bill, 37, 40
Covert, "Dad," 14
cow-milking contests, 71
Craft, Jerry, 139
Crane affair, 39
Crane (Millionaires player), 39
Creamer, Theodore A., 28, 33
Cree, Birdie, 35, 36
Cross, Lave, 18
Crosscutters, Williamsport
   franchise, 90
   1999 season, 164
   2000 season, 165–66
Crowley, William, 14
Crum, R. H., 16, 17, 45
Cuban players, 114–16
Cuban X-Giants, 27–28
Cubs, Chicago, 90, 159–63. *See also* Cubs, Williamsport
Cubs, Geneva franchise, 53, 74, 159
Cubs, Williamsport
   long-term commitment to Williamsport, 159–60
   1994 season, 160
   1995 season, 160–61
   1996 season, 161–62
   1997 season, 162
   1998 season, 162–63
Culler furniture factory, 100
Culp, Ray, 134, 136
Curry, Tony, 131
Curtin Middle School, 16
Cutright, Larry, 133

Dalkowski, Steve, 136
Danville, 19
Darcy, Pat, 143
Darkstones, 22
"Dave Bresnahan Award," 71
"Dave Bresnahan Night," 71
Davis, Harry, 118
Davis, Jacke, 131
Davis, John "Red," 148
Day, Leon, 95
Decker, Al, 144
Delahanty, Joe, 33, 35
Delucia, Rich, 154
Delycure, Frank, 96
Demarest, Carlton, 99
Demorests, 21, 22, 24
Demorest Sewing Machine Company, 21, 22

Dempsey, Tom, 73
Denehy, Bill, 139
Desautels, Gene, 118
Deshler, Dave, 17
Dessau, Frank, 33
Detore, George, 118
Detroit, 28
Detroit Tigers, 86, 87, 93, 117–22
Devine, Bing, 139
"Diamond Dig Night," 74
Diaz, Diogenes, 164
DiGregorio, Joe, 137
Dixon, Don, 105
Doby, Larry, 95
Donovan, Jerry "Ironman," 28, 30
Donovan, Wild Bill, 28
Doumit, Ryan, 166
Dozier, D. J., 155
Drauby, Jake, 18
Drennen Brothers Construction Company, 80
drinking, associated with baseball, 11
Drum and Bugle Corps competitions, 95
DuBoistown Stars, 22
Dugan, Jim, 42
Duke, Willie, 112
Duncan, Courtney, 162
Dunkle, Davy, 151
Dyer, Duffy, 141

Eagles, Newark, 95
Eastern League (EL)
   demise of, 103
   divisions of, 128–29
   Grays departure from, 113
   Johnson as president of, 65
   1967 play-offs, 138
   NYPL as, 107
   promotions and, 59–60
   reclassification of, 136
   silver anniversary of, 118
   support for Williamsport "Bills," 149
   suspension of 1961 play-offs, 134
   Williamsport affiliation with, 3, 40, 52, 154, 155–57
   Williamsport population and support for, 73
Easton, John, 129
EL (Eastern League). *See* Eastern League (EL)
Elia, Lee, 132
Elite Giants, Baltimore, 95
Ellis, "Monk," 14
Elmira Pioneers, 57, 104, 110, 112, 142, 161
Embree, Charles "Red," 110
Engel, Joe, 64
Erie City club, 8
Erie Excelsiors, 12
Ernst, Jack, 106

Estes, Doug, 74, 160
Estes, Susan, 74
Eutermarks, John, 8
Evans, Al, 71
Excelsiors, Erie, 12
exhibition games, 29, 67, 68, 83, 115, 123, 137–38

Faatz, Charles, 18
fans. *See* kranks (fans)
Faries, Ed, 14
Farley, Bob, 137
Farnsworth, W. C., 28, 33
Farnsworth Cup, 29, 30, 31, 36
Farrell, John, 97
Farrell, Percy B., 83
Federal League, 29
Feighner, Eddie, 95
Feldman, Chic, 116, 118
Feller, Bob, 150
Fernandez, Aurelio, 116
Ferrell, Kerby, 138
Fichman, Mal, 72, 147, 148
Fields, Charlie, 133
Figard, Gordy, 131
Fisk, Carlton, 143
Fitzpatrick, Jack, 127
Fitzpatrick (1886 Williamsport player), 18
Flater, Jack, 36
"Flood Repair Night," 70
Foran, Steve, 144
Ford, Lambert, 142
Ford, Whitey, 95
Forsch, Bob, 142
Foster, Andrew "Rube," 28
Foster, Eddie, 36
Foulk, Dudley, 98, 99
Foulkrod, Frank, 18
Four Tops, 95
Fowle, Charles, 12
Foxx, Jimmy, 83
Foytack, Paul, 93
franchises
    Bowman support for, 45
    conditions for success of, 4, 5, 166–67
    Geneva Cubs, 53, 74, 159
    instability of, 19, 28–29
    mobility of, 53
    promotions in financial health of, 66–71, 137
    purchase of Williamsport Tigers, 122–23
    raiding of players by, 25, 29, 36
    sale of Williamsport Tri-State League team, 40
    Waterbury, 53
    Williamsport Crosscutters, 90, 164, 165–66
    Williamsport Grays loss of Phillies, 135
free agency, 13, 29

French, Walter, 97, 99
Frey, Dunbar, 19
Fulweiler, Harold, 98, 99
Funk, Art, 107

Gallardo, Frankie, 115
Gardiner, Mike, 153–54
Gaspar, Rod, 141
Gass, Ed, 21
Gehrig, Lou, 83
Gehron, Carl, 107
Gehron, Dutch, 107
Gehron, Jimmy, 107
Geneva Cubs franchise, 53, 74, 159
Gentry, Gary, 141
George, Thomas "Lefty," 99, 100
Gera, Bernice, 145
Ghelfi, Andy, 152
Ghelfi, Tony, 152
Giants, New York, 22, 27, 28, 103
Giants, Philadelphia, 27
Giants, Springfield, 129, 131, 136
Gibson, Josh, 95
Giddens, Charlie, 118
Gigon, Norm, 131
Gilbert, Jess, 99
Gillick, Pat, 136
Ginsburg, Joe, 133
Gleason, Harry "Rabbit," 33
Gleason, Irvin W., 48–49, 80, 81, 83
Gleason, James B., 48, 49–50, 80, 107
Gleason, William "Kid," 19
Godfrey, Paul, 42
"Go-Go Grays," 131, 132
Gohl, Jess, 21
Goicochea, Leonard, 115
Golden, William "Pop," 21
Goldklang, Marvin, 73, 74, 153, 154, 155
Gomez, Orlando, 149, 151
Gontkosky, Bob "Gunner," 129, 130, 136, 137
Gonzalez, Geremi, 160–61
Gonzalez Echevarria, Roberto, 114
Goodman, Dave, 109
Goodyear Tire Company team, 107
Governor's Cup, 133
Graff, Milt, 126
Grand Division Championship Series, 41
Gray, Thomas, 26, 30–31, 46–47, 48, 97, 99
Grays, Homestead, 95
Grays, Williamsport
    affiliation with Detroit Tigers, 117–22
    affiliation with New York Mets, 136–41
    affiliation with Philadelphia A's, 123
    affiliation with Philadelphia Phillies, 128–36
    affiliation with Pittsburgh Pirates, 123–28

Grays (*continued*)
  boosters (*see* boosters)
  brawl with Wilkes-Barre Barons, 110–12
  championships, 99–100, 105–7, 112
  Cuban players, 114–16
  departure from Eastern League, 113
  financial problems of, 103, 104, 125, 127–28, 135
  first game in Bowman Field, 81
  "Go-Go Grays," 131, 132
  Little League and, 109
  loss of Phillies franchise, 135
  naming of, 99
  1924 season, 99–100
  1925 season, 100–101
  1926 season, 101
  1927 season, 101
  1928 season, 101
  1929 season, 101–2
  1930 season, 102
  1931 season, 102
  1932 season, 102–3
  1933 season, 103, 104
  1934 season, 83, 105–6
  1935 season, 107
  1936 season, 107
  1937 season, 107
  1938 season, 107–8
  1940 season, 109
  1941 season, 109–12
  1942 season, 112–13
  1944 season, 113–15
  1945 season, 115–16
  1954 season, 124–25
  1955 season, 125–26
  1956 season, 126–27
  1958 season, 128–29
  1959 season, 129, 131
  1960 season, 131–33
  1961 season, 133–34
  1962 season, 134–36
  origin of name for, 47
  promoters, 54–66
  promotions and public relations (*see* promotions)
  Sunday games, 105
"Great Potato Caper," 71, 95, 150–51, 152
Grier Street diamond, 41
Griffey, Ken, Jr., 151
Griffin, Alfredo, 148
Griffin, Jerry, 136
Griffith, Clark, 113–14
Grit, 49, 63
Grit Publishing Company, 80
"Groundskeeper," 51
Guehrer (1886 Williamsport player), 18
Guise, Frank P., 14
Gumpert, Randy, 108

Haas, George "Mule," 56, 83, 97, 98
Hall, Irv, 110, 113
Halstead, Earle E., 117, 118
Hanner, Ray, 42
Harder's Sporting Good Store, 80
Hargrove, Mike, 151
Harris, Dick, 131
Harrisburg, 35, 37, 104
Harrisburg Colored Giants, 81, 95
Hasney, Pete, 18
Hazel, John, 37
Hazelton, 26
Hearn, "Bunny," 105, 106
Heinz, J. J., 41
Heller, Frank, 118, 119
Hemperly, Eli, 14
Hennessey, Joe, 35, 36
Herdic, Carl, 26
Herdic, Peter, Jr., 26, 45
Herdic Hotel, 12
Hernstein, John, 131, 132, 133
Hidalgo, Chino, 115, 116
Higgins, Josh, 166
Higgins, Mark, 149
Hinchman, Bill, 30, 31, 98
Hinchman, Harry, 98–99, 100, 101, 102–3, 134
"Hinchmanites," 99
Hinske, Eric, 162, 163
Hinsley, Jerry, 137
Hipps, Bobby, 106
Hoffman, Myron, 125
Hollingsworth, Al, 71
Homestead Grays, 95
honorary nights, 69
Hope, Bob, 58
Hopke, Fred, 131
Huffman, Henry "Lefty," 99
Hughes, Ed, 133
Hulbert, William, 12
Humphrey, Ken, 118, 121
Humphrey (1886 Williamsport player), 18
Hunnefield, Bill, 99
Hunsicker, Gerry, 155
Hunsinger, Louis, Jr., 4
Hurdle, Clint, 155
Hurricane Agnes, 144
Hurricane Donna, 131

immigrants, baseball and acculturation of, 2
Imperial Teteques, 67, 81
Indians, Cleveland, 103, 147–48
Indians, Pawtucket, 138, 140
Indians, Reading, 85, 127
Indians, Shamokin, 101
Indians, Watertown, 162

Industrial League, 42
injuries, 40, 129, 131, 148
"Instant Vacation," 74
International League, 16, 19, 61, 148
Iron and Oil League, 16

J. C. Dressler Construction Company, 81
J. K. Mosser Tannery, 50
Jackson, "Blondy," 28, 30
Jacobsen, Landon, 166
Jaffe, Irving "Bud," 50
Jaffe, Max, 50, 51, 80
James V. Bennett Construction Company, 80
Jenkins, Ferguson, 136
Jersey Shore Centrals, 42
"Joel Garrison Day," 95
Joe Ottenmiller's Brewery Colts, 22
John, Tommy, 134
Johnnies, 31
Johnson, Adam Rankin, Jr., 64–67, 70, 142
Johnson, Adam Rankin, Sr., 54, 63, 64
Johnson, Ban, 25
Johnson, Joan, 64
Johnstown club, 31
Jones, Art, 109, 111, 112
Jones, B. C. "Red," 128
Jones, Calvin, 152
Joseph H. Mosser Leather Company, 50

Kast, Charley, 21
Kato, Takkaki "Tiger," 162, 163
Keds, 42
Keegan, Ed, 129, 133
Keister, William, 40
Kempf, Clarence "Harry," 84
Kensecke, Len, 110
Kettle, Jerry, 133
Keyes, Ray, 56–57, 57, 93, 123, 131
Keystone League, 16
Keystones, 8, 22
Keystones [Foundry] Team, 21
Keystone team, 42
"Kid Cub," 160
Kids Day, 95
Kiess, Howard, 21
Killinger, Glenn, 49, 101, 103
Kimber, Sam, 18
Kiner, Ralph, 95
"Knot-Hole Gang" program, 50, 68, 74
Kobritz, Jordan, 149
Kolberg, Irv, 109
Kolp, Ray, 70, 114, 115
Koosman, Jerry, 141
Krall, Johnny, 115
Kranepool, Ed, 137

kranks (fans). *See also booster clubs*
    attendance at amateur games, 20
    attendance at early games, 14
    attendance at EL games, 59–60
    attendance at games, 74, 102, 120, 135, 142, 145, 147,
        148, 166
    attendance at night games, 81, 83
    attendance at Tri-State League games, 40
    behavior of, 10, 22, 24
    preference for professional baseball, 24–25
    super, 94
    support for NYPL, 155
    views on social role of baseball, 2
Kretlow, Lou, 118, 121
Kroll, Gary, 134, 136
Kuban Joint Club, 22
Kubek, Tony, Jr., 107
Kubek, Tony, Sr., 107
Kuhn, Bowie, 63
Kuzma, Dick, 116

Lackawanna County Commissioners, 148
Lackawanna County Multipurpose Stadium, 149
Ladies Day, 67
Laedlein, John, 30
Lafferty, Frank "Flip," 14
Lancaster, 17, 19, 26, 35
Lancaster Ironsides, 17
Landreth, Jason, 164
Langley, Jim, 115
League Alliance, 16
Leavitt, Roy, 98, 99
Lebanon, 26
Lemon, Bob, 95, 110
Lennon, Patrick, 152
Lentz, Mary Louise, 81
Leon, Eddie, 148
Leonard, Buck, 95
Lewistown, 17
Life Magazine, 55
Lindemann, Bob, 30
Lindheimer, Max, 30, 33
Lipscomb, Gerald "Nig," 118
Little League Baseball, Inc., 3, 60, 87, 107–8, 109
Lloyd, Thomas W., 14, 15
Locke, Ron, 140–41
Lock Haven, rivalry with Williamsport, 8, 14, 15, 17, 18,
    20, 22, 24
Lock Haven College, 95
Longmire, Marcel, 162
Lopez, Hector, 123
Lopez, Marcelino, 134
Lucas, Charles "Chet," 126
Lucchesi, Frank, 71, 93, 129, 131, 133, 134
lumber barons, evolution of baseball and, 1–2, 15

Lundblade, Rick, 150–51
Lundy, A. D., 9, 91
Lunsford, Ed, 133
Luppachino, Frank, 72, 147
Lush, Johnny, 26, 28, 30, 31
Lutz, Barney, 113
Lutz, John, 21
Lycoming College, 95
Lycoming County Central Labor Council, 71
Lycoming Creek, 83, 86, 118
Lycoming Foundry, 42
Lycoming Motors, 42, 56
Lycoming Rubber Works, 21
Lyon, Howard, 14

Mack, Connie, 58, 59, 61, 64, 67, 123
Madigan (1910 Williamsport player), 40
Madura, Frank, 110
Maglie, Sal "The Barber," 110, 112
Mahaffey, Art, 129
Mahoning Valley Scrappers, 165
Maine Guides, 148
Maitland, Edgar, 28, 36
Major Leagues
    agreements with National Association of Professional
        Baseball Leagues, 4
    American League and, 25–26, 36
    minor league players upgraded to (*see* players, minor
        league to Major Leagues)
    ownership of minor league clubs, 61, 103 (*see also*
        franchises)
    Tri-State League and, 29
Maley, Jack, 26, 28
Malone, Fergy, 19
Manlove, Charley, 18
Manning, Nate, 162
Manning, Walter "Rube," 30, 31, 36, 42
Manno, Don, 69, 104–5, 121, 122
Mansfield, Larry, 142
Mansfield College, 95
March, Ed, 118
Marhefka, Tony, 40
Marichal, Juan, 95, 129
Mariners, Vermont, 151
Maris, Roger, 85, 95
Marquart, Ollie, 106
Martin, Homer, 8
Martinez, Tino, 153, 154
Mason, Henry, 134
"Massachusetts game," 9
Mazeroski, Bill, 124, 126
McAndrew, Jim, 141
McBride, Horace "Red," 83, 105, 106, 107
McClure, Harold, 14
McConnell, Bob, 163

McCracken, Jack, 134
McGough, Tom, 148
McHale (1904 Williamsport player), 30
McIlveen, Henry "Irish," 30
McManus, Marty, 108–9
McMunn, Bill, 21
McNally, Mike, 104
McQuinn, George, 109
McVaugh, Bill, 42
Medina, Luis, 149
"Meet the Cubs Night," 160
Mejia, Oscar, 151
Memorial Field, 79, 80, 81
Mertz, Joseph, 21, 41
Mets, New York, 4, 52, 67, 74, 89, 136–41, 154–55
Mets, Williamsport, 136–41
Mifflinburg, 84
Mileto, Jimmy, 94
Miller, John, 136
Miller, "Punch," 98
Millionaires, Williamsport
    1906 season, 33
    1907 season, 35–36
    1908 season, 36–37, 38
    1909 season, 37, 39
    1910 season, 40
Mills, Art "Jockey," 106
Milton, 24
Miner, George, 106
Miners, Scranton, 110
minor leagues, 24–28. *See also* players, minor league to
        Major Leagues; *specific leagues and teams*
Mitchell, Max, 100
Mize, "Big" Johnny, 95
Montelongo, Joe, 160
Montilla, Felix, 164
Montoursville, 41
Moran, Herb, 102
More, Allie, 21
Moreno, Mike, 162
Moss, Charley, 30
Mosser, Joseph H., 42, 50–52, 89, 128
Mowrey, Mike, 30
"Mr. Baseball," 51. *See also* Mosser, Joseph H.
Mt. Carmel, 26
Mullen (1904 Williamsport player), 30
Murphy, Johnny, 137
Murtaugh, Danny, 63
Mustaikis, Alex, 109, 111, 112, 113
Myers, Frank, 106
Myers, William, 33
Myron Noodleman, 70

NAPBL (National Association of Professional Baseball
        Leagues), 25, 90, 103, 136

National Association of Independent Clubs, 27
National Association of Professional Baseball Leagues
    (NAPBL), 25, 90, 103, 136
National Baseball Agreements, 18, 29
National League of Professional Base Ball Clubs
    (National League). *See also specific teams*
    American Baseball Association and Northwestern
        League agreement of 1883, 15–16, 25
    American League and, 25
    Chicago teams of, 27
    founding of, 12–13
    League Alliance, 16
    "reserve clause" of, 13, 18
    rule changes and, 9–10
Nationals, New York, 17
Navarro, Tito, 155
Negro Leagues, 95. *See also* black teams and players
Neiger, Al, 131
Nelson, Jeff, 153, 154
Ness, Jack, 40
Newark Eagles, 95
Newberry, 22, 41
New Orleans Pelicans, 123
New York Giants, 22, 27, 28, 103
New York Knickerbockers Baseball Club, 9
New York Mets, 4, 52, 67, 74, 89, 136–41, 154–55
New York Nationals, 17
New York–Pennsylvania League (NYPL)
    championships and, 83
    establishment of, 97
    fan support for, 155
    1968 relocation to Williamsport, 53
    Richardson as president of, 107
    Williamsport affiliation with, 4, 40, 46, 53, 141–45,
        159–67
"New York rules," 9
New York Yankees, 103
Nicholson, "Big Bill," 108
Night games, 27, 81, 102, 104
Nine-County Baseball Booster Association, 52, 72
Nine-County Baseball Boosters, Inc., 128, 129, 135,
    137, 139, 141, 142
Noradukian, Taleen, 162, 163
normal schools, 21
Norris, William, 9
Northeast Baseball, Inc., 72, 148, 149
Northern Division, of Eastern League, 128–29
Northey, Ron, 109, 112
NYPL (New York-Pennsylvania League). *See* New
    York–Pennsylvania League (NYPL)

O'Dell, Jon, 141
Office of Defense Transportation, 112
O'Hara, Tom, 35, 36, 37
Old Oak Park racetrack, 14

"Old Tymer," 29
Oliver, Dick, 101
Oliver, Harry, 134
"Olympic Day," 70
O'Neill, Dick, 21
Orioles, Baltimore, 92
Orso, Mike, 91
Ott, Ed, 142
Ottenmiller, Joe, 22
Otto, H., 9
Otto, Luther M., 8, 9
ownership groups, 72–75

Pacific Coast League, 16
"Pack the Park Nights," 74
Pagan, Jon, 166
Pagan, Jose, 148
Page, Ed, 14
Page, Sam, 125
Paige, Satchel, 95, 96
Panko, Emil, 126
parades, 31, 35–36, 67
Parkes, Chant, 102, 104
Parra, Danny, 115, 116
Passeau, Claude, 106
Patkin, Max, 70
Pawtucket Indians, 138, 140
Pelicans, New Orleans, 123
Pelter, Nate, 113
Penn College, 95
Pennsy League, 26
Pennsylvania Department of Labor and Industry, 85, 87
Pennsylvania Historical and Museum Commission, 77
Pennsylvania–Ontario–New York (PONY) League, 117
Pennsylvania Railroad League (PRL), 41, 42, 56
Pennsylvania Sports Hall of Fame, 63, 66
Pennsylvania State American Legion Convention, 95
Pennsylvania State Association, 16, 17–20
Pennsy team, 42
Peploski, Henry, 107
Peterman, Bill, 112
Philadelphia Athletics, 54, 113
    agreement with Williamsport Grays, 103, 123
    Billtowners with, 19
    City League and, 22
    1885 Billtowners versus, 17
    exhibition games at Bowman Field, 83
    games played in Williamsport, 67
    1931 team, 68
    Richardson and, 61
    Stovey and, 15
Philadelphia & Erie (P&E) Railroad club, 8
Philadelphia Giants, 27
Philadelphia Phillies, 57, 67, 97, 128–36
Philadelphia Stars, 95

Phillies, Philadelphia, 57, 67, 97, 128–36
Phillies, Reading, 147, 148, 150
Phillie Phanatic, 70
Pickelner, Louis, 52, 115–16
Pickelner, William "Bill," 52–53, 89, 116, 137, 139, 141, 149, 159
Piersall, Jimmy, 90
Pinckney Division, 165
Pioneers, Elmira, 57, 104, 110, 112, 142, 161
Pirates, Pittsburgh, 67, 97, 98, 103, 123–28, 163, 166
Pirates organization, 57
Pitcairn team, 42
Pittsburgh, 27
Pittsburgh Pirates, 67, 97, 98, 103, 123–28, 163, 166
Plankenhorn, Fred, 21
players, minor league to Major Leagues, 173–76
   Allen, 134, 135, 136
   Applegate, 21, 26, 30, 37
   Ashburn, 95, 116
   Barnhart, 42, 56
   Bishop, 42, 56
   Blair, 30, 36
   Boley, 42, 56
   Boswell, 141
   Bunning, 93, 95, 122
   Burba, 153, 154
   Burnitz, 155–56
   Cater, 132, 133, 134
   Colavito, 123
   Cross, 18
   Culp, 134, 136
   Day, 95
   Doby, 95
   Dyer, 141
   Elia, 132
   Faatz, 18
   Ford, 95
   Forsch, 142
   French, 97
   Gaspar, 141
   Gentry, 141
   Gleason, 19
   Gonzalez, 160
   Griffey, 151
   Griffin, 148
   Haas, 56, 83, 97, 98
   Hernstein, 131, 132, 133
   Hinchman, 30, 31, 98
   Jenkins, 136
   Kiner, 95
   Koosman, 141
   Kroll, 134, 136
   Lemon, 95, 110
   Manlove, 18
   Manning, 30, 31, 36, 42
   Marichal, 95, 129
   Martinez, 153, 154
   McAndrew, 141
   Mize, 95
   Nelson, 153, 154
   Rice, 142, 144
   Ryan, 95, 138, 140, 141
   Savage, 131, 132, 133
   Stovey, 14–15
   Stroud, 37
   Swoboda, 138, 141
   Tiernan, 17
   Troy, 18
   Virtue, 18
   Warhop, 36, 37, 102
   Wood, 161
   Wyckoff, 42
   Yasztremski, 132
   Zoldak, 113
Plummer, Jake, 106
Poff, W. Herbert, 41
PONY League. *See* Pennsylvania–Ontario–New York (PONY) League
Poole, Arnold "Bucky," 98, 99
Portboys, Williamsport
   1875 season, 13–14
   1876 season, 14
   1877 season, 14–15
Porter, "Red," 37
postgame celebrations
   after 1905 pennant win, 31, 33
   after 1907 pennant win, 36
   after 1924 pennant win, 100
   parades, 31, 35–36, 67
   rituals of, 12
Potter, Scott, 152
Powell, Fred, 14
Powers, Johnny, 85
"President's Cup," 42, 61
press, on baseball, 13, 16, 116, 141, 144. See also *Williamsport Gazette & Bulletin* (*WG&B*); *Williamsport Sun-Gazette* (*WS-G*); *specific radio stations; specific sportwriters*
Price, Jackie, 70
The Pride of Havana (Gonzalez Echevarria), 114
Prince, Bob, 63
printers, 21
PRL (Pennsylvania Railroad League), 41, 42, 56
promoters, 54–66, 110
promotions, 59–60, 66–71, 137

Quebec City Metros, 148
Quick, Hal, 109
Quicksteps, Wilmington, 14

racism, in baseball, 2, 115, 116, 124
radio broadcasts, 102. *See also specific radio stations*
raiding, by franchise owners, 25, 29, 36
Railroaders, 8
Ramblers, 22
Reading, 26, 28, 133
Reading Indians, 85, 127
Reading Phillies, 147, 148, 150
recruitment of players, 14, 16, 30. *See also* raiding, by
    franchise owners
Red Barons, Scranton-Wilkes-Barre, 72
Reder, Johnny, 107, 151
Reds, Cincinnati, 67
Red Sox, Boston, 67, 142, 144
Red Sox, Scranton, 120
Red Sox, Williamsport, 142–45
Red Stockings, Cincinnati, 12
Reese-Sheriff Lumber Company, 80
Rehkopf, Rob, 160
Renovo, 15, 22
Repasz Band, 31, 33, 35, 67
reporters, 22
"reserve clause," 13, 18, 29
Revelo, Manny, 166
Revo, Larry, 73, 152
Revo, Stuart, 73, 152
Rhone, M. C., 26, 27
Rice, Jim, 142, 144
Richards, W. D., 16
Richardson, Joe, 57
Richardson, Ken, 109, 112, 113
Richardson, Thomas H. (Tommy), 51
    agreement with Philadelphia A's, 123
    death of, 63
    on financial support for professional baseball in
        Williamsport, 104
    Halstead ouster and, 118
    Johnson as secretary to, 65
    as president of NYPL, 107
    profile of, 57–61
    promotions and, 67
    at renaming of Bowman Field, 81
    super fan Mileto and, 94
Richardson Buick, 61
Rickley, Chris, 18
Richmond, Don, 109, 110, 112
Rickey, Branch, 103
Ritchie, "Lurid Lou," 30, 31
Rittenhouse, William, 18
River League, 22
Riversides, 22
Robert M. Sides Music Company, 89
Robinson, Sheriff, 138
Roche, Ray, 112
rock concerts, 95

"Rocking Horse," 24
Rohr, Les, 137, 139
Rojas, Chris, 164
Romano, Joe, 53, 66, 141, 142, 145
"Ron Blackburn Night," 70
Ross Club, 100
Roulan, Mike, 74, 159
Rowe, Lynwood "Schoolboy," 121–22
Roy, Emil, 56–57
"Rubber Collection Night," 69
Ruch, Larry, 14
Rusie, Amos, 22
"Rusty Roughcut," 74, 164
Ruth, Babe, 83
Ryan, Nolan, 95, 138, 140, 141

SABR (Society for American Baseball Research), 4
St. Louis Americans, 27, 28
St. Louis Browns, 67
St. Louis Cardinals, 103
salaries
    Crane affair and, 39
    early semipro, 14
    first professional team, 16–17
    for minor league players, 25, 27
    Tri-State League and, 29–30
Sales, Eddie, 24
Sallee, "Slim," 35
Sanders, Bobby, 134, 137
Sandherr (1903 Williamsport player), 28
Savage, Ted, 131, 132, 133
Sawyer, Ken, 151
Schacht, Al, 70
Schaedler, Bill, 116
Schmidt, Henry, 21
Schreckengost, Ossie "Rocking Horse," 24
Schudder, "Scoops," 28
Schultz (1903 Williamsport player), 28
Schweiker, Mark S., 91
Scranton, 17, 19, 26
Scranton Miners, 110
Scranton Red Sox, 120
Scranton–Wilkes-Barre Red Barons, 72
Scrappers, Mahoning Valley, 165
Searfoss, Bobby, 21
season ticket sales, 72, 104, 128, 129, 137
Sebring, Jimmy, 26, 30–31, 33
Seibler, Dwight, 133
Seminick, Andy, 133
semipro periods, 13–17, 41–43
Sesquicentennial Pageant, 95
Shamokin, 24
Shamokin Indians, 101
Shaughnessy, Frank "Shag," 61
Shaw, Jeff, 152

Shean, Dave, 36
Shepard, Larry, 125, 126
Shipley, Jack, 106
Showalter, John, 111
Siebert, Sonny, 134
Simmons, Curt, 129, 130, 131
Sinicropi, Gabe, 74, 160
Slate, Hyman, 8
Sloan, William, 9
Smaldone, Ed, 74, 159
Smith, Bernie, 141, 164
Smith, D. Vincent, 82
Smith, Edgar, 107
Smith, Zach, 106
Snyder, Bernie, 106
Society for American Baseball Research (SABR), 4
Sons of Italy, 93
Sorrell, Bill, 136
South Atlantic (Sally) League, 136–37
Southern League, 16
South Side, 41
Spahn, Warren, 137
Spalding, Alfred G., 12
Spencer, David, 22
Spencer, Glenn, 108
Spotts, Dick, 102, 106
Springfield Giants, 129, 131, 136
stadiums, guidelines for, 4. *See also* Bowman Field
Stallard, Tracey, 137
Stansbury, Jack, 40
Stars, Philadelphia, 95
Steinecke, Bill, 107
Steinhilper, Robert "Bob" J., 54, 56, 93, 118
Stell, Charles, 98
Stengel, Casey, 52, 136, 137, 138
Stetler, Percy, 26
Stotz, Carl, 3, 61, 107–8, 109
Stovey, Harry, 14–15
Stowe, Harry. *See* Stovey, Harry
Stradley, Otto, 93
Strang, Evelyn, 89
Strauss, "Blondy," 42
Street, Charles "Gabby," 33, 42
"Stroehmann's Cake Night," 70
Stroud, Ralph "Sailor," 37
Sunbury, 24
Sunday games, 105
Susquehanna Boom Festival, 95
Swain, Rob, 150
Swiftford club, 8
Swisher, Steve, 149
Swoboda, Ron, 138, 141

Tauscher, Walter, 101
Taylor, Joe, 123

Telgheder, Dave, 156
Terleckey, William (Bill), 72, 149, 151
Texas League, 16, 137
Therre, George, 40
Thomas, Bill, 106
Thomas, Ira, 104
Thomas, Luther "Bud," 106, 107
Thorne, Ralph "Pat," 51, 80, 103
Three Dog Night, 95
Tiant, Luis, 134
ticket sales, 27, 67, 72, 104, 126, 128, 129, 137
Tiernan, Mike, 17
Tigers, Detroit, 86, 87, 93, 117–22
Tigers, Williamsport, 54, 55
    franchise purchase, 122–23
    name change from Williamsport Grays, 118
    1948 season, 118–21
    1951 season, 122
    1952 season, 122
Tighe, Jack, 69, 121
Tinsman, Garrett, 14
Tomahawks, Williamsport, 72, 147–48
Tompkins News Agency, 60
Townsend, Jack, 36, 37
Trautman, George, 92
Travis, Randy, 95
Trenton, 17
Trillo, Manny, 162
Triplets, Binghamton, 67, 101–2, 103, 133
Tri-State League
    bidding wars and, 33, 39
    Billies and, 30–33
    championships, 31, 34, 35–36, 37, 38
    exhibition games and, 29
    fan attendance at games of, 40
    Major Leagues and, 29
    Millionaires, 33–40
    Millionaires emblem and, 33
    National Agreement and, 35
    1904 season, 30
    1905 season, 30–31, 33
    origin of, 28
    as outlaw league, 3, 29
    playoffs and, 31
    "reserve clause" and, 29
    salaries and, 29–30
    sale of Williamsport franchise, 40
    semipro team, 41–43
    Williamsport team and, 20, 33, 35–36
Trolley League, 41–43
Troy, John "Dasher," 18
Trusty, Shep, 27
Turbeville, George, 107
Turn Verein Vorwaerts, 22

Feb. 02

Tyrone, 22
Tyson, Cecil "Turkey," 115, 116

Ullman, S. E., 50
umpires, 145
Unglaub, Bob, 33
Union Park Diamond, 21–22
Union Park Fairgrounds, 23
United States Rubber Company, 42
Utica Blue Sox, 115

Valdes, Rogelio, 115
Vallamont Athletics, 41
Valo, Elmer, 63
Van Dusen, Fred, 129
Vannucci, Putsee, 86, 88
Velte, Paul, 74, 159, 160
Vermont Mariners, 151
Vickers, Rube, 35
Virdon, Bill, 138
Virtue, Jake, 18

Waddell, "Rube," 24
Wahl-Braun Furniture, 50
Wakefield, Bill, 138
Walker, Ron, 162
Walters, Bucky, 102
Walton, Jack, 42
Walton, Jim, 143
Ward, John Montgomery "Monty," 14, 15
Warhop, Jack, 36, 37, 102
Warren, Malcolm "Bunky," 137, 138
Waterbury franchise, 53
Watertown Indians, 162
Way, J. Roman, 80
Weeks, Fred, 40
Weigand, Curt, 30
Weisman, Skip, 73, 74
Welteroth, Dick, 115
West Branch Bulletin, 8
West Branch League, 42
West End, 41
West Haven Yankees, 147, 148
Westrum, Wes, 138
WG&B (Williamsport Gazette & Bulletin), 10, 18, 19, 26, 46–47, 81, 99, 102, 104
Whalen, Jimmy, 35
Wheaton, Woody, 107
White, Ernie, 137
White Roses. *See* York White Roses
Whitney, Mert, 35
Whyte, William, 27
Wilkes-Barre, 17, 18, 19, 26, 37, 54
Wilkes-Barre Barons, 110–12
Williams, Clarence, 27

Williams, Dewey, 109, 133
Williamson, Leo, 94
Williamsport. *See also specific teams*
    amateur teams in, 11, 16, 20–24
    ballpark construction projects (*see* Bowman Field)
    corporate teams, 20–24
    Eastern League affiliation with, 3, 40, 52, 154, 155–57
    first professional team, 16–20
    minor league tradition and, 2–3
    New York Mets 1991 purchase of baseball franchise in, 4 (*see also* New York Mets)
    NYPL affiliation with, 4, 40, 46, 53, 141–45, 159–67
    origins of baseball in, 7–8
    in Pennsy League, 26
    Pennsylvania State Association affiliation with, 17–20
    player names in very early baseball in, 8
    player occupations in very early baseball in, 8–9
    rivalry with Lock Haven, 8, 14, 15, 17, 18, 20, 22, 24
    semipro teams, 13–17, 41–43
Williamsport Area Community Baseball Association, 71–72
Williamsport Athletic (Baseball) Club, 8, 9, 12, 13, 22, 40
Williamsport Athletic Club, 26, 27
Williamsport Baseball Association, 10, 11
Williamsport Baseball Club, 19–20, 84
Williamsport Booster Club, 54, 74
Williamsport Bowman Field Commission, 75
Williamsport Cubs Booster Club, 160
Williamsport Gazette & Bulletin (*WG&B*), 10, 18, 19, 26, 46–47, 81, 99, 102, 104
Williamsport High School, 95, 100
Williamsport High School Athletic Field, 42, 78
Williamsport High School band, 67
Williamsport-Lycoming Foundation, 90
Williamsport School District, 83
Williamsport Sun-Gazette (*WS-G*), 4, 123
Williamsport Water Company, 78
Willig, Ed, 21
Willig, Henry, 21, 26
Willig, Lou, 26, 28
Williner, Carl, 46
Willman, Lefty, 21
Wilmington Quicksteps, 14
Winter Baseball Banquet, 137
Witman, William Abbot, 26
Witmer, Bill, 125–26
Wolf, Sol "Woody," 69, 107
Wolff, Roger, 109, 110, 112
Wolgamot, Earl, 111
Wolverton, Charles, 35, 36
Wolverton, Harry, 33, 37
women, involvement with baseball, 67, 89, 94, 145, 162, 163
Wood, Kerry, 161

Woodsman's Rally, 95
Works Progress Administration (WPA), 84–85
World War II, 69, 112–13
WPA (Works Progress Administration), 84–85
WRAK, 102, 104
WS-G (Williamsport Sun-Gazette), 4, 123
WWPA, 72, 151
Wyckoff, "Weldy," 42

Yankees, New York, 103

Yankees, West Haven, 147, 148
Yasztremski, Carl, 132
YMCA team, 21
York White Roses, 30, 31, 33, 83, 99, 100
Young Champions, 22
Young Men's Republican Club, 22

"Zafar Grotto Night," 71
Ziegler, Scott, 151
Zoldak, Sam, 113